SAGE was founded in 1965 by Sara Miller McCune to support the dissemination of usable knowledge by publishing innovative and high-quality research and teaching content. Today, we publish over 900 journals, including those of more than 400 learned societies, more than 800 new books per year, and a growing range of library products including archives, data, case studies, reports, and video. SAGE remains majority-owned by our founder, and after Sara's lifetime will become owned by a charitable trust that secures our continued independence.

Los Angeles | London | New Delhi | Singapore | Washington DC | Melbourne

Advance Praise

It is a welcome development that academic and action interest in Gandhi and his period, as well as in the lives and works of the associates of his movement and various campaigns, is on the rise.... Joseph Chelladurai Kumarappa, better known as J. C. Kumarappa or JCK, may have been comparatively a lesser known Gandhian for long, but not any longer. This has changed, especially after the arrival of a few others and this meticulously conceived and appreciably written book by Chaitra Redkar. Chaitra Redkar has made a brilliant attempt in tracking JCK's contribution to Gandhism during and after Gandhi's lifetime as well as right into our contemporary times. The resurgent interest in JCK's life and work, and thereby in Gandhian economic thought, is due to several recent developments, some of which are well taken note of in this book. The significance of this book nevertheless lies in tracing the germination and blossoming of this thought at an ideational as well as some praxis level during and after Gandhi. The Gandhian economic discourse is critically summarized. From every critical appraisal it can be stated that this book has potential to become a landmark piece of academic work.

—Priyavadan M. Patel
Professor and Former Head, Department of Political Science,
The Maharaja Sayajirao University of Baroda

Dr J. C. Kumarappa was a prominent Gandhian economist who attempted 'green' critique of both capitalism and communism as both followed the development policies, enhanced inequality and deprived a large number of people from their livelihood. His critique was based on the Gandhian critique of sustainable development. Kumarappa criticized capital because of its money economy, mechanized industrialism, centralization of power and production fuelled by consumerism. Instead, he advocated development of a network of village industries, the khadi and skill-based handicrafts, and agriculture based on farmers' collectives. He criticized the Bhoodan movement for distributing land to the farmers instead of forming their collectives. The Gandhian environmentalism of Kumarappa is deeply rooted in Gandhian ethics and development concerns of the Third-World countries. Dr Chaitra Redkar has admirably brought out the main features of Kumarappa's ideas as well as their contemporary relevance.

—Ashok Chousalkar
Former Professor, Department of Political Science,
Shivaji University

The present volume which is built around the socio-economic ideas of J. C. Kumarappa acquires seminal importance, particularly in the context where Kumarappa's contribution has been inadequately covered by scholars. One has to also appreciate the intellectual importance of this volume for another, perhaps more important reason—that it opens up a new dimension of Gandhian economics. The volume manifests to the readers the formative influence of the Western intellectual tradition that shaped Kumarappa's thought. But this, as the volume suggests, does not leave an everlasting impact on Kumarappa's thought. Gandhian influence had determinative impact on the ideas of Kumarappa. More interestingly, the volume brings forth the reflective character of Kumarappa's thought which is critical of the Western economy and also the modernist economic thinking within the Congress Party. Of course, the vantage point of this double critique is the Gandhian moral/political economy.

—Gopal Guru
Professor, Centre for Political Studies,
Jawaharlal Nehru University

The world is going through a difficult period. On the one hand the world seems to be progressing, but at what cost?... One can find some answers to such difficult questions in J. C. Kumarappa's thinking. He was a true Gandhian in all sense. He believed in 'small is beautiful'. It is Antyodaya (uplift of the last), base of Gandhian economic thinking. Today it is all the more relevant. Unfortunately, after Independence many intellectuals like J. C. Kumarappa were forgotten. It is time to remind the young generations born after partition what kind of socio-political-economic thinking our freedom fighters had and what kind of society they visualized.... My sincere opinion is this book by Chaitra will contribute in a big way. Such a book in the 150th birth anniversary of Mahatma Gandhi will make all the more impact.

—Jatin Desai
Veteran Gandhian activist, journalist, Former General Secretary of Pakistan–India Peoples' Forum for Peace and Democracy and Ex-Bureau Member of South Asians for Human Rights

Gandhian Engagement with Capital

Gandhian
Engagement
with
Capital

Perspectives of **J. C. Kumarappa**

Chaitra Redkar

Los Angeles | London | New Delhi
Singapore | Washington DC | Melbourne

First published in 2019 by

SAGE Publications India Pvt Ltd
B1/I-1 Mohan Cooperative Industrial Area
Mathura Road, New Delhi 110 044, India
www.sagepub.in

SAGE Publications Inc
2455 Teller Road
Thousand Oaks, California 91320, USA

SAGE Publications Ltd
1 Oliver's Yard, 55 City Road
London EC1Y 1SP, United Kingdom

SAGE Publications Asia-Pacific Pte Ltd
18 Cross Street #10-10/11/12
China Square Central
Singapore 048423

Published by Vivek Mehra for SAGE Publications India Pvt Ltd and typeset in 10/12.5 pts ITC Stone Serif by Zaza Eunice, Hosur, Tamil Nadu, India.

Library of Congress Cataloging-in-Publication Data

Name: Redkar, Chaitra, author.
Title: Gandhian engagement with capital: perspectives of J.C. Kumarappa/ Chaitra Redkar.
Description: New Delhi, India: SAGE Publications India, 2018. | Includes bibliographical references and index.
Identifiers: LCCN 2018049038| ISBN 9789353282288 (hbk) | ISBN 9789353282295 (e-pub 2.0) | ISBN 9789353282301 (ebook)
Subjects: LCSH: Gandhi, Mahatma, 1869–1948—Political and social views. | Economics—India. | Capitalism—India. | Kumarappa, Joseph Cornelius.
Classification: LCC HB126.I43 G449 2018 | DDC 330.0954—dc23 LC record available at https://lccn.loc.gov/2018049038

ISBN: 978-93-532-8228-8 (HB)

SAGE Team: Abhijit Baroi, Vandana Gupta, Shaonli Deb and Anupama Krishnan

To Aai, Baba

Thank you for accepting me the way I am, for supporting my decisions and for loving me unconditionally.

Thank you for choosing a SAGE product!
If you have any comment, observation or feedback,
I would like to personally hear from you.

Please write to me at **contactceo@sagepub.in**

Vivek Mehra, Managing Director and CEO, SAGE India.

Bulk Sales

SAGE India offers special discounts
for purchase of books in bulk.
We also make available special imprints
and excerpts from our books on demand.

For orders and enquiries, write to us at

Marketing Department
SAGE Publications India Pvt Ltd
B1/I-1, Mohan Cooperative Industrial Area
Mathura Road, Post Bag 7
New Delhi 110044, India

E-mail us at **marketing@sagepub.in**

Subscribe to our mailing list
Write to **marketing@sagepub.in**

This book is also available as an e-book.

Contents

Preface

On the eve of Mahatma Gandhi's 150th birth anniversary, is there anything that is unknown about him? It would be unrealistic to make such a claim and, yet, at the same time, revisiting Gandhi in different theoretical and methodological frameworks has always brought out certain new dimensions. The present work revisits the Gandhian understanding and critique of capitalism from the location of J. C. Kumarappa (1892–1960). This is done with a view to understand both Gandhi and Kumarappa in a fresh light, but more so, there is also a hope that it will contribute to enhance our understanding of capital itself. The unfolding of capital has been an important development in the modern world. Gandhi and Kumarappa raise a very pertinent question: Can capital be cast off when we prefer continuing with its conventional organization and its paraphernalia? When the processes of production and distribution are going to remain the same, when the organization of political life would be the same, can the nature of capital even be repaired? This work analyses how Kumarappa problematizes the political and economic organization of capital, and how he provides for an alternative from the Gandhian perspective.

This work is an exploration in the history of ideas and not a systematic analysis of any economic model. Such journeys normally provide interesting reflections and creative inputs for building models later. This journey begins on the premises provided by the existing scholarship on Gandhi as well as on Kumarappa and brings out alternate ways to approach their ideas.

Acknowledgements

This book originated in 2013 at the Department of Politics & Public Administration, Savitribai Phule Pune University (SPPU). Therefore, first and foremost I want to thank my supervisor, the late Professor Yashwant Sumant, for his insights, supervision and guidance, not only during my PhD but right from my post-graduation days and beyond. His teaching made the domain of Indian political thought an interesting and promising area for research. He always encouraged all his students to take up studies on lesser known personalities in modern India; the decision to take up research on Kumarappa resulted from the same rationale. Initially, in 2001, when I began exploring Kumarappa, there was hardly any studies on his ideas. Working in a single-person department at SNDT Women's University did affect the speed of my research. But Professor Sumant's training enabled me to search beyond what had meanwhile been explored from Kumarappa's ideas. I'm grateful to Professor Sumant for this training. I am equally grateful to him for helping me realize my potentials. His untimely demise in 2015 is a big loss for many like me. He would have been very happy to see me publish this work.

This book wouldn't have been possible without my dear friend Dr Papia Sengupta (Jawaharlal Nehru University (JNU), New Delhi), who untiringly kept on pushing me to write and publish in English. I am grateful to her for the unconditional love, the academic and personal support, and her faith in me.

During the course of writing this work, I interacted with a number of scholars and activists with my queries. I am thankful to them for giving me their valuable time and for sharing with me their insights. I am thankful to Professor Suhas Palshikar (SPPU) for his insightful inputs. I am grateful to the senior Gandhian Professor Sudarshan Iyengar for the informal discussion on Kumarappa and Gandhian economics. I am indebted to the senior Gandhian activist, Mr Vijay Diwan, who lives in Vinoba's birthplace at Gagode (Raigad district, Maharashtra) tanning leather from dead cattle. He has devoted his life to bringing the issue of equality to the centre stage of the Gandhian movement. He introduced me to various Gandhian organizations and to the crucial issues that came up in the Gandhian movement after Gandhi's assassination. I am grateful to him for his unconditional support. I am equally grateful to Mr Kishor Bedkihal, a senior scholar and activist from Satara, associated with progressive social movements in Maharashtra. He has written extensively in Marathi. The interactions with him were very fruitful and thought-provoking. My association with the activists of 'Mahatma (Phule) to Mahatma (Gandhi) Samata Abhiyan' that aimed at searching spaces of dialogue between Gandhi and Ambedkar, and with the 'Sevagram Collective' that aimed at presenting Gandhi in consonance with the contemporary concerns was extremely enriching.

There are some senior scholars who supported me in successfully completing this work and constantly encouraged me to write and publish; I am greatly thankful to them. I want to express my deep sense of gratitude towards Professor Priyavadan Patel (retired from the MS University of Baroda) for reviewing my work and constantly reminding me to publish it. I am extremely grateful to Professor Ashok Chousalkar (Shivaji University, Kolhapur), Professor Gopal Guru (JNU), Professor

Usha Thakkar (Mani Bhavan Gandhi Museum, Mumbai), senior journalist Mr Jatin Desai (Mumbai) and Dr Deepti Gangawane (Pune) for their generous support and affection.

I was greatly assisted by the archives and libraries I visited during the course of this work: Nehru Memorial Museum & Library, New Delhi; Gandhi Seva Sangh Library, Sevagram, Wardha; Magan Sangrahalaya & Kumarappa Memorial Library, Maganwadi, Wardha; Mani Bhavan Gandhi Sangrahalaya and Library, Gamdevi, Mumbai; Dhananjayrao Gadgil Library of Gokhale Institute of Politics & Economics, Pune; the Asiatic Society of Mumbai's library, Town Hall, Mumbai; Snehasadan Library, Pune; Union Biblical Seminary Library, Pune; University Library, SNDT Women's University, Mumbai; Bai Jerbai Wadia Library, Fergusson College, Pune; Jayakar Library, Pune; and Department of Politics & Public Administration Library, University of Pune. I am grateful to their respective librarians and staff. I am particularly grateful to Mr Kanakmal Gandhi (Wardha) for the access and assistance.

The help and affection of friends Arati Khatu, Chitra Lele and Chinmay Dharurkar are truly precious. I could freely voice my thinking aloud with them and discuss my dilemmas while writing this work. I am thankful to them for the time they gave in reading the manuscript and for giving candid feedback while preparing the final draft of this work.

I wish to express my deep sense of gratitude towards Madhuri Sumant for always being there with all her love, affection and support. I treasure our friendship.

My parents, Leena and Vilas Redkar, and brother Niket and sister-in-law Swanandi have always stood by me in all my decisions and in good and bad times. I wish to extend my deepest gratitude to them and love to my dearest nephew Malhar for their love, care and faith in me.

Finally, I would like to thank Abhijit Baroi, Vandana Gupta and the entire team at SAGE Publications for their helpful assistance. Any inadequacies that remain are my own.

In Search of Gandhi
Known and Unknown

A large number of studies have been conducted on Gandhi and his ideas. An overview of these studies not only exhibits the multiple dimensions of Gandhi's ideas, but also presents a historical account of how the academic studies about Gandhi have changed over the years. An overview of some of the major studies is given here.

In the Gandhi Birth Centenary year, the Khadi and Village Industries Commission organized a round table on 'Research on Gandhian Thought'. Eminent personalities such as Jayaprakash Narayan (JP), P. C. Joshi, D. K. Bedekar and Sriman Narayan, along with others, contributed in this round table and reflected upon the possibilities of exploring Gandhian thought at the academic level. While JP pressed the need to explore Gandhian concept and mechanism for revolution,[1] P. C. Joshi insisted on exploring Gandhi's economic model with a more scientific approach. He also pressed the need to explore Gandhi as an interpreter of tradition.[2] D. K. Bedekar pointed out the need to explore and understand Gandhian concepts like 'Ram Raj'

---

[1] *Round Table on Research Programme on Gandhian Thought: Papers and Proceedings*, 1970, 19–28.
[2] Ibid., 59–66.

beyond their conventional meaning. He also underlined the need to explore Gandhian thought on the one hand in the context of the intellectual tradition of nineteenth-century Indian thinkers such as Ranade and Gokhale, while on the other in the Western intellectual tradition of thinkers such as Herbert Marcuse, C. Wright Mills, Sartre and Marx.[3] The round table by and large pressed the need to explore the revolutionary potential of Gandhian thought and thereby highlighted the significance and relevance of Gandhian ideas for everyone in the society. An official statement on the possibilities of exploring Gandhian thought was also published by the national seminar committee of the Gandhi Centenary Celebration Committee of the Government of India. This committee identified a number of areas around which Gandhi's political thought could be explored. This broadly included Gandhian values such as non-violence and purity of end and means as well as strategies[4] such as Satyagraha. The list is indicative of how 'political' as a term was understood and how Gandhi as a 'political thinker' was perceived officially. In the past 40 plus years, Gandhian thought has been explored across numerous conceptual as well as thematic frameworks and a great number of biographies (politico-historical, intellectual, spiritual, psycho-analytical and so on) presenting different aspects of Gandhi's personality are available.

The studies that attempted to explore and construct the Gandhian concepts of truth, non-violence and Satyagraha are in huge numbers. Raghavan Iyer's work *Moral and Political Thought of Mahatma Gandhi*[5] is one of the pivotal studies on the Gandhian concepts. Iyer has discussed the significance of the concepts of truth and non-violence, freedom and obligation as well as Gandhi's views about ends and means. Iyer's discussion of the Gandhian concepts of relative truth and absolute truth is especially illuminating in recognizing the particular and the universal in Gandhi as well as the dialogue between the

---

[3] Ibid., 79–81.
[4] Achuthan, *Taking Gandhi to People through Seminars*, 53.
[5] Iyer, *Moral and Political Thought of Mahatma Gandhi*.

two. The Gandhian concept of non-violence has also received wide attention from pacifists and psychoanalysts to anthropologists. In fact, during Gandhi's lifetime itself, Gandhi's idea of non-violent resistance had been presented in support of pacifism. Richard Gregg's book *The Power of Non-Violence*,[6] with a foreword by none other than Martin Luther King (Jr.), presents the power of non-violent resistance in an idealist, utopian and yet a pragmatic manner. In recent years, Martin Green's work *The Origins of Non-Violence: Tolstoy and Gandhi in Their Historical Settings*[7] has explored the intellectual sources of Gandhi's idea of non-violence. Green traces how the idea of non-violence emerged and evolved in Tolstoy and Gandhi. He locates the origin of the idea of non-violence in the religious ideas of Tolstoy and Gandhi. He maintains that their religion was not theological or ecclesiastical, but existential. Their sense of the divine was aroused by something they encountered at the furtherest limit of their own experience—their moral experience—not by religious mysteries or miracles, not by temples and rituals, not by creed and theologies, and not primarily by beauty of nature. But that sense of the divine was something they persistently aroused in themselves, and something to which they responded dutifully once it was aroused.[8] He maintains that Tolstoy and Gandhi represent the purest form of 'religious radicalism', that is, they were radically religious—their thought contained an anti-political, anti-cultural element. Green presents the idea of non-violence as a virtue challenging and transcending Anglo-Saxon rationalist modernity.

Gandhi's idea of Satyagraha has also been explored and constructed in different ways. Jean V. Bondurant's study *Conquest of Violence: The Gandhian Philosophy of Conflict*[9] reviews Gandhi's five different Satyagraha campaigns and identifies certain moral prerequisites that Gandhi considered essential for staging

[6] Gregg, *The Power of Non-Violence*, 1318–1348.
[7] Green, *The Origins of Non-Violence*.
[8] Ibid., 19–20.
[9] Bondurant, *Conquest of Violence*.

Satyagraha. Bondurant maintains that for Gandhi one of the chief prerequisites for breaking law on moral grounds is to respect law and to abide by law at other times. But do liberal democracies recognize law-abiding citizen's right to disobedience? Vinit Haksar[10] discusses Gandhi's views on civil disobedience in the light of this question. He points out that modern liberals have differed heavily on the validity of citizen's right to disobey the law. While Joseph Raz maintains that in liberal democracies there is no need for the right to disobedience considering there are constitutional devices and legal ways for pursuing further on the matters of dissent. Ronald Dworkin expects the State to be tolerant to the disobedient after examining if disobedience is integrity-based, justice-based or policy-based. As against this, John Rawls looks at civil disobedience as the final device to maintain the stability of the constitution. Haksar maintains that Gandhi's ideas of civil disobedience show deep affinity with those of Rawls, since Gandhi considers disobedience as the sacred duty of a citizen when the State has become lawless or corrupt. Haksar thus presents a 'liberal' Gandhi.

A completely different interpretation of the Gandhian idea of Satyagraha could be found in Richard Fox's *Gandhian Utopia: Experiments with Culture*.[11] Fox points out that with colonization the world system of cultural domination became operative in India. This system had started dominating the perception of the self among the other things. Fox rejects the arguments developed by Ashis Nandy and Partha Chatterjee that a part of the traditional culture had remained un-dominated and untamed by colonialism. He therefore insists that it is unthinkable that Gandhi could have resisted the cultural domination from outside. Fox points out that Gandhi's originality and 'authorship' lie in the fact that he reversed the logic of orientalism and presented, what he calls, 'affirmative orientalism'. Fox writes:

> Gandhian utopia built cultural resistance by accepting the pejorative indignations of India encoded in the world system

[10] Haksar, *Rights, Communities and Disobedience.*
[11] Fox, *Gandhian Utopia.*

and making them affirmative. What appeared in Orientalism as India's ugliness now became India's beauty; her so-called weakness turned out to be her strengths. Otherworldliness became spirituality, an Indian cultural essential that promised her a future cultural perfection unattained in the West. Passiveness became at first passive resistance and later non-violent resistance; the age-old Indian character thus provided a revolutionary technique by which to bring on that future perfection ....[12]

Fox thus presents Satyagraha as a product of Gandhi's experiments with culture.

In recent years, Gandhi's ideas have also been explored and presented as alternatives that transcend the limits of liberal democratic values such as freedom, tolerance and pluralism. Ronald J. Terchek's study *Gandhi: Struggling for Autonomy*[13] is an interesting example. Terchek maintains that in Gandhi's political discourse, autonomy stands as a greatest good that precedes in importance to his other social goals. He problematizes the question of autonomy. First, he insists that Gandhian autonomy is the state of affairs when a person governs himself or herself in such a way that he or she becomes active in the preservation of autonomy not only in himself or herself but also in the polity. Autonomy understood in this way faces many obstacles. Terchek connects the issue of struggle here. The journey to overcome the obstacles takes the form of struggle. Hence struggle becomes an inherent aspect of maintaining autonomy. Terchek insists that with a combination of inner character, virtue and spiritual training, an appropriate institutional arrangement is essential for maintaining autonomy. Autonomy thus presented transcends the liberal notion of freedom.

Anthony Parel in his work *Gandhi, Freedom and Self-Rule*[14] maintains that Gandhi's idea of Swaraj or self-rule makes a fundamental contribution to the ongoing debate on the idea

---

[12] Ibid., 103.
[13] Terchek, *Gandhi: Struggling for Autonomy*.
[14] Parel, *Gandhi, Freedom and Self-Rule*.

of freedom. Parel maintains that to Gandhi the concept of freedom appears with four different meanings: freedom as sovereign national independence, freedom as the political freedom of the individual, freedom as emancipation from poverty, and freedom as the capacity for self-rule or spiritual freedom. Gandhi taught that human well-being, both for the individual and for the collective, requires the simultaneous enjoyment of all four of these aspects. They provide a vantage point from which to assess the adequacy of the reigning theories of liberalism in the West—such as the Western divisions of rights from duties and individual political freedom from spiritual freedom. Likewise, they throw useful light on the dangers inherent in the ascendant Indian ideology of Hindutva (Hindu-ness), which concentrates on national independence and economic freedom and subordinates the freedom of the individual.

Margaret Chatterjee, who had earlier studied Gandhi's religious thought, in recent years has come up with two interesting works.[15] As a student of comparative religion, Chatterjee's concern is how to initiate and sustain inter-religious communication. Plural societies do provide public spaces where people of different religions interact with each other. However, such an interaction does not necessarily lead to inter-religious communication. In this context, she asks a very fundamental question: *Is it possible to understand without sharing, or to share without understanding?*[16] Chatterjee maintains that Gandhi provides a space and a method to generate such a dialogue since he encourages knowledge of one's own religion as well as that of the other's. He expects this to be followed by introspection and self-critique which will not encourage scepticism, but will eventually lead to self-purification. Such self-purification, Chatterjee insists, provides the moral and emotional foundation of inter-religious communication in plural societies.

The discussion of various recent works on Gandhi and Gandhian ideas is but suggestive and certainly not exhaustive.

[15] Chatterjee, *Gandhi and the Challenge of Religious Diversity*, 2005; *Inter-religious Communication*, 2009.
[16] Chatterjee, 2009.

The diverse nature of such studies is indicative of the promise that the study of Gandhi offers to the scholars across countries, across disciplines and across ideological orientations. In addition to such conceptual explorations, Gandhi has also been explored across numerous themes, sociopolitical transformation being one of the dominant themes of them all.

Thomas Pantham has classified the numerous interpretations of Gandhi around the theme of sociopolitical transformation into five categories. They are:

1. Gandhian values and strategies as a factor modernizing tradition and traditionalizing modernity
2. Gandhian values and strategies as a factor contributing to the political appropriation of subaltern masses
3. Gandhian thought as a strategy for Total Revolution
4. Gandhian thought as ideas subserving the cause of Hindu nationalism
5. Gandhian programme as an alternative to liberal democratic as well as Marxist–Leninist paradigms of development and governance[17]

More than 15 years have passed since the publication of Pantham's work that took a critical survey of the literature on Gandhi. In the past 15 plus years, a number of new studies have come up on the themes discussed by Pantham. In certain cases, scholars can also be found altering their own argument. The study conducted by Rudolph and Rudolph on Gandhi[18] has been cited by Pantham as a study representing the modernity of tradition argument. In the recent times, the Rudolphs have explored postmodernist traits in Gandhi from an epistemological point of view. They present postmodernist Gandhi as an antithesis to the modernist politics of Nehru.[19] The second theme, that is, Gandhism as an ideology for political appropriation of the peasantry, has also been debated

---

[17] See Pantham, *Political Theories and Social Reconstruction*, 102–125.
[18] Rudolph and Rudolph, *The Modernity of Tradition*.
[19] Rudolph and Rudolph, *Post-Modern Gandhi and Other Essays*.

widely. The supporters of this position have developed this argument against numerous sub-themes, though not necessarily from the same theoretical position. There are certain nuanced differences in their arguments and sharp differences in their theoretical positions. But at a broader level, they agree that Gandhi's sociopolitical thinking provides a space for the appropriation of oppressed sections of the Indian society without doing much harm to the established hierarchical order and thus weakening the movement for equality. Sujata Patel, for instance, has shown how Gandhi's construction and reconstruction of womanhood is essentialist, how it includes only the elite, upper class–upper caste women and excludes the experiences of lower caste–lower class women. She therefore insists that the image of new woman as developed by Gandhi was a product of a particular historical times and had a particular political goal to serve. This she believes cannot serve the cause of women's liberation in the contemporary times.[20] If Sujata Patel finds Gandhi's ideas unfit for women's liberation, Gail Omvedt has found them unfit to serve the democratic aspirations of Dalits as well. Omvedt has shown how Gandhi's anti-caste discourse doesn't transcend the limits of Brahminical reformism, but uses these masses only for political purposes.[21] She therefore denounces Gandhism as an ideology devoid of any revolutionary potential.

Interestingly, while these sociologists have found Gandhism devoid of any revolutionary potential for the liberation of women or Dalits, certain other scholars have found Gandhism full of potential to build an alternative model of economic development that will be sensitive to the issue of equitable distribution, employment generation and environment protection. At least three historical moments could be identified in the evolution of scholarship that analysed the Gandhian model of economic development and its implications for capitalism. The first historical moment occurred with the publication of

---

[20] Patel, 'Construction and Reconstruction Woman in Gandhi', 377–387.
[21] Omvedt, *Dalits and the Democratic Revolution*, 266–267.

Bhikhu Parekh's much-debated work *Colonialism, Tradition and Reform: An Analysis of Gandhi's Political Discourse*. Parekh's work includes a chapter titled 'Gandhi and Bourgeoisie' that attempts to construct Gandhi's economic discourse. He identifies four aspects of Gandhi's critique of capitalism.[22] First, for Gandhi, capitalism, socialism, communism and all such 'economically' oriented ideologies rested on the 'materialist' view of man, which equated the human being with the body and saw him as an essentially self-centred being who found his fulfilment in the gratification of his ever-increasing and inherently insatiable wants. Second, Gandhi argued that the concept of private property underlying capitalism was logically incoherent. It was based on a misguided notion of self-ownership. Third, for Gandhi, capitalism was an exploitative system propelled by greed and based on the survival of the fittest. It created large-scale unemployment and condemned millions to miserable lives. Fourth, Gandhi thought that the economic order should be embedded in and subordinated to the civilization of the wider society. Indian society was historically unique and different from the Western. India should evolve its own 'humane' and 'spiritual' economy based on values, motivations and self-understanding characteristic of its own people.[23] Parekh also enumerates the principles on which Gandhi's spiritual alterative to capitalism rested. First, every adult had a right to work. Work for him was essential to acquire the basic human qualities such as sense of self-respect, dignity, self-discipline, self-confidence, initiative, and the capacities to organize energies and shape personalities. Second, the economic life should be in harmony with and create conditions necessary for moral and spiritual development. Third, the nature, pace and scale of industrialization should be determined by and subordinated to the requirements of village communities. Fourth, the means of production of the basic necessities of life should be collectively owned. Fifth, since all socially useful activities were equally important, the wage differentials should be reduced to the minimum. And finally,

[22] Parekh, *Colonialism, Tradition and Reform*.
[23] Ibid., 301–302.

since a healthy moral community was impossible in a grossly unequal society, the State had to embark on a programme for levelling up the poor and the oppressed and levelling down the rich.[24] Parekh, thus, provides a convincing explanation of Gandhi's economic ideas. He, however, maintains that Gandhi did not provide a realistic alternative to capitalism. He insists that Gandhi's ideas have enough resources to criticize and transform capitalism radically, but they do not provide a viable alternative to the capitalist model of economy.[25]

Ajit Dasgupta's work *Gandhi's Economic Thought*, which could be seen as the second historic moment in the evolution of the scholarship on Gandhian economic discourse, presents very interesting insights to look at the Gandhian model of economic development.[26] Dasgupta rejects the charge that Gandhi does not provide a realistic alternative to capitalism. He writes:

> ... Gandhi was trying to describe an economic ideal to strive for rather than simply an economic plan to implement. To that extent his economics was utopian. However, 'utopian' can also refer to something 'impractical' or even 'impossible'. Gandhi's economic thought was not 'utopian' in that sense. It was certainly meant to apply to an actual society, that of rural India in particular. It would still apply only to a few selected aspects of that society while neglecting others, but that is true of all economic models.[27]

Thus Dasgupta presents Gandhi's economic discourse as a postulated ideal that can help in achieving clarity in thought and in solving real-life problems. He identifies six foundational principles of the Gandhian model of village-centric economic development. First, though religious terminology is a kind of a 'signature tune' of Gandhian writings, Gandhian worldview in general and economic views in particular are not religious, but ethical in nature. Second, Gandhi insists that economics

[24] Ibid., 302–304.
[25] Ibid., 322.
[26] Dasgupta, *Gandhi's Economic Thought*.
[27] Ibid., 2.

cannot be separated from ethics, but interestingly he also insists that even ethics cannot be separated from economics. Dasgupta insists that Gandhi did not support carrying out of good policies by the method of involving continuing economic loss.

> Gandhi, who worked all his life for the cause of protecting animals, and cows in particular, regarded schemes for conducting tanneries on sound economic lines as essential for the cause to succeed.... Similarly Gandhi strongly opposed the proposal that cotton spinners should also be encouraged to weave, for he believed that this involved economic disadvantage.[28]

Third, according to Dasgupta, Gandhian economic theories were consequentialist rather than deontological; that is, his ideas asserted that the righteousness of a choice depends upon the goodness of its effect on the world and disagreed that the righteousness of an action is intrinsic to the action itself. Gandhi, however, did not subscribe to the consequentialism in the form of utilitarian theories. He rather rejected utilitarianism by saying that there is more to human welfare than pleasure, happiness or preference satisfaction. Fourth, Gandhi's view of the welfare of the society was individualistic rather than collectivist. It was individuals, rather than caste, class, tribe, race or state, who mattered. At the same time, at the level of economic analysis, individual's preference was understood as a preference modified by reflection, corrected by knowledge and experience, and regulated by ethical principles. The natural consequence of this assumption was his assertion for the limitation of wants and adherence to Swadeshi. Fifth, Gandhi did accept altruism and charity as principles for macroeconomic policies but at the same time warned about the harm of misplaced benevolence. 'Such (misplaced) charity actually contributed to poverty, idleness, hypocrisy and crime because if food is available without effort those who are habitually lazy remain idle and become poorer.'[29] This leads to the sixth foundational principle, that is,

[28] Ibid.
[29] Ibid., 33.

the doctrine of bread labour. Gandhi insists that bodily labour is a duty imposed by nature on mankind. Therefore, one must earn one's bread by the sweat of one's brow. Seventh, Gandhi's belief in the primacy of duty does not imply a passive view of rights. He was a supporter of the Fundamental Rights accepted by the Congress in its Karachi Session in 1931. More importantly, he emerges as a supporter of welfare rights (sometimes described as positive rights) such as nutrition, shelter, education and health care which guarantee a decent, minimum level of material welfare for the individual.[30] Naturally, his economic model necessitates availability and accessibility of these rights to all the individuals in the society. And finally, Dasgupta insists that Gandhi's hostility to industrialization and to the use of machinery needs to be interpreted in a large measure as a response to the specific problem of a hugely populated, poverty-ridden society.[31]

Dasgupta thus brings the Gandhian economic discourse out of the duality of realism and idealism as well as that of capital-intensive and labour-intensive models by providing a convincing explanation of its underlying assumptions. He, thereby, attempts to relieve Gandhi from the charge of playing merely a corrective role towards capitalism. Despite this commendable contribution, Dasgupta's comprehension of the ontological principles of the Gandhian economic discourse raises certain issues. Dasgupta has insisted that Gandhi had adhered to methodological individualism,[32] that is, Gandhi's view of the welfare of society was individualistic rather than collectivist. It was individuals, rather than caste, class, tribe, race or state, who mattered. Dasgupta does qualify his position about Gandhi's methodological individualism by adding that Gandhi's individual economic choice is supposed to be an enlightened choice modified by reflection, corrected by knowledge and experience, and regulated by ethical principles. However, in the final analysis he places Gandhi in the

[30] Ibid., 59.
[31] Ibid., 70.
[32] Ibid., 181–183.

framework of methodological individualism. This placement is rather problematic in two ways. First, it tends to ignore Gandhi's insistence on recognizing the context-specific and society-specific nature of social phenomena and the corresponding need to incorporate this historical–geographical difference in the models of development. Second, in the context of a caste-ridden society like India, methodological individualism may also imply indifference towards the role of caste as a collective social phenomenon in shaping economic behaviour. Gandhi's position on caste can be interrogated and debated, but to believe that his model is unsympathetic towards a collective social phenomenon of caste would be unrealistic. Besides, this would conveniently allow ignoring the macro-level transformations that the Gandhian model necessitates.

A more recent work *Gandhian Political Economy: Principles, Practice and Policy* by B. N. Ghosh helps to resolve and transcend this problem; hence it is regarded as the third historic moment in the scholarship on Gandhian economic discourse. Ghosh has preferred to explore Gandhian political economy (henceforth referred to as GPE) over Gandhian economics. He writes:

> Political economy has taken a broader view of the world than economics. If economics is the study of scarcity, wants, equilibrium and competition linked to a narrow theory of human rationality, (heterodox) political economy is more an interdisciplinary analysis of the material and immaterial reproduction of humanity's everyday life set within a geo-social environment.[33]

This position enables Ghosh to recognize the historically different context in which Gandhi developed his economic ideas and thereby relieve Gandhi from the burden of fulfilling the criteria of viability rooted in the Eurocentric models. As far as the methodological premises of GPE are concerned, Ghosh insists that GPE seems to have rationalized transcending the dualism of methodological individualism and methodological

[33] Ghosh, *Gandhian Political Economy*, 7.

collectivism, and incorporating it into its methodological framework. He writes:

> Although methodological individualism becomes the fundamental basis of GPE, it does not remain an isolated or segregated entity. In the social structure that Gandhi was contemplating, no doubt individuals were the ultimate explanatory or ontological units but simultaneously, society or collective welfare was equally a predominant consideration. In the social structure contemplated by Gandhi, life will be like an oceanic circle whose centre will be the individual who will be ready to make sacrifices for the whole society. The integration of individual and society at the collective level is a type of unique methodological specificity of GPE, and here lies one of its fundamental methodological characteristics. Without such integration, the methodological structure would have suffered from the blemishes of methodological dualism.[34]

Ghosh identifies six characteristics of Gandhi's economic ideas. First, the model of economic development needs to be rooted in the historically specific character of society. Second, it needs to address maximization of social welfare in such a way that it would invariably include individual welfare. Third, it needs to oppose concentration of wealth beyond a point of necessity as wealth does not necessarily mean welfare. Fourth, it needs to provide for self-sufficient villages where ecological balance is maintained. Fifth, it should facilitate the promotion of village industries where production, consumption and distribution are confined within villages, and where there is strict control over large-scale industries whenever inevitable. And finally, there would be strict opposition to labour-supplanting machinery.[35]

The Gandhian models of economic development that can be discerned from these three crucial commentaries also necessitates a particular kind of polity. Gandhian theory of State

[34] Ibid., 91.
[35] Ibid., 12–17.

or Gandhi's ideal polity rarely addresses and incorporates his economic ideas. Nor does the discussion of Gandhi's economic ideals necessarily include his critique of parliamentary democracy or his views on State. The understanding of Gandhi's view on capital thereby gets affected. Gandhian critique of capital, his model economic development and his ideal polity are inherently connected with each other. Approaching them in a fragmented manner hampers approaching Gandhi as a system-builder.

From the perspective of the student of political thought, this entire gamut of debate over Gandhi and his ideas is like the proverbial 'Pandora's box'; there are a number of themes—those that are parallel to each other and also those that cross each other's path! Those that complement each other and also those that interrogate each other! When this box is so full of themes, what is it that has not been explored?

The focus of these studies has largely been either on exploring the complex and multifaceted nature of Gandhi's political/economic thought or on making sense of Gandhian themes in the context of the post-1970 theories of social transformation, State, nation and civil society, and on the discourses of secularism, feminism, environmentalism, cultural politics, pacifism and economic development. What is missing from this discourse is the major contributions made by the leading Gandhian stalwarts such as Vinoba Bhave, Acharya Javdekar, Dada Dharmadhikari, Kakasaheb Kalelkar, JP, Shankarrao Deo, J. B. Kripalani, Kishorelal Mashruwala, Sriman Narayan Agarwal, Dhirendra Majumdar, Mira Behn, Prema Kantak and, of course, J. C. Kumarappa, among others, to modern Indian political ideas in general and to Gandhism in particular. These stalwarts still await scholarly attention. A handful of works on Vinoba, JP, Khan Abdul Gafar Khan, J. C. Kumarappa and Prema Kantak have come up, but the framework in which they have been explored and analysed is not essentially that of Gandhism. These Gandhian scholars not only reflected on a variety of issues in political thought, but also substantially contributed to the enrichment of Gandhian thought. The spectrum of their contribution is not only broad, but, contrary to the common understanding, it is also divergent in nature. Despite the divergence what binds the contributors together into a discourse is not only their love for and association with Gandhi but acceptance of two rules. First, all of them agree that the goal which has to be attained needs to accommodate the aspirations of all the sections of the society rather than any particular class, caste, gender group or creed. The goal must address the concerns of each and every section of the society. And second, the means to attain this end has to be non-violent. Beyond adherence to these two rules, this discourse is characterized by divergence in the form of the starting points, concerns, emphases, approaches towards State, party politics and other ideological streams and in a couple of other ways.

A brief overview of the divergence in Gandhism and Gandhi will give an idea of how stupendous and significant the task of exploring this discourse is. Vinoba Bhave (1895–1982), for instance, explores the *sadhak* (seeker) in Gandhi and looks at the public life as another site for attaining the ideal of seeker. He locates the genius in Gandhi in his ability to address the contemporary issues as part of his sadhana. He writes:[36]

> Normally proselytization and revolution are distinct phenomena. Saints and seers have often preached about *samanya dharma* (routine religious practices), but when the need of the hour coincides with the saintly preaching, revolution takes place…. The one who is able to connect the inner strength of religious thought with that of the external circumstances, no longer remains a religious person or merely a pious soul, he emerges as the person of the epoch. Gandhiji was a person of the epoch in this sense.[37]

Vinoba insists that the post-Gandhi period is drastically different than what it was during Gandhi's lifetime. Political

[36] The quotations from the Marathi and Hindi works cited here have been translated into English by the author, except those otherwise mentioned.

[37] Bhave, *Gandhi: Jase Pahile–Janile Vinobanni*, 14–15.

independence, establishment of democratically elected government and advancements in science and technology are the three factors that have changed the context significantly.[38] In such a situation, Vinoba insists that the ideals cherished and practised by Gandhi may require certain alterations to suit our times. He identifies this need specifically in case of the technique of Satyagraha which he insists to develop in a more constructive and subtler manner. He insists that in democracy the technique of Satyagraha is not to be used 'against' someone; it needs to be seen as a complementary tool which can be used at the individual level with love and sacrifice to reform the other. Therefore, there is rarely room to resort to Satyagraha as a tool of mass action.[39] He recommends that the term *agraha* (insistence) be removed from Satyagraha and the practice of *Satya* be made part of the daily routine rather than insisting for it occasionally. Vinoba thus replaces the confrontational dimension of Satyagraha with that of persuasion.

With this viewpoint, Vinoba addressed the issue of land redistribution. While deemphasizing this issue as an issue of confrontational politics, Vinoba gestated *Bhoodan* (land donation) as an aspect of constructive programme to reorganize social relations. To *Bhoodan* he later on added *Sampatti-dan* (donation of wealth), *Sutanjali* (donation of hand-woven yarn), *Shram-dan* (donating one's labour) and *Gram-dan* (donation of the entire village land and its redistribution through Gram Sabha).[40] Though Vinoba always endeavoured to develop a sphere of constructive activities independent of the State, he also stood for the consolidation of the State in Indian society. The placement of persuasion over confrontation also complemented and facilitated the process of consolidation of state in India. Vinoba never joined or even supported any confrontational/ agitational activity in the post-independence period; whether it was Pandharpur Temple-Entry Satyagraha of Sane Guruji (on

---

[38] Ibid., 65.
[39] Ibid., 67.
[40] Bhave, *Sarvodaya Vichar ani Swarajya-Shastra*, 108–112. Also Bhave, *Gramswarajya*.

the eve of Independence, May 1947), Telangana agitations, Samyukta Maharashtra Movement or the anti-Emergency agitations. Vinoba had deeper faith in *Advaita-vad* (unity of being). The practical implication of this faith was his total adherence to the principle of *sarvesham avirodhen* (renunciation from every contradiction and confrontation). Vinoba passionately pleaded for the unity of religions. The numerous tracts that he wrote on Islam (*Kuran-Sar*), Christianity (*Christ-Dharma-Sar*), Sikhism (*Japuji*), Buddhism (*Dhamma-Padam*) as well as on the different religious traditions within Hinduism are testimony to his faith in the unity of religion. In this entire endeavour, however, the issue of eradication of caste-based exploitation and oppression got side-tracked. In his address to the Uttar Pradesh Sarvodaya Conference in November 1951, Vinoba had said, '...even if there cannot be absolute equality, there should not be disproportionate inequality; but there should be equity, even though there is inequality....'[41] With this kind of dialectical approach, Vinoba endeavoured throughout his life for equity and equanimity; this also saved him from any kind of confrontational politics. Vinoba thus emerges as the chief exponent of the non-confrontational Gandhian thought.

Another prominent Gandhian who contributed to this development of Gandhism after Gandhi was Dada Dharmadhikari (1899–1985). He supported most of Vinoba's ideas as well as programmes. Like Vinoba, Dharmadhikari also endeavoured for *vichar-shuddhi* (purity of thought) in the public sphere. The major difference between Vinoba and Dharmadhikari, however, lay in the way they looked at the process of *vichar-shuddhi*. While for Vinoba the path to *vichar-shuddhi* goes through spiritualism, for Dharmadhikari it goes through reason. This is not to say that Vinoba's spiritualism or religious discourse is devoid of rationality; rather reason and rationality is an integral part of Vinoba's life and thought. However, since Vinoba anchors himself in spiritualism, his entire discourse is characterized by some amount of mysticism. Dharmadhikari, on the other hand, speaks more in terms of *buddhi-nishtha* (faith in

[41] Kumarappa, *Sarvodaya: The Welfare of All*, 152–153.

and commitment to reason). He insists that Gandhi's transition from 'God is Truth' to 'Truth is God' is a testimony to his commitment towards *buddhi-nishtha*. He writes, 'Gandhi was committed to Truth, consequently he underwent the process of individuation. The one, who undergoes the process of individuation, transcends singular personality and thus cannot be typified.'[42] He further adds, '*Satya-nishtha* (faith in and commitment to truth) entails in it, commitment towards reason, rather than commitment towards the thought. The commitment for thought leads to sectarianism ... which ultimately gets developed into arrogance.'[43] For Dharmadhikari, the two essential aspects of *buddhi-nishtha*—'spirit of enquiry' and 'humility'—are inherently linked to Gandhi's *satya-nishtha*. Dharmadhikari's apprehensions in accepting one's commitment towards thought, however, does not prevent him from accepting Vinoba's idea of *vichar-shasan* (rule of thought). He accepts this idea but at the same time insists that *vichar-shasan* is characterized by *buddhi-nishta* and *buddhi-pramanya* (rationality).[44] *Vichar-shuddhi* and *vichar-shasan* thus occupy central position in Dharmadhikari's endeavour to realize Sarvodaya.

It is interesting to see that despite the faith in reason and rationality, Dharmadhikari was well aware that mere rationality is not likely to create deeper bonding between members of society. Hence, he insisted for reorganization of society on the principle of humanity rather than material prosperity. He also pleaded for reconstruction of man with an integrated approach. He writes, 'Human personality should become integrated; hence the presence of the two streams of science and poetry should not remain segregated in human mind.'[45] He holds that Indian tradition can play significant role in facilitating such integration at the individual level. At the social level, Dharmadhikari believes that it is the responsibility of Sarvodaya economics to facilitate this integration by organizing economic activities on the

---

[42] Dharmadhikari, *Samagra Sarvodaya Darshan* Vol. 4, 760.
[43] Ibid.
[44] Dharmadhikari, *Sarvodaya Darshan*, 1–15.
[45] Ibid., 92.

principle of fraternity. He identifies three stages in Sarvodaya economics that facilitate organization of fraternity in society. In the first stage, the non-productive classes seize control over the means of production. In the second stage, non-productive occupations cease to exist; while in the third stage nobody in the society remains unproductive.[46] This is possible only when physical labour is contributed as a vow, as a religious duty rather than as a compulsion. Dharmadhikari points out that Sarvodaya considers physical labour as a respectable activity; at the same time, Sarvodaya reorganizes the entire process of production and engages itself with culture to make physical labour a delightful activity.[47] Therefore, he insists that Sarvodaya economics is not only about self-sufficiency, it is also about coexistence.

Dharmadhikari has also paid sufficient attention to the agency through which the Sarvodaya Samaj is to be realized. He considered youths as the agency to realize the Sarvodaya Samaj and conducted a number of workshops for youths and activists, in order to orient them towards the process of change and their role in it. He firmly believed that the person who practices social values religiously gets an insight for recognizing the revolutionary potentials in the situation. Despite Dharmadhikari's attention towards the mechanism and agency of realizing Sarvodaya Samaj, the structural prerequisites of Sarvodaya Samaj did not occupy much of his attention. On the political scene, Dharmadhikari stood by Nehru and despite differences did not find any problem in legitimizing him as Gandhi's heir;[48] but he seems to have concentrated more on the normative content of Sarvodaya Samaj than on the political arrangements and their significance for realizing Sarvodaya Samaj. Unlike Vinoba, Dharmadhikari didn't keep himself totally aloof either from electoral politics or from confrontational politics. He was elected to the Central Legislature in 1945 from Kamathi Parliamentary Constituency (Nagpur) on the instructions of Gandhi, but did not complete the term and

[46] Ibid., 108.
[47] Ibid., 125.
[48] Dharmadhikari, *Samagra Sarvodaya Darshan* Vol. 4, 760.

resigned in the backdrop of a controversy.[49] He was a member of India's Constituent Assembly. The Samyukta Maharashtra Movement had nominated him as the deputy secretary of the Samyukta Maharashtra Committee. He worked on this committee, but at the same time maintained that reorganization of states on linguistic lines doesn't facilitate cooperation, and hence pleaded for equal status to the other languages in the province.[50] Thus, though Dharmadhikari played a crucial role in demystifying the meaning of Sarvodaya, he remained and represented the sceptic overtone within the Gandhian discourse, which, although recognized the necessity and significance of State in facilitating the constitution of Sarvodaya Samaj, never engaged itself either intellectually or politically to shape it.

An approach to Gandhism, distinctly different from the above two approaches, could be located in Acharya S. D. Javdekar (1894–1955), who engaged himself with Gandhism for developing a theory of non-violent State-building and that of revolution. He writes:

Gandhism is a synthesis of spiritual idealism (*adhyatmik adarshvad*) and a pragmatic philosophy of revolution (*vyavaharic krantivad*).... Europe witnessed the evolution of two different revolutionary philosophies in the past three centuries; namely democracy and communism. These philosophies generated optimism in Europe, that by resorting to political violence people can avail their freedom, can establish democracy or communism, and State can be reconstituted on the founding principles of liberty, equality and fraternity. Rousseau, Mazzini and Marx are considered as the founding fathers and proponents of this European philosophy of revolution. In Europe, counter-revolutionary philosophy emerged in the form of nationalism which opposed democracy and communism in the name of religion and spirituality. Today by resorting to violent means, it has created havoc all over the world in the form of capitalism, militarism and imperialism.

[49] See Dada's correspondence with Gandhi in Dharmadhikari, *Manishichi Snehgatha*, 125–132.
[50] Ibid., 146.

The history of Indian nationalism is completely different. By educating nationalism into Satyagraha, Mahatma Gandhi transformed it into a non-violent philosophy of revolution. Under the auspices of this type of nationalism, India is witnessing the rise of democracy and communism, which is constituted on the foundation of *atma-bal* (strength of the soul). When in Europe, democracy and communism have almost been extinguished, there is increasing optimism in India that we shall be able to realise the social goals associated with democracy and communism on the basis of our *atma-bal*. The entire credit for this goes to Gandhism.[51]

Thus, Javdekar provides an interesting interpretation of Gandhism that engages itself intellectually to reconstitute the dominant models of democracy, socialism and nationalism on the principle of non-violence. The rejection of the prevailing models is done, not because these models are alien to this land, but because these models (both democratic as well as communist), based on force, have shown their inherent limitations in the form of Fascism–Nazism as well as through the World Wars. Javdekar points out that at this hour in history, it has been well established that the models of constitutional democracy are useful only for minor reforms. To bring about revolutionary change in the society, these models have become irrelevant, thereby directing people to resort to violent means. On the other hand, the communist model of proletarian revolution culminates into a reign of uncontrolled bureaucracy. The failure of both these models makes it necessary to search for a process of change that transcends the limitations of both these models and ensures a more permanent transformation. Satyagraha as a non-violent technique of revolution provides for an alternative.[52] It is this revolutionary technique that has transcended nationalism.[53]

The thrust on self-purification in the Gandhian discourse is explained by Javdekar by associating it with the traditional

---

[51] Javdekar, *Gandhivad*, 30–31.
[52] Ibid., 40–43.
[53] Ibid., 52.

notion of *yati* (one who practises self-mastery through yoga and austerity). Javdekar points out that in Indian tradition the class that rules is different from the class that has the power of amending the laws of ruling. The responsibility of amending laws was entrusted to the class of *yati*, because they had the *atma-bal* to generate change. As long as the class of *yati* is devoid of the sufficient amount of *atma-bal*, there is bound to remain violence in the society. Javdekar writes:

> As long as the *atma-bal* of the class of *yati* is unable to promote Truth and non-violence in the society, the state-craft [loose translation of the term *raj-dharma*; mine] is bound to remain violent; it is inevitable. In order to remove violence from the state-craft, the prevalence of truth and non-violence in the people has to be intensified. How to constitute citizenship in a non-violent way is a serious question. While the *yati* attempts to raise non-violence with emotive measures, the rulers do it in a negative way, that is, by preventing violence and falsehood. Since the *atma-bal* of the *yati* is insufficient, the rulers are required to resort to the violent means and they become uncontrollable due to the violent force at their disposal. Consequently, it becomes necessary for the people to search for the science of revolution. The science of revolution emanating from violence has proved inadequate in establishing justice in the society, hence there emerges, non-violent science of revolution. The responsibility to lead this revolution rests with the *yati*.[54]

Although Javdekar had some serious reservations in accepting the violent science of revolution approved by the Marxists and communists, he never denied its significance in explaining and analysing the nature of exploitation and inequality in the society. In fact, he strongly asserted the need to integrate the insights emanating from Marxism with Gandhism in order to deepen the egalitarian content of the latter. Similarly, he also asserted the incorporation of the ethical premises of Gandhism

[54] Ibid., 39–40.

into Marxism in order to make it a more holistic philosophy. In his renowned work *Adhunik Rajya-Mimansa* published in 1941, Javdekar raised certain fundamental questions about Gandhism and pointed out that the natural culmination of some of the Gandhian ideas is bound to reach Marxist view on the same issue. In case of the idea of trusteeship, for instance, Javdekar points out that the foundational principle of this idea is the Gandhian belief that the factories cannot be considered as private property of the industrialists, nor can the workers be seen as the personal servants of the capitalists. Gandhism looks at both these classes (owners as well as the workers) as the servants of the society and attempts to reorganize their relations on a more just grounding through the idea of trusteeship. However, this does not mean that Gandhi looks at the idea of trusteeship as an all-time truth. If the strategy of trusteeship fails to establish justice, it will be not be antithetical to the spirit of Satyagraha to withdraw the property rights of the industrialists and establish social ownership of the means of production.[55] Similarly, the Gandhian concept of *asteya* (non-stealing) can also be developed further with Marxian insights.

> ... The three ways of wealth creation—tenancy fees, interest and profit—cannot be eliminated as long as *zamindari*, usury and industrialism persist. Through all of these three ways of wealth creation, wealth is generated without putting any physical labour by the one who appropriates it. A Satyagrahi social order cannot allow these types of mechanisms of wealth-creation which resort to stealing and violence.

In view of this, Javdekar attempts to integrate socialist economics with the philosophy of Satyagraha through his concept of *Satyagrahi Samajvad*.

In Jp (1902–1979) and in his transition from the idea of 'party-less democracy' to that of Total Revolution, Gandhi's quest for the simultaneous growth of the inner self and outer

[55] Javdekar, 'Satyagraha va Samajvad', 215–216.

world could be identified. But more importantly, the lacuna in Javdekar's thought, resulting from the absence of praxis, is overcome by JP with his idea of Total Revolution. At the intellectual level, Javdekar had shown a number of spaces to bring together the two revolutionary philosophies of Gandhism and Marxism, but this formulation did not get transmitted into praxis. Neither the Gandhian movement under the leadership of Vinoba found it necessary to engage itself a bit more positively with the 'materialist' philosophy of Marxism, nor could the Indian communists keep aside the suspicion of counter-revolution and approach Gandhism freely. JP was probably the only thinker–politician who allowed himself to engage and move freely between the two, ideologically as well as politically. In the pre-Independence period, JP had not thought very positively of Gandhi's economic ideas and was more inclined towards socialism. In the post-Independence period, however, he engaged himself with Gandhism in a more serious way. Jayaprakash Narayan's politics played at least three important political functions. First, he attempted to impinge upon the socialists the need to integrate Gandhi's visions of social change into socialism at the level of philosophy, strategy and programme. He asserted that Gandhi was not a social reactionary as seen by the communists; in fact, he was a social revolutionary. In the article entitled 'Socialism and Sarvodaya', written in 1951, JP went to the extent of appealing to the socialists to act as an instrument for the implementation of Sarvodaya Plan developed by the Sarva Seva Sangh.[56] At this point, he did not succeed in bringing Sarvodaya and socialism together politically. However, at a time when the Nehruvian model of heavy industrialization had received almost unconditional acceptance, he reminded the socialists as well as the Congressmen of the need to take Gandhi and Sarvodaya seriously for India's economic regeneration. In his letter to the prime minister on Minimum Programme for National Regeneration, JP could be seen advocating for 'establishing, encouraging and protecting small-scale industries' and

[56] Prasad, *Socialism, Sarvodaya and Democracy*, 93.

for 'promoting the spirit of Swadeshi'.[57] Few years later, this assertion became more constructive, and he started emphasizing the need to implement the model developed by Gandhi and Kumarappa.[58] At the political level, however, by this time JP had started advocating the idea of party-less democracy. He was doubtful about the role political parties could play in creating a new man. Very soon he decided to renounce power politics and joined the Bhoodan Movement. He gave almost 20 years to the Bhoodan Movement as a *jeevandani* (one who has devoted his life to the cause) activist.

The second important function performed by JP is his assertion of the need for lokniti. The idea of *lokniti* was of course conceived by Vinoba. JP saw it as an attempt to generate social revolution. The idea of *lokniti* was in a way an extension of JP's idea of party-less democracy, but it certainly had a more positive and meaningful content. He maintained that confining oneself to the politics only within the corridors of State power ultimately results in making the State more and more powerful. The measure of redistribution adopted by a socialist State in the form of nationalization of means of production overpowers the bureaucracy; while in a democratic State, due to electioneering and parliamentary politics the parties become powerful. Such a power-mongering State can hardly be considered democratic or pro-people. In this context, *lokniti* plays the role of balancing the State power with people's power. JP insists that *lokniti* does not necessarily mean keeping oneself away from politics, but more positively it means engaging oneself in people's politics.

The third crucial function performed by JP was through the contribution of the idea of Total Revolution. He observed that the working class has lost its revolutionary potential and has become a dominant interest. It is inclined to think more in terms of trade unions than in terms of wider social interests. The peasants, on the other hand, do not have realistic understanding of the situation in the country. In such a situation, only

[57] Ibid., 83.
[58] Ibid., 219.

students can take lead in staging a revolution. JP endeavoured incessantly to awaken the students in India to make them realize their constructive role in India's social reconstruction. JP insisted that so far revolutions have concentrated only on changing the external conditions and ignored the necessity to change the human being internally. Total Revolution would aim at bringing about revolutionary change in every aspect of both individual and social life. Jayaprakash Narayan's genius lies in the fact that he attempted to link the dissatisfaction and anger, generated due to the issues such as corruption and black marketing, to a wider issue of social transformation. More importantly, he attempted to revive and reinstate the confrontational dimension of Gandhism.

An overview of the post-Gandhi debates in Gandhism reveals that the Gandhians did share many of the academic concerns on which a wide of range of scholars have conducted their studies in Gandhism. The issues pertaining to the right of disobedience in a democratic society as reflected in Vinit Haksar's work discussed earlier in this chapter appear in Vinoba as practitioner and interpreter of Gandhism. The concerns for radical transformation of Indian society discussed thematically by Pantham occur in the ideas Jawadekar, Dharmadhikari and JP. The ideas of these Gandhians could be analysed and made intelligible in the various theoretical and paradigmatic frameworks as has been done in case of Gandhi himself. However, the way these creative minds have engaged themselves with Gandhism, Gandhism itself emerges as a framework of making sense of their reflections. So rather than presenting a 'liberal Vinoba' or a 'socialist Jawadekar' one may choose to problematize these Gandhian ideas in the framework of Gandhian discourse itself. Present work approaches J. C. Kumarappa from the same viewpoint. Kumarappa has been understood and interpreted in the framework of environmentalism and ecological concerns. Present work attempts to make Kumarappa intelligible in the framework of Gandhism itself. Gandhism thus approached is not a rigid framework of ideas but an evolving discourse shaped by the reflections and practices of Gandhians.

J. C. Kumarappa, a close associate of M. K. Gandhi in all his economic endeavours, was an ignored figure throughout the post-Independence period till recently when historian Ramachandra Guha referred to him as a 'Green Gandhian'.[59] Since then a number of studies have taken cognizance of Kumarappa. Most of these studies have presented him as an advocate of sustainable development, proponent of green economics or supporter of the 'Small is Beautiful' viewpoint. By thus presenting Kumarappa, these studies have shown how contemporary concerns are echoed in Kumarappa's economic ideas. The present work has approached Kumarappa in his own context and has analysed the meaning generated through his dialogue with his contemporaries. Kumarappa's Gandhian colleagues such as Vinoba Bhave, Kishorelal Mashruwalla, JP, Shankarrao Deo, Kaka Kalelkar, Shriman Narayan Agarwal and Vaikunthbhai Mehta reflected on many of the common themes and came up with their own interpretations of Gandhi, his ideals, programmes and strategies. A close reading of various Gandhian journals such as *Young India, Harijan* and *Gram Udyog Patrika*, and both places suggested other published works as well as the correspondence with Gandhi present an interesting interplay of narratives. This intertextuality enables to understand Gandhi in a fresh new light. The present work endeavours to construct and analyse the meaning of Gandhian ideals as generated through this exercise. The rationale for selecting Kumarappa's stand point for this exercise will be clear after knowing Kumarappa's life and works. The next chapter gives a comprehensive overview of the making of J. C. Kumarappa's persona and ideas as well as his location in the galaxy of Gandhians.

---

[59] Guha, *An Anthropologist among the Marxists and Other Essays.*

2

Life and Times of J. C. Kumarappa

Joseph Chelladurai[1] (aka J. C. Kumarappa) was born at Thanjavur (in the then Madras Presidency) in a Protestant Christian Tamil family on 4 January 1892. The Kumarappa family originally belonged to Madurai. The family was living in Thanjavur (in present-day Tamil Nadu) when Kumarappa was born. Thanjavur or the anglicized Tanjore was the capital of the Cholas, Mutharayars, Nayaks and Marathas when they were at the peak of their power. Since then, Thanjavur was one of the chief political, cultural and religious centres of South India. Thanjavur, from the administrative point of view, was a municipality since 1866. It had a first grade college, a training school, a technical institute and a hospital attached to a medical school. Drainage system (since 1840) and pumped drinking water (since 1880)[2] were its urban features, while the

---

[1] Kumarappa was the original name of the family before their ancestors converted to Christianity. Joseph and two brothers decided to keep this family name and made the corresponding declaration in 1929. Since then he was famous as J. C. Kumarappa. Here, he will be referred to as Kumarappa.

[2] Oddie, 'Protestant Missions, Caste and Social Change in India, 1860–1914', 244.

prominence of agriculture as the main occupation of people was its rural characteristic. Thus Thanjavur was a multi-cultural, semi-urban township by the end of the nineteenth century when Kumarappa was born. At the time when Kumarappa was born, it had a population of 54,390 (1891 Census), of which Christians numbered 4,796.[3] It included both the Roman Catholics and the Protestants. Though the Catholics outnumbered the Protestants, the latter were more prominent in the city. This was precisely due to the fact that the Lutheran missionary of the famous Tranquebar Mission, Christian Friedrich Schwartz (1726–1898), had been receiving State patronage from the Maratha King of Thanjavur, Amar Singh Maharaj, and later from his son, Raja Sarbhojee. Schwartz had also received benefaction from the British East India Company and later received patronage from the British imperial government. He was one of the ministers appointed by the British to advise the Thanjavur king.[4] Schwartz had such a close association with Raja Sarbhojee that after his death the king erected a marble monument in the memory of Schwartz in the church within the fort and personally composed the epitaph engraved on the stone.[5] Schwartz had a deeper impact on the public life of Thanjavur. He was the first to translate the Bible into Tamil.[6] He had started a school in Thanjavur. Chandra Mallampalli in his book *Christians and the Public Life in Colonial South India* takes note of Schwartz's impact on the entire Tamil culture. He maintains that by translating Bible into Tamil, Schwartz had indirectly contributed to the formation of Tamil consciousness and thus along with others was actively responsible for the formation of the subnational or regional identity.[7]

Schwartz's presence and his association with the Hindu king speak a lot about the cultural milieu in Thanjavur at the

[3] *The Imperial Gazetteer of India*, Vol. 23, 242.
[4] Thomas, *Christians and Christianity in India and Pakistan*, 160.
[5] Ibid.
[6] *Christian Friedrich Schwartz: Apostle to South India*.
[7] Mallampalli, *Christians and Public Life*, 110.

time of Kumarappa's birth. Besides Schwartz, other Christian missionaries were also active there. The Society for the Propagation of Gospel, the Methodists, the Lutherans and the Roman Catholics had mission stations there.[8] As far as the caste composition of Thanjavur city is concerned, exact figures are not available. As per the 1901 Census (a decade after Kumarappa's birth), when the total population of the Thanjavur district was 2,245,029, the proportion of the non-Brahmin castes was about 50 per cent of the population. It comprised of the labouring castes of *Pariyans* (310,000) and *Pallans* (160,000) as well as the middle-level peasant castes of *Pallis* (235,000), *Vellalas* (2,12,000) and *Kallans* (188,000).[9] Christians were 4 per cent of the population and 86 per cent of them were converted by the Catholic missions.[10] Kumarappa's family being Protestant was in a sense a minority within the minority, albeit, with a considerable influence. The Protestant Christians of Thanjavur came mostly from the *Vellala* caste.[11] The *Vellalas* were landlords, who often collaborated with priestly Brahmins to exert their social dominance over Tamil-speaking localities. They had a unique understanding of Protestant Christianity, fully anchored in the classical traditions of Tamil culture.[12] Even after converting to Christianity, the consciousness of caste distinction was very much present among the Christians of South India. This was true in case of both Roman Catholics as well as Protestants. Irrespective of the continuous attempts made by the Church to declare caste as an aspect of Hinduism and thus heathen, caste practices were observed by the converted Christians. While elsewhere in South India the Church's approach towards caste was of 'extreme concern' and it had declared the 'Heathen' practice of caste as incompatible with 'the spirit of the Gospel', the Lutheran mission (which, as mentioned earlier, was dominant in Thanjavur) had taken

[8] *Gazetteer*, 243.
[9] Ibid., 225.
[10] Ibid.
[11] Mallampalli, *Christians and Public Life*, 8.
[12] Ibid.

conciliatory attitude on the issue. Hence, even the Anglican churches in Madras and Thanjavur had joined them.[13] The survey conducted in the Tanjore Mission in 1828 revealed that in the church the Christians of the high caste sat on the left side of the pulpit, while lower castes sat on the right. The same chalice was used for separate castes, but they went up at different times to the altar. The high-caste Christians refused to intermarry or to eat with the lower-caste converts.[14] The situation had not changed much even at the beginning of the twentieth century. As G. A. Oddie has shown in her paper 'Protestant Missions, Caste and Social Change in India, 1850–1914', various missionary conferences were still showing concern over the presence of caste practices among the Christians.

At the time of Kumarappa's birth, throughout the Madras Presidency, agriculture was suffering from stagnation and impoverishment due to over-assessment of land. It was felt even in the comparatively prosperous district of Thanjavur.[15] As a result of the famine of 1876–1878, the progress of agricultural classes in affected districts and of the landless classes in other parts of the Presidency received a severe check. The Ramine Commission of 1898 in its report had mentioned that the *rayats* of Madras Deccan were still very poor and without resources. In spite of the much publicized reduction and remission in land-revenue assessment, the rate of tax per acre in the *rayatwari* area of Madras was still the highest in India in 1901.[16] Another report of 1904 shows that the number of registered mortgages was particularly high in Coimbatore (645), Madurai (628), Tirunelveli (621) and Thanjavur (517).[17] In the absence of adequate famine-relief measures, heavy migrations took place. From Thanjavur the estimated emigration during the decade

---

[13] Oddie, 'Protestant Missions, Caste and Social Change in India, 1860–1914', 262.

[14] Ibid., 261.

[15] Bhatia, 'Growth and Composition of Middle Class', 343–344.

[16] Ibid., 344–345.

[17] Rajendran, *National Movement in Tamil Nadu*, 20.

1891–1901 was 208,000.[18] Around the same period (in 1904) the Kumarappa family also migrated from Thanjavur to Madras. Mr Solomon was working as an officer in the Public Works Department of the Government of Madras. From Thanjavur he was transferred to Madras.[19] Incidentally, this migration coincided with the migrations that were taking place all over the Madras Presidency due to the famine.

Madras, as compared to Thanjavur, had a purely urban set-up, with trade and commerce as the main source of occupation of its population. Madras was the headquarters of the Madras Presidency (the Presidency of Fort Saint George). As per the 1901 Census, the population of Madras city was 509,346, that is, about 10 times more than that of Thanjavur (57,175).[20] Since 1639, it was the headquarters of the East India Company on the Coromandel Coast. When the East India Company gradually assumed the governmental and judicial functions, the number of officials and their clerical assistants in Madras increased proportionately. A new class of professionals and petty bourgeoisie distinct from traders and craftsmen grew in Madras. In the later half of the nineteenth century, large textile mills were established in the northwest of the city. This again added to the population with the growth in numbers of the industrial workers. The city, however, never became a highly industrialized unit like Bombay due to the absence of any convenient supply of fuel for industries, and the majority of its population remained dependent on commerce and trade.[21]

While Thanjavur with its numerous craftsmen was a centre of inland trade for many years, Madras, on the other hand,

[18] Ibid., 24.
[19] While Kumarappa's biography published during his lifetime mentions that the family moved to Madras due to Mr Solomon's transfer, a recent intellectual biography maintains that the family moved to Madras due his retirement. Govindu and Malghan, *The Web of Freedom*, 13.
[20] *Gazetteer.*
[21] Ranson 'The Growth of the Population of Madras', 321.

being a port was a centre of international trade for centuries. Thanjavur's contact with the foreigners came mainly through the Christian missionaries, while in Madras foreign traders and administrators were numerous, in addition to the missionaries. The commercial and industrial enterprise as well as the banking sector in Madras was dominated by the Europeans and sparsely also by Brahmins; while in Thanjavur, trade, commerce and banking were in the hands of the upper castes and modern mechanized industry was yet to make its appearance there.[22] In Madras, the pace of capitalist development was slow as compared to the cities such as Bombay and Calcutta, but it was certainly rapid in comparison to Thanjavur.[23] Though Thanjavur was not totally unaffected by the capitalist developments, the feudal set-up was very much a part of its socio-economic milieu. In Madras, on the other hand, mercantile capitalism was in the process of paving the way for industrial capitalism. Madras was also a centre of high learning. The Madras University was constituted as early as in 1840, and by the turn of the century the number of students graduating from its colleges was the second highest in the entire country.[24] The migration as well as the depressing surroundings must have made the already compassionate Kumarappa family more sensitive about the society at large and also about the gross inequalities that had emerged around these times. When the Kumarappa family migrated to Madras, Joseph Kumarappa was about 12 years old. The agricultural recession and poverty, the migration as well as the difference between the two social set-ups seem to have left lasting impressions on his mind.

Joseph Kumarappa's mother played a very crucial role in developing his sensitive mind. J. C. Kumarappa has written how his mother always insisted on donating at least one-tenth of the income for charity.

[22] Bhatia, 'Growth and Composition of Middle Class', 345–346.
[23] Ibid., 347 and 349.
[24] Ibid., 352. (Number of graduates from 1857 to 1888: Bengal Presidency 6,142, Madras Presidency 3, 886, Bombay Presidency 1,471.)

[...]Once when I was spending a summer holiday with her at Kodaikanal in the early twenties, on a Sunday at Church announcement was made that China was visited by a terrible famine. That day the noon dinner was a perfect feast. We could not assign any reason for this. When we enquired mother smilingly replied 'I shall explain later.' We enjoyed our nap. Then at tea time, mother called us together and told us of this famine in China and contrasted it with sumptuous meal we ourselves had enjoyed and invited us to help in feeding the distressed in China. She brought out a subscription list with amounts set against our several names according to her conception of our respective ability to pay the sum immediately. She had put me down for fifty rupees and took it too. Besides such personal contributions, she made us go round and collect from our friends also. She used her mother-love to goad us on. This was the home-training.[25]

Both of Joseph's parents were devout Christians. From both maternal as well as paternal ancestors Kumarappa had a deep affinity with Christianity. His mother was a descendent of the famous Vednayaga Sastriyar family.[26] Vednayaga Pillai (1774–1864), later given the title of *Sastri*, was a prominent figure in the Protestant Tamil Christian community. He had enacted Christian teachings through the medium of Tamil folk and classical traditions, thus playing a pivotal role in spreading the message of Jesus in the Tamil-speaking region of the Madras Presidency.[27] J. C. Kumarappa's paternal lineages also had deep association with Christianity. His paternal grandfather, John Cornelius, was a reverend. J. C. Kumarappa's father was the Secretary of the Indian Christian Association and the Indian Christian Provident Fund.[28] J. C. Kumarappa's affiliations on the one hand with the Vednayaga Sastri tradition and

[25] Vinaik, *The Gandhian Crusader*, 35.

[26] Ibid., 34.

[27] Mallampalli, *Christians and Public Life*, 116–117. Also see 'Brief History of Sashtriyars'.

[28] Vinaik, *The Gandhian Crusader*, 34–37.

on the other with a Christian clerical tradition are of crucial significance. These affiliations placed him at the hotbed of the debates that were taking place within the Tamil Protestant Christianity in the mid-nineteenth century—the debates in which if the Church represented the Eurocentric view of Christianity, Vednayaga Sastri stood for its Indianized avatar.[29]

Throughout his life Christianity continued to dominate Kumarappa's worldview. The way Kumarappa approached and comprehended the issue of inequality and exploitation in his later life, and the virtue of dispassionate service that he practised all his life with a missionary zeal showed his deep association with Christianity. Kumarappa had written a number of essays reinterpreting Christian dogma. Moreover, the typology[30] of socio-economic systems developed by Kumarappa, among other factors, also echoes Christian humanitarian ethos. The roots of this anchorage could be traced to his parental and familial religious convictions. His parents inculcated in Kumarappa typically Christian humanitarian values.

The impact of Christianity, initiation from mother into social service and migration from a small town to a metropolis at a sensitive age are some of the factors that help us understand the evolution of the personality of Joseph Cornelius Kumarappa. These factors throw light on why Kumarappa, a successful chartered accountant, left his practice in the middle of his rising career and joined Gandhi in his experiments in village reconstruction; how a person from urban middle-class back-ground developed deep concern about the agonies of Indian

---

[29] See Peterson, 'Between Print and Performance'.

[30] A fully developed version of this classificatory scheme appeared in Kumarappa's *Why the Village Movement?* (1936) and *Economy of Permanence* (1945), but its indicators could be sensed in Kumarappa's postgraduate dissertation 'Public Finance and India's Poverty' written in 1928 before meeting Gandhi. Kumarappa's professor at the Columbia University, Herbert J. Davenport, had used similar terms in his work. Davenport's role in Kumarappa's intellectual development has been discussed later in this chapter.

villages. The familial upbringing and peer-group socialization had developed the core of Kumarappa's personality into a sensitive being. His social commitment, however, was not a product of mere emotional orientation; it had a definite cognitive and evaluative base generated from his education and intellectual development. The study of economics equipped Kumarappa with the tools of analysing and explaining the dynamics of British colonialism and the consequent impoverishment of the Indian economy.

Kumarappa attended the Christian College at Madras for his undergraduate studies. The management of the college was supportive of the British imperialism; however, a section of students of the Christian College were active in the nationalist movement. The developments in the Swadeshi Movement of 1905 were given publicity in the annual college magazine. The CID files of that time report of an incidence in the debating union of the college when a student talked of the British despotism.[31] The management of the college being unsympathetic to such nationalist activities immediately expelled those students from the college. Kumarappa later wrote that he was drilled to believe in 'the trusteeship of the British Government, their well-meaning bureaucracy and their God-sent mission'.[32] There is no record of Kumarappa participating in any nationalist activity during his college years, which in fact was in correspondence with the general trend in Christian community of South India at that time.[33]

In 1912, Kumarappa went to London and became a chartered accountant. He practised there in 1918–1919 in a firm of accounts and auditors. In 1919, after the end of the First World War, he returned to India. Initially, he started working with a Bombay-based accounting firm as an employee and also as a lecturer in accountancy in Davar's College of Commerce. Around 1924 he opened his own firm in Bombay named

[31] Rajendran, *National Movement in Tamil Nadu*, 76–77.
[32] Vinaik, *J. C. Kumarappa and His Quest for World Peace*, 9.
[33] Mallampalli, *Christians and Public Life*, 87–100.

'Cornelius & Davar'.[34] He ran his practice in Bombay until 1926 when he left India for the USA. Kumarappa's elder brother J. M. Cornelius[35] was in the USA for his studies. Kumarappa joined him for holidays. He, however, could not sit idle for long. After a month or so, he wanted some concrete work for himself and joined the Syracuse University for the BSc degree in business administration. His studies included a course in public finance. He graduated successfully from this university in 1928.[36] His professor of public finance, Professor Harvey W. Peck, found in him an excellent student and a man of mature judgement, wide experience and broad culture. Professor Peck recommended that Kumarappa should pursue his further studies at Columbia University.[37] Thus Kumarappa moved to the Columbia University, New York, to study public finance.

Kumarappa's stay in New York is crucial in understanding his intellectual development precisely for two reasons. First, his economic ideas got consolidated during this period through the interactions with two of the professors of Columbia University—Professor Herbert Joseph Davenport (1861–1931) and Professor Edwin Robert Anderson Seligman (1861–1939). Second, his impressions about the benevolence of the British Empire (inculcated by the studies at Doveton College, Madras) drastically changed during this period. Both the professors at the Columbia University were well-known economists. Herbert J. Davenport was a leading, albeit somewhat iconoclastic, economist of his day.[38] He had a broader intellectual background compared to other economists. He had studied law and written

---

[34] Ibid.

[35] Like J. C. Kumarappa, two of his brothers also later took up the name Kumarappa. Elder brother J. M. Kumarappa (1890–1954) later worked as a faculty member of Tata Institute of Social Sciences, Mumbai. He was also a member of the Rajya Sabha between 1952 and 1954. The younger brother, Bharatan Kumarappa (1896–1957), was part of the Gandhian Movement and activities at Wardha.

[36] Vinaik, *The Gandhian Crusader*.

[37] Lindley, *J. C. Kumarappa*, 6–7.

[38] Samuels, 'Davenport, Herbert Joseph', 749.

on language and logic in addition to his study of economics. He had acted as the president of the American Economic Association in 1920. He was a close friend of the famous economist Thorstein Veblen and was also influenced to a large extent by his ideas. Professor Davenport like Veblen considered human desires and productive capabilities as the real forces in economy and insisted that market is not governed merely by the law of demand and supply. In the book *The Economics of Enterprise* (1914), Davenport had argued, 'Institutions [...] are a working consensus of human thought or habit, a generally established attitude of mind and a generally adopted custom of action, for example, private property, inheritance, government, taxation, competition, credit.'[39] Davenport thus challenged the market-centred understanding of economics and supported a more human-centred view. Davenport, however, held that the purpose of production was to increase purchasing power and no moral or social considerations should be applied to it. Kumarappa had serious reservations about this view. He was not ready to accept that man is merely a wealth-producing agent; he strongly believed that man is essentially a member of society with political, social, moral and spiritual responsibilities.[40] There were a number of incidences of arguments between Professor Davenport and Kumarappa in a seminar over the purpose of production.[41] Kumarappa insisted that morality and ethics cannot be bifurcated from economics. Despite these differences, Kumarappa looked upon Davenport as a great contributor to his thinking, someone who 'drove him from complacently being a party to capitalistic and imperialistic organisations'.[42]

Davenport's contribution in Kumarappa's intellectual development is twofold. First, Davenport introduced Kumarappa to a non-Marxist critique of market economy.

[39] Davenport, *Economics of Enterprise*.
[40] Vinaik, *J. C. Kumarappa and His Quest for World Peace*, 11–12.
[41] Vinaik, *The Gandhian Crusader*, 41.
[42] Ibid.

Second, and more importantly, the classificatory scheme of the economic systems that Kumarappa developed in his later life[43] was influenced to a very large extent by Professor Davenport. The nomenclatures of the first three types—Parasitic Economy, Predatory Economy and Economy of Enterprise—were borrowed from Professor Davenport.

Another important personality at the Columbia University that influenced Kumarappa was Professor E. R. A. Seligman,[44] someone who combined a life of distinguished scholarship with philanthropy and active participation in a variety of reform causes.[45] Seligman seems to have influenced Kumarappa's thinking in a still deeper way. He influenced Kumarappa's views about public finance, but more crucially he shaped Kumarappa's notion of the 'economic'. Seligman's influence on Kumarappa is hitherto understood mostly in the context of taxation policies.[46] Seligman was Kumarappa's supervisor for his master's degree dissertation entitled 'The Contribution of Public Finance to the Present Economic State of India'.[47] Hence, it was but natural that Kumarappa's views on taxation were influenced by Seligman. At the same time, however, Seligman's views on the process of social change also seem to have had a deeper impact on Kumarappa directly and indirectly.

Seligman was known for his contribution to public finance; at the same time, he had his own understanding of the evolution of human history. He was a strong exponent of economic historicism. In an article named 'Economic Interpretation

[43] In *Economy of Permanence* (1945), Kumarappa classified economies into five types: Parasitic Economy, Predatory Economy, Economy of Enterprise, Economy of Gradation and Economy of Service. All these have been discussed later in this work.

[44] Incidentally, Professor Seligman also happened to be the supervisor of Dr B. R. Ambedkar's doctoral thesis.

[45] Coats, 'Seligman, Edward Robin Anderson', 300.

[46] Lindley, *J. C. Kumarappa*, 15–19.

[47] This dissertation was serialized in the *Young India* between November 1929 and January 1930, and later published in book form with the title *Public Finance and India's Poverty*.

of History', published in *Political Science Quarterly* in 1901, Seligman had critically reflected upon various historicists such as Hegel, Henry Thomas Buckle[48] and Karl Marx. In this article, Seligman rejects Hegel's idealist interpretation of history as unscientific and something that is not in sync with the ethos of the age. He frequently quotes Buckle's geographical interpretation of history, but rejects it in want of an explanation for the unequal distribution of wealth. He accepts Marxist interpretation of history, but insists that the Marxist notion of the 'economic' needs to be understood in a wider sense. For him, the term 'economic' includes not merely the means of production but also the geographical, natural (= environmental) and social factors as well as the production relations. To substantiate his arguments in addition to *Das Kapital*, Seligman cites German correspondence of Engels between 1890 and 1894. Seligman criticizes the commentators of Marx for reducing Marxist approach to history to a deterministic and tool-centric view. He discards it as technology-centred approach to history and propounds a more comprehensive view to include nature.[49] For Seligman, physical environment and geography emerge as part of the structural aspects of economy. It is necessary to note that Seligman was well-versed in German and French in addition to English. He had taught at German and French universities and had access to Marx's original writings. Interestingly, in this article, Seligman refers to some of the early writings of Karl Marx, which became available to the English-speaking world only around the 1950s. Seligman also refers to some of the German commentaries on the early writings of Marx. In this article he makes a clear distinction between young Marx

[48] Henry Thomas Buckle (1821–1862) was a British historian and author of the incomplete work 'History of Civilization'. He had considered climate, soil, food and other aspects of nature as the primary sources of intellectual progress.

[49] Seligman, 'Economic Interpretation of History', 16 (1901): 612–640; 17: 71–98, 284–312.

and old Marx.[50] Seligman insists that Marx (and even Engels) has used the term 'economic' in a very wider sense to include the geographical and environmental aspects. From the above essay, it becomes evident that the sources of Seligman's environmental awareness[51] lie in an eclectic understanding of Marx and these concerns are therefore very much 'material' in nature. As far as Kumarappa's approach towards nature and environment is concerned, similar traits could be found. His concern for environment is very much rooted in the material aspects of human life and is anthropocentric in nature.

Seligman's allegiance to Marx was however limited in nature. In fact, in a public debate 'Capitalism vs. Socialism' with Professor Scott Nearing on 23 January 1921, Seligman had clearly rejected socialism in favour of capitalism.[52] The discussion of his argument for capitalism and against socialism will be out of place here. However, the crucial point that emerges from this debate is: Seligman's thrust on progressive taxation was an attempt to remove the weaknesses of capitalism. In this debate, he insists that for the abolition of that leisure class which emerges under capitalism the State must levy high taxes on the rich, propertied classes.[53] This he called as progressive taxation. He believed that if, in addition to this, the other measures suggested by him are followed there will emerge what he calls 'progressive capitalism'.[54] Kumarappa in his writings has often insisted on progressive taxation.

---

[50] The terms 'young Marx' and 'old Marx' became popular in the late 1950s when Nikita Khrushchev initiated the process of de-Stalinization of Marxism. It is interesting and surprising that Seligman had used the same terms more than 50 years before. Seligman locates young Marx in the tradition of anthropology and German historicism, while old Marx he believes was more occupied in aligning himself with socialism. See 'Economic Interpretation of History'.

[51] According to Mark Lindley, Seligman was actively involved in the forest conservation movement.

[52] *Public Debate between Prof. ERA Seligman and Prof. Scott Nearing.*

[53] Ibid., 14.

[54] Ibid., 41–42.

The purpose of discussing E. R. A. Seligman's writings at length is threefold: First, it provides a framework to comprehend Kumarappa's awareness towards the significance of natural resources. Second, it deciphers his influence on Kumarappa's taxation policies. And third, it also provides a point of reference to understand Kumarappa's views on Marxism–socialism. As far as the first two dimensions of Seligman's influence are concerned, Kumarappa's postgraduate dissertation 'Public Finance and India's Poverty'[55] proves to be an ideal case though not the only case. This work characteristically represents Seligman's influence on Kumarappa's thinking, particularly in the context of environment protection and that of taxation. In the introduction to this work, Kumarappa has specifically insisted on the need to protect natural resources. He writes, 'With its aid (the aid of the science of Public Finance) the Government should husband resources of the land, as short-sighted private ownership might waste and exhaust them in a brief period of time.'[56] He also adds that the loss of natural resources is a loss of the entire humanity and not merely of the country which owns them. The idea of progressive taxation has also paved the way for itself in this work. Kumarappa writes:

> [...] the taxes should rise as the vapour from sea, from the section of the populace who could best pay, and should be precipitated like rain on the needy, as when the rich taxed to pay for the education of the poor [...] It would be sheer folly to extract a rupee from a man on the subsistence level, to whom that unit represents great marginal utility, and to spend it so as to afford benefit to one who is much better off. There would be a waste of national income rupee by rupee [...].[57]

In this work, Kumarappa has shown how the colonial government 'wasted national income rupee by rupee' through

---

[55] The quotations cited with reference to this dissertation are from its published version 'Public Finance and Our Poverty'.
[56] Kumarappa, *Public Finance and Our Poverty*, 1.
[57] Ibid., 3–4.

its anti-people tax regimes and 'imperial' expenditure. Interestingly, while writing about the flaws in the colonial taxation policy, Kumarappa has categorically criticized the salt tax; its significance is well evident considering his later association with Gandhi.[58]

After completing this dissertation and securing the degree in business administration, Kumarappa returned to India in 1928. He wanted to publish his dissertation. One of his friends Mr C. H. Sopariwalla suggested him to see Gandhi in this regard.

Kumarappa met Gandhi for the first time in 1929. Kumarappa had written to Gandhi seeking his advice on the publication of the thesis and had sought a consultation on 'the way he could best serve the country'.[59] Gandhi met Kumarappa at the end of May 1929. He appreciated Kumarappa's work and told him that his thesis would be serialized in *Young India*.[60] In this meeting Gandhi told Kumarappa to undertake an economic survey of rural areas of Gujarat. He was asked to meet Kaka Kalelkar, the then Vice Chancellor of Gujarat Vidyapeeth,[61] and Shankarlal Banker, the then Secretary of All India Spinners' Association (AISA), regarding his prospects of joining either of the institutions. Kalelkar invited him to join the Vidyapeeth. At the suggestions of his elder brother and partner Dorab Davar, Kumarappa decided to join the Vidyapeeth on probation.[62] Kumarappa joined Gujarat Vidyapeeth at the end of 1929 which opened a new chapter in his life. Under the auspices of the Gujarat Vidyapeeth, Kumarappa undertook the survey of the Matar taluka of Kheda district (Gujarat). For this survey a committee was appointed under the chairpersonship of

[58] Ibid., 34–35.
[59] Kumarappa Papers, NMML, Subject File No. 5, 56.
[60] 'Public Finance and Our Poverty' was serialized in *Young India* from 28 November 1929 to 23 January 1930.
[61] Gujarat Vidyapeeth was a national university established by Gandhi in 1920 to impart national education. Gandhi was its lifelong chancellor.
[62] Kumarappa Papers, NMML, Subject File No. 5, 58–60.

Vallabhbhai Patel. The committee comprised of Mahadevbhai Desai and Narhari Parikh as its secretaries while Kumarappa as the director. The Vidyapeeth made available the sum of ₹4,000 for this survey.[63] Mahadevbhai Desai wrote about this survey in *Young India* on 28 November 1929 and explained the reasons for choosing Matar taluka. He mentions three reasons for choosing Matar: First, due to its debatable history of revenue settlement; second, its impoverished conditions and third, because of government's ignorance despite official acknowledgement of poverty.[64] Desai points out that the first revenue settlement for the district took place in 1862–1863 and revision in 1893–1894 when the assessment was enhanced. In 1913, the commissioner recognized that the revised assessment in Matar and Mehmadabad was higher than lands can generally bear. Hence he ordered a fresh resettlement. In 1916 the settlement officer reported that from 1898 to 1915, there were only five normal years when rainfall was adequate and for five years (1899, 1901, 1904, 1914 and 1915) there was general crop failure. Despite these crop failures 799 penalty notices, 88 distrains and 306 forfeitures were issued in the year 1913–1914. Desai further mentions that the percentage of land lying fallow went up from 8.21 per cent in 1893 to 21.46 per cent in 1916. There was a steady decline in the produce of rice from 21.44 per cent in 1893 to 13.73 per cent in 1916, while the population went down strikingly from 79,080 in 1891 to 61,522 in 1901 and to 58,705 in 1911.[65] Mahadevbhai Desai then cites a list of remarks of government officers ranging from the local settlement officer to district settlement commissioner, who though acknowledged that the assessment was high, still did not reduce the tax. Mahadevbhai Desai makes a very pertinent comment here; he writes, 'The wonder is that there has not been an agrarian rebellion.'[66]

---

[63] Kalelkar, prefatory note in Kumarappa, *A Survey of Matar Taluka*, iv.
[64] Desai, 'An Economic Survey', 389–390.
[65] Ibid.
[66] Ibid., 390.

Mahadevbhai Desai's observations and comments sufficiently explain why Gandhi must have found it necessary to undertake such survey despite and amidst the political turmoil that was taking place around this time. The survey, the serialization of 'Public Finance and Our Poverty' and the very encounter between Gandhi and Kumarappa at that particular historical juncture had its own role in the general transition of Gandhi's political position that was taking place around this period.[67] A brief discussion of this transition is therefore necessary.

Throughout 1929 (around the time when Kumarappa met Gandhi for the first time), Congress and Gandhi were debating over the issues of dominion status versus complete independence, the formula for communal representation, the nature of the federation and so on. There were a large number of divisions even within the Congress on these issues but the common context of the debate was that of power sharing. At the end of January 1930 (when 'Public Finance and Our Poverty' was getting serialized in *Young India* and the preparations for the rural survey were on its way), Gandhi formulated 11 demands, which, he insisted, epitomized independence. They concerned the liquor trade, exchange rate, land revenue, salt tax, custom duties, coastal shipping, military expenditure, civil service salaries, political prisoners, the criminal expenditure department and the embargo on armaments. These 11 demands made no reference to constitutional issues which were getting widely debated at that time.[68] On the other hand, these demands summed up the essence of Britain's economic exploitation of India and the violent methods by which she enforced it. Motilal Nehru saw this transition 'more like surrender than anything

[67] For a detailed discussion of this transition, see Moore, *The Crisis of Indian Unity*.

[68] In the introductory note to the first part of the serialization of the 'Public Finance and Our Poverty' in *Young India*, Gandhi pre-empts this transition when he writes, 'So long this crushing burden is not removed there is no Swaraj, *whether one calls it by the name of Dominion Status or Independence.*' (Emphasis added). See *Young India* 11, no. 48: 391.

else'. In his letter to Jawaharlal Nehru he had lamented about the fact that after the grand Lahore independence resolution and the pledge, Gandhi seemed to have 'gone back to the Delhi Manifesto only in greater details, with perhaps the addition of one or two fresh items'.[69] Gandhi, however, wrote to Jawaharlal Nehru, 'I never thought you would miss the importance of the 11 points.'[70] As anticipated by Gandhi this 11-point agenda proved instrumental in creating a sense of common interest against the British. It bridged the fissures within the nationalist movement. Even the Federation of Indian Chamber of Commerce and Industry extended its support to the Civil Disobedience Movement. Not only G. D. Birla, but also Sir Purushottamdas Thakurdas[71] resigned from the assembly when an ordinance to reimpose the Press Act (1910) was introduced. Sir Thakurdas, in one of his letters, has mentioned that the views of his electorate—'the vast Indian commercial community'—had forced him to the decision that he must resign from the assembly.[72]

It is thus clear that by emphasizing and articulating the economic aspect of the colonial exploitation Gandhi removed the clog over the issue of power sharing from the path of the nationalist movement, thereby taking it to another pedestal. This amounted to the widening of the support base for the movement. The significance of Kumarappa's association with Gandhi could be understood in this particular context. It's not that the economic dimension of the colonial exploitation was brought to the notice for the first time. Starting from Dadabhai Naoroji and Mahadev Govind Ranade, the economic drain had been highlighted by many others before Kumarappa. Even Gandhi had written a number of times in

[69] Ibid., 167.
[70] Ibid.
[71] The resignation of Purushottam Thakurdas is specifically significant because Sir Thakurdas was one of the forerunners of the Anti-Non-Cooperation Society set up in 1920. See Bhattacharya, *Cotton Mills and Spinning Wheels*, 1828.
[72] Ibid., 173.

Young India and elsewhere about India's deindustrialization, its social implications, the unfair free trade policy and the need for tariff protection and so on. Hence what Kumarappa put forth through his thesis was not unknown to Gandhi. But with Kumarappa joining in, Gandhi found a dependable hand for articulating his economic ideas in greater details and in a disciplined manner. In Kumarappa he found an ally who even after walking on a different path had arrived at the same conclusions as he had. The 'truth' that the training in economics and faith in Christianity had unleashed before Kumarappa was no different than what Gandhi had realized through his interactions with the masses. It was, therefore, quite natural that Kumarappa's association with Gandhi, which had started with the publication of the former's thesis, became deeper and stronger over the years.

As mentioned earlier, the first task that Gandhi assigned to Kumarappa was that of the economic survey. Kumarappa along with the two students of the Gujarat Vidyapeeth (from the rural service course) personally visited 54 villages in the Matar taluka between December 1929 and March 1930 to collect data. Kheda district with its richly fertile *charotar* tract[73] was a comparatively well-irrigated and prosperous district. Since the 1890s, a high acreage of land was under non-food crops—tobacco and cotton in particular—which had brought prosperity to the entire district. But despite prosperity the agriculturalists had suffered heavily in the famine in the years between the two Wars. As mentioned earlier, the peasants had complaints about the land revenue policy of the government. Land under cultivation was relinquished as the revenue assessment was too high. On the political front, the peasants in this district had had the experience of Gandhi's 1918 Peasant Satyagraha. The Bardoli Satyagraha (1928) was a more recent example of peasant unrest in the adjoining district when Kumarappa was planning for a survey. In addition to the peasant agitations at Bardoli,

[73] Kheda was traditionally known as Charotar. It had rich fertile soil and was sufficiently irrigated with the rivers Shedhi, Vatrak and Mahi.

the overall environment was generally charged as Gandhi had already started the first phase of the Civil Disobedience Movement. Peasants of Matar had participated in the Civil Disobedience Movement. In fact, the government repression had worked with a special virulence in the Matar taluka.[74] During the period when Kumarappa was visiting the villages to collect data, Gandhi was planning for the Dandi March. Matar was one of the halting points in the Dandi March.[75] Naturally, with this survey Kumarappa was exposed to the hotbed of the political activities along with the plight of rural India. He got first-hand information about the agricultural practices, crop patterns and indebtedness in the Indian agriculture. But more importantly, with this survey, Kumarappa was exposed to the causes of rural unemployment, the necessity to provide opportunities for rural employment supportive to farming and the colonial government's complete unresponsiveness towards the masses.

Another interesting aspect of this survey would be Kumarappa's sensitivity towards the caste dimensions in the agricultural relations in this part of Western India. He mentions Patidars and Dharalas as the main agricultural castes in the Matar taluka.[76] He takes note of the presence of Muslim agriculturalists in good numbers 'in amity and goodwill with other communities'. Similarly, he also identifies the presence of the Rajputs (known as Garasias by the locals), Brahmins, Banias, Thakkars, Shepherds, Dheds, Chamars and Barbers in small numbers in agriculture. In addition to being aware about the social composition of the Matar taluka, Kumarappa also takes note of the class dimension of these castes and result-ant benefits that these castes are able to extract from their economic activity. While pointing out the sheer apathy of the British agriculture department towards the issues of rural credit, availability of seeds, manure and so on, Kumarappa writes:

[74] Kalelkar, prefatory note in Kumarappa, *A Survey of Matar Taluka*, vi.
[75] *Collected Works of Mahatma Gandhi* (CWMG), 1930, Vol. 48, 392–393.
[76] Kumarappa, A Survey of Matar Taluka, 3.

The Banias who supply seeds on credit expect 25 per cent more grains returned to them by way of interest. The transaction, as it requires no cash capital, is more attractive to the farmers generally. As a rule, the Patidars who form the better class of farmers, preserve part of their previous year's grain for seeds, while the Dharalas and others, who are financially weak, find the claims for food too heavy on their stock of grain to enable them to save their own seeds.[77]

From later studies it has been found that around the same period when Kumarappa surveyed these villages, the contradictions between the Patidars on the one hand and the Rajputs, Kolis, Dharalas on the other were coming to the forefront.[78] The Dharalas from amongst whom most of the agricultural labour came were categorized as criminal by the British. As against this, by adapting to the market forces, the Patidars who were at arm's length from the Dharalas in the caste hierarchy[79] had risen high, leaving behind their traditional competitors. This deeply affected a number of socio-economic and political processes. The traditional patron–client relationship was particularly absent between the Patidar landowners and Dharala labourers.[80] As Epstein rightly observes, the apathy of the Dharalas towards the nationalist movement was characterized by the dimension of caste contradictions between the middle castes and the toiling castes. Similarly, it had also affected the unfolding of the rural labour processes in this part.

The focus of Kumarappa's study was to assess the economic dimension of rural and agricultural practices in the context of the British colonial policies; obviously he did not indulge into sociological analysis of the patterns of political mobilization. It is also necessary to remember here that the sociological

[77] Ibid., 15.
[78] See, for instance, Hardiman, *Peasant Nationalists of Gujarat, Kheda District 1917–1934*. Also Gidwani, 'The Quest for Distinction', 145–168.
[79] Epstein, *The Earthy Soil*, 28.
[80] Ibid.

categories which are readily available to the later historians for analysing the unfolding of various events were not present in Kumarappa's period. The significance of Kumarappa's survey lies in the fact that it exposed the apathy of the British colonial administration towards Indian agriculture and thus substantiated the nationalist critique of the colonial administration. Second, it exposed the myth of the prosperity of the Charotar tract by highlighting the imbalances and variations even within this small geographical locality. Third, it gave an insight into the degree of commercialization of agriculture in this period and its possible contribution in bringing prosperity to the region. Finally, at a personal level it impinged in Kumarappa the dire need for rural economic regeneration.

As mentioned earlier in this chapter, Christianity was one of the crucial factors that shaped Kumarappa's worldview right from his childhood. The Civil Disobedience Movement launched by Gandhi was essentially a moral appeal to one's sense of justice in the midst of the repressive policies of the colonial rulers. This stirred Kumarappa to reflect on how a faithful Christian should response to the call of civil disobedience from one's sense of justice. In the midst of the Civil Disobedience Movement, Kumarappa wrote a number of articles in the weekly journal *Indian Social Reformer* about the duties of the true Christians towards the Civil Disobedience Movement. A debate was going on in the *Indian Social Reformer* since mid-1929 regarding the role of Christianity and the Church in India. Kumarappa joined the debate by appealing to Christian workers and missionaries to condemn the brutalities against the non-violent activists of the Civil Disobedience Movement.[81] Kumarappa's appeal generated intense debate about Christianity and civil disobedience in which a number of missionaries from all over India participated. In response to this debate, Kumarappa wrote:

---

[81] Kumarappa, 'Police Violence: An Appeal to All Christian Workers and Missionaries', 553.

[...] Perhaps you do not wish to follow Christ to the extent of non-violence. You'll forgive me if I say most of our missionaries and other leaders of the Christian Church seem to be Britishers first and Christians afterwards if convenient. They themselves are a product of a civilisation based on violence and so are not able to fully appreciate and interpret Christ's teaching on the subject.[82]

Kumarappa's approach to Christianity is discussed in Chapter 5 of this work. This episode was the first expression of his unique engagement with the religion of the Christ.

Kumarappa's interpretation of Christianity in the context of the Civil Disobedience Movement, along with his approach to the economic survey of Matar taluka, brought him closer to Gandhi. In April 1930, Gandhi asked Kumarappa to write regularly for *Young India* and help Mahadevbhai Desai in editing the newspaper, which eventually Kumarappa did. When Mahadevbhai Desai and later Gandhi were arrested in the Civil Disobedience Movement, Kumarappa shared the editorial responsibility of *Young India* with Jayaramdas Doulatram, Mira Behn and others.[83] Kumarappa's writings in *Young India* during this period amounted to a powerful critique of colonialism. This critique was rooted on the one hand in an astute analysis of the British economic policies, while on the other in moral foundations of the Christian dogma. Some Gandhians however did not approve of Kumarappa's style of writing. Mira Behn, for instance, felt that Kumarappa's writings were unnecessarily

[82] Kumarappa, 'Christianity and Civil Disobedience', 619–620.
[83] Gandhi was arrested on 5 May 1930. Kumarappa shared the editorial responsibility of *Young India* from May 1930 till his own arrest in February 1931. Kumarappa's name appears as editor (pro. tem.) only on the 15 May 1930 issue (Vol. 12, no. 20) of *Young India*. For the rest of the issues, the editor was Jayramdas Doulatram. In July 1930 the press was confiscated by the government. From 10 July 1930 cyclostyled issues of *Young India* were published without the name of any editor till Gandhi's release on 26 January 1931.

aggressive.[84] There is no doubt that Kumarappa's style of writing was blunt. In the article 'Who Pays the Piper', for instance, he has compared the revenue systems of Great Britain, Japan and India. While mentioning the prevalence of Death Tax only in Britain and its absence in India, Kumarappa writes, 'Fortunes made here pay duty in England.'[85] At another place, he describes the Indian officials working under the British as those who are committing the offence of 'prostituting our motherland for personal gain'.[86] Mira Behn found this bluntness untrue to the non-violent spirit. In jail when Gandhi came to know about the differences between the two, he wrote to Kumarappa to introspect about the character of his writing style. 'Is it *satvik* or is it *rajasik?*'[87] he wrote. To Mira Behn on the other hand he wrote, 'Charity is our best talisman. I should let him (Kumarappa) do as he pleases.'[88] In another letter to Mira Behn, Gandhi wrote:

... The golden rule is not to fret if things go contrary to one's wishes and to yield where resistance is useless or likely to be misunderstood, where there is no principle at stake and where in an organization responsibility is not solely one's own. The virtue of charity comes into play when one comes in contact with a variety of opinion and conduct.[89]

The differences between Kumarappa and Mira Behn, however, grew sharper when in July 1930 *Young India*'s printing press was confiscated by the government and cyclostyled issues of *Young India* were published without the name of editor or place of publication. Mira Behn felt that as a true Satyagrahi Kumarappa needs to inform the government where the paper was typed and cyclostyled. Kumarappa, however, believed that it is the responsibility of those who were out of jail to publicize

[84] Vinaik, *The Gandhian Crusader*, 7.
[85] Kumarappa, 'Who Pays the Piper?', 66.
[86] Kumarappa, A Call and a Lead to Indian Officials', 193.
[87] Letter to Kumarappa, 8 September 1930, CWMG Vol. 50, 38.
[88] Letter to Mira Behn, 28 September 1930, CWMG Vol. 50, 89–90.
[89] Letter to Mira Behn, 1 December 1930, CWMG Vol. 50, 283–284.

about Satyagraha, hence they need not disclose the place of publication.[90] Gandhi supported Kumarappa's views and disagreed with Mira Behn on this matter. He wrote to her:

> ... As to secrecy, there seems to be some confusion of thought as expressed by you. If a butcher asks me in which direction the cow has gone, I am in no way bound to disclose the information to him. I may not mislead him but nor may I lead him to where the cow is. Not only that I may even hide away the cow. Indeed it would be my duty to do so.[91]

With the same spirit of duty, Kumarappa continued the publication of *Young India* almost singlehandedly till the time Gandhi was released from Yervada Jail on 26 January 1931.

On 3 February 1931, Kumarappa was served with a show-cause notice for writing seditious articles in *Young India*, which were alleged to cause feelings of contempt and dissatisfaction among the public against the government. Kumarappa gave a bold and fearless statement before the magistrate. Gandhi published this statement in *Young India* (on 26 February 1931) with a word of praise. Kumarappa in this statement says:

> ... I am not going to take part in the proceedings of this court beyond submitting this statement.... A Govt. founded on the free will of the people it governs, can be said to be a 'Govt. by law established'. Has the Govt. of India any pretence to be styled so? The Govt. of India is established by an Act of Parliament of Great Britain and the British Parliament represents the will of the British people. So this Govt. can function only as a legal body in London, but not in Peking, Timbuktu or Delhi in which places it becomes an illegal association.... As regards this statement that I am causing the feelings of contempt I am afraid you are totally misinformed. It is not I who cause contempt; it is the accredited agents of this Govt. that bring it into disrepute.... Now a word as to your

[90] Vinaik, *The Gandhian Crusader*, 8.
[91] Letter to Mira Behn, 7/12 January 1931, CWMG Vol. 51, 23–24.

jurisdiction! As the Govt. of India is a usurper of the people's rights and at best its laws are but executive mandates or ordinances under disguise as the Legislatures have not the power to pass a bill against the executive's wish, you have no power arising from the people in whom rests the sovereignty. You are an arm of the executive and hence you have no jurisdiction over me and it is not for me to participate in this farce of a judicial proceeding....[92]

His hearing continued till the end of February, and thereby he was sentenced to one year simple[93] imprisonment.[94] Kumarappa has written about his first trial. He writes:

The trying magistrate was personally good, national minded man, but he was part of a huge soulless machine. When I made my statement to the court he sat with his head down supported by his hand. People in the court remarked that he looked the accused in the court and I the presiding judge pronouncing the judgement.[95]

Kumarappa was ceremoniously escorted to the prison. He however was not required to serve the full term. After the Gandhi–Irwin Pact, he was released from jail within a few days in March 1931.

Out from his first imprisonment, Kumarappa was now entrusted with a few other significant responsibilities. In the Karachi session of the Indian National Congress, held in March 1931, a select committee was appointed to scrutinize the details

[92] *Young India* 13, no. 9, 25–26.
[93] On 5 March 1931, *Young India* announces that J. C. Kumarappa is sentenced to one year's simple imprisonment; however, in his personal memoir *Stone Walls and Iron Bars* Kumarappa states that all his sentences had been rigorous (5). His official biographer mentions that he was sentenced to one and half years' rigorous imprisonment in 1931. Vinaik, *The Gandhian Crusader*, 22.
[94] *Young India* 13, no. 10, 28.
[95] Kumarappa, *Stone Walls and Iron Bars*, 2–3.

of the financial obligations between India and Britain up to that time. J. C. Kumarappa was appointed as the convener of this committee. The committee prepared its report within two months. It looked into the expenditure incurred by the colonial power before 1857 (that is, by the East India Company) and after 1857 (that is, by the British Crown). The committee found that the cost of the external wars including the Abyssinian War (1867), the Second Afghan War (1878) and even the expenditure to suppress the 1857 'Mutiny' was charged to the Indian pockets. The legacy of the East India Company of burdening India with defence expenditure was continued by the Crown. The amount of around 400 crore[96] rupees used for the First World War (then known as the European War) was charged to the Indian pockets.[97] Gandhi often referred to this report in his speeches at the Second Round Table Conference. In the statement made on 25 November 1931 before the Federal Structure Committee of the Round Table Conference, Gandhi emphatically referred to this report and refuted the claim made by the colonizers that their financial decisions were in the interest of India. Gandhi says:

> If I remember rightly, Your Lordship used the words 'obviously it was in the interest of India'. I was waiting to find some illustrations, but no doubt you took it for granted that we would know these matters or those illustrations which you had in mind. I had really converse illustrations in mind while you were speaking…. Take, for instance, so many wars. Take the war of Afghanistan…. most of these wars were certainly not in the interest of India; not only that the Governor-General had bungled over these wars … the history of British

[96] The Congress Select Committee Report mentions this amount as 400 crore. The Congress Golden Jubilee Brochure *Public Debt of India* authored by Kumarappa, and published in 1935, is more specific in mentioning the amount as 397.7 crore (14–15).

[97] *Report of the Congress Select Committee on Financial Obligations between Britain and India*, 24–26.

Finance in India was history of muddle and bungling where it was not also one of exploitation of India.[98]

While leaving for the Round Table Conference, Gandhi entrusted the responsibility of looking after *Young India* to Kumarappa.[99] Kumarappa regularly wrote in *Young India* mostly on the pressing economic issues of the time. In addition to such analytical writings, this time Kumarappa also explored the philosophical foundations of some of the Gandhian economic ideas. In one of his articles of this period, Kumarappa reflected upon the philosophical foundations of the idea of trusteeship vis-à-vis the purpose of private property. Kumarappa maintains that thinkers from Plato to Sir Thomas More thought of removing the evils attached to private property. Soviet Russia came up with its own experiments, but all these attempts could not bring about equality. The failure of these attempts, Kumarappa believes, lay in the fact that all of them carried an element of compulsion or violence. Kumarappa insists that the religious preachers did not denounce private property as an evil in itself, but whenever they found that riches become stumbling block to certain characters, they advised to consider it as a trust given by God. He then concludes, the way feeling of possessiveness and lust cannot be removed by creating 'Community of Wives' (as visualized by Plato), similarly evils of wealth cannot be removed by communism. He writes:

Wealth is a grave responsibility but at the same time it is a great opportunity [...] The remedy for the evils of capitalism is not in dispossessing persons of their wealth but rather in bringing about or cultivating an attitude of mind which will control selfish enjoyment and harness one's surplus production to serve other's needs.[100]

[98] Rajagopalachari and Kumarappa, eds., *The Nation's Voices*, 63. Also in CWMG Vol. 54, 206.

[99] Gandhi's letter to Kumarappa, 28 August 1931, CWMG Vol. 53, 295.

[100] Kumarappa, 'Great Possessions', 253–254.

The echoes of Gandhian influence could be clearly heard from such writings of Kumarappa. At the same time, interestingly, these writings also reflect Christian leanings as Kumarappa often cites from Christian religious scripture in support of his argument. In addition to such contemplative writing during this tenure with *Young India*, Kumarappa also continued his mission of exposing the exploitative character of the British economic policies, the irresponsiveness of its bureaucracy and overall undemocratic character of the British government in India. In the article 'The Financial Crisis', he criticized the currency exchange policy of the British government.[101] In another article, he scrutinizes the British textile policy and its implications for the Indian agriculture.[102] Such writings invited the wrath of the British government, and Kumarappa was put under house arrest in the beginning of 1932. In the statement before the court Kumarappa reiterated his views about the British government, which he had expressed earlier before the court in 1930, and expressed his firm commitment to the Civil Disobedience Movement.[103] This time he was sentenced with two and a half years' rigorous imprisonment. He served his term in the Central Jail, Nasik. Morarji Desai, B. G. Kher and Kishorelal Mashruwala were the some of the other jail inmates during this imprisonment. Kumarappa was released at the end of 1933.

On 15 January 1934 Bihar was shaken by earthquake. The Indian National Congress set up an earthquake relief committee for rescue and rehabilitation work. Donations and help came from all over the world. Kumarappa was made financial advisor of the earthquake relief committee. Dr Rajendra Prasad in his autobiography has gratefully recognized Kumarappa's contribution to the relief work. He writes:

I cannot forget the help rendered by J. C. Kumarappa.... It would be no exaggeration to say that but for him we would have been in a terrible mess. We had more than 2,000 workers

[101] Kumarappa, 'The Financial Crisis', 291.
[102] Kumarappa, 'Exorcising Demon', 375.
[103] Vinaik, *The Gandhian Crusader*, 30–31.

spread over twelve districts. Few of them knew accounting and the nature of work was multifarious and separate accounts had to be kept for each kind of work. Our task was assuming formidable proportion but, thanks to Kumarappa, we were able to manage it.[104]

From his experiences in Bihar, Kumarappa wrote a booklet 'The Organisation and Accounts of Relief Work'.[105] This booklet is an insightful code for disaster management. The most crucial aspect of this manual is its assertion for transparency and accuracy as the vital norms for using public money. While Kumarappa was occupied in the relief work in Bihar, Congress was deliberating over the true definition of Swadeshi while Gandhi was busy giving concrete shape to the All India Village Industries Association (AIVIA). The concern about the definition of Swadeshi and the urgency in reviving Village Industries had, among other things, the background of Swadeshi League.[106]

In June 1934, a delegation of the All India Swadeshi League had approached Gandhi for a comprehensive definition of Swadeshi. The delegation included K. M. Munshi, Lalubhai Samaldas, J. A. D. Naoroji, Vaikunth L. Mehta, Purushottamdas Thakurdas and Dhirajlal Modi.[107] The context of this meeting was the clear apprehensions expressed by both Gandhi and Nehru over the exhibition of the mill-made products under the nomenclature 'Swadeshi Exhibition'. In November 1933, Gandhi in his speech at the All India Swadeshi Exhibition at Raipur insisted that Khadi must be the centre of the Swadeshi Exhibitions.[108] In December 1933, at the Madras Swadeshi Exhibition, Gandhi reiterated:

[104] Prasad, *Autobiography*, 367–368.

[105] Kumarappa, *The Organisation and Accounts of Relief Work*.

[106] All India Swadeshi League was established around 1914 with Madan Mohan Malaviya as its president and Lilavati Munshi as secretary. It was largely supported by a faction of mill owners, traders and bankers from Mumbai and Ahmedabad.

[107] CWMG Vol. 63, 74.

[108] CWMG Vol. 62, 212–213.

You cannot have everything that grows or is manufactured in India exhibited [...]. I object to open the exhibitions where mill clothes, may be hundred per cent Swadeshi, are exhibited.... I do not want to pit myself against mill-cloth. What I want to say is this. If you go into the history of mill industry in India, you will discover it does not need a Swadeshi exhibition for its distribution.[109]

In this speech Gandhi also linked the issue of Swadeshi with that of caste. He insisted that hand-spinning and hand-weaving generated employment for millions of Harijans and mill-made cloth doesn't necessarily guarantee such kind of employment to the millions of downtrodden.[110] In the same month Nehru is reported to have said at Kanpur Swadeshi Exhibition:

I have no time to waste over Swadeshi League exhibitions.... I do not subscribe to the policy of encouraging exhibitions where mill-cloth is allowed either for sale or for display. I have no sympathy for mill-owners. They try to fill their pockets at the expense of labourers.[111]

In this background, the members of the Swadeshi League had approached Gandhi for a comprehensive definition of Swadeshi. Gandhi clarified:

Swadeshi covers useful articles manufactured in India through small scale industries which are in need of popular education for their support and which will accept guidance of the All-India Swadeshi League in regulating prices and in the matter of wages and welfare of labour under their control. Swadeshi will, therefore, exclude articles manufactured through large and organised industries which are in no need of services of the All-India Swadeshi League which can or do command State aid.[112]

[109] Ibid., 305–306.
[110] Ibid.
[111] Ramagundam, *Gandhi's Khadi*, 167.
[112] CWMG Vol. 64, 74.

Gandhi also appealed to the members of the Swadeshi League to stop being 'self-appointed advertising agents' of the large and organized industries.

The Congress Working Committee (CWC) deliberated on the meaning of Swadeshi in July 1934 at Banaras, where Kumarappa was chosen as arbitrator.[113] After listening to the arguments from both the sides, Kumarappa summed up that Swadeshi is the best utilization of the whole of the manpower of India. He warned that any plan which neglected the raw materials of a country and the potentially more powerful manpower was lopsided and could never tend to establish human equality. CWC had also prepared an outline for constructive programmes, which was then discussed by the Provincial Congress Committees. Interestingly, in the Bihar Provincial Congress Committee, JP 'while not disapproving of the constructive programme' found it 'inadequate for the achievement of independence'. He said in his speech:

> I'm not opposed to Khadi or untouchability, which are good enough in their own way—Khadi as a means of unemployment relief and untouchability as social service. These items do help in establishing contact with the people and create in them a sort of awakening. But a Congressman is a soldier of freedom and the question is whether he should concentrate on these items to the extent it was being done.[114]

Thus, the socialists represented by JP were doubtful about the efficacy of the Constructive Programme even as a political strategy; considering it as a tool of economic regeneration was for them almost out of question. The Congress was, however, determined to support the Constructive Work Programme, leaving it on history to unfold whether as a mere political strategy or as a tool of economic re-generation!

---

[113] Vinaik, *The Gandhian Crusader*, 61.
[114] Prasad, ed., *Selected Works of Jayaprakash Narayan*, Vol. 1, 77–78.

In the Banaras session (October 1934), the Congress proposed to establish the AIVIA in order to give concrete shape to the ideals of Swadeshi and of Constructive Programme. The resolution moved by Pattabhi Sitaramayya states:

> Whereas organizations claiming to advance Swadeshi have sprung up all over the country with and without the assistance of Congressmen and whereas much confusion has arisen in the public mind as to the true nature of Swadeshi and whereas the aim of the Congress has been from its inception progressive identification with the masses and whereas village reorganisation and reconstruction is one of the items in the constructive programme of the Congress and whereas such reconstruction necessarily implies revival and encouragement of dead or dying village industries besides the central industry of hand-spinning, and whereas this work like reorganization of hand-spinning is possible only through concentrated and special efforts unaffected by and independent of political activities of the Congress, Shri J. C. Kumarappa is hereby authorized to form, under the advice and guidance of Gandhiji, an association called the All India Village Industries Association as part of the activities of the Congress. The said organization shall work for the revival and encouragement of the said industries and for the moral and physical advancement of the villages, and shall have power to frame its own constitution; to raise funds and to perform such acts as may be necessary for the fulfilment of its objects.[115]

The resolution was passed by the Congress, but there were certain resentments. These resentments were expressed through the amendments to the resolutions. Two amendments were proposed, although they lost after the vote. The first amendment proposed by Basant Kumar Majumdar wanted to replace the words 'unaffected by the political activities of the Congress' with 'under the supervision and control of Congress'.

[115] Zaidi and Zaidi, eds., *The Encyclopedia of Indian National Congress*, Vol. 10, 330–331.

This amendment refers to one of the crucial debates within Gandhism, that is, the structural mechanism for realizing Gandhian ideals; particularly the relationship between the political organization and constructive work. This debate and Kumarappa's views on this issue will be dealt with at length in later in this work. The second amendment proposed by Majumdar insisted that Congress must stand by the country's industries and help them grow.[116] The relationship between heavy industries and the cottage industries was another crucial issue of debate during this period. This debate and Kumarappa's position on this matter is discussed in Chapters 3 and 4.

The idea of setting up AIVIA is considered to be Gandhi's way of providing structural foundation to the idea of constructive programme. AIVIA is also seen as the extension of the AISA established in 1925. There is no doubt that Gandhi tried to institutionalize Constructive Programmes through these organizations, but the entire idea went far beyond mere employment generation, village reconstruction, moral-spiritual growth or even the promotion of Swadeshi for that matter. The institutionalization of AIVIA was an attempt to develop a deeper critique of capitalism and pave way for non-capitalist form of industrialization and non-feudal village system. Kumarappa's association with the AIVIA needs to be understood in the light of this wider context.

The members of the AIVIA met for the first time on 14 December 1934 where organizational structure of AIVIA was finalized. AIVIA was constituted of seven bodies: the board of management, the members, the agents, the honorary workers, the paid whole-time workers, the associates and the board of advisors. The work of AIVIA fell in five categories: research, production, training, extension and organization, propaganda and publication.[117]

[116] Ibid.
[117] AIVIA: Object and Constitution, CWMG Vol. 65, 457–458.

For conducting research into village industries, numerous processes were initiated simultaneously. Attempts were made for identifying existing village industries. Suggestions were invited on the possible new areas that can either be developed as village industries or could be complimentary to village industries. Gandhi's correspondence of this period shows that he was in regular contact with the scientists and researchers from all over the undivided India, who were experimenting in newer technology useful in agriculture without replacing human labour. Gandhi would write them to contact Kumarappa and exhibit their product before him and the other officials of AIVIA. Scientists were encouraged to conduct research on nutritional values of unpolished rice, jaggery and other food products that AIVIA was producing.

The second aspect of AIVIA work, that is, production, was initially limited to Khadi and unpolished rice. But very soon the list became longer. In March 1936 when AIVIA organized exhibition at the Lucknow Congress, 12 items of village industries, 16 items of Khadi processes and 21 items of arts and crafts were included.[118] For the purpose of training, a school namely 'Gram Sevak Vidyalaya' was started to train the village workers. The training school offered one training programme of 12-month duration in Hindi medium.[119] Kumarappa's brother Bharatan Kumarappa joined him to share the responsibilities and be part of the staff.

For the purpose of propaganda and extension, Kumarappa travelled throughout the country addressing different groups at different places. A few of his outstanding speeches are collected in a book entitled *The Philosophy of the Village Movement*.[120] A year after this publication, Kumarappa came up with *Why the Village Movement?*[121] Both these works systematically put forth

[118] Vinaik, *The Gandhian Crusader*, 73.
[119] *Harijan* 3, no. 43, 7.
[120] Subba Rao, ed., *The Philosophy of the Village Movement*.
[121] Kumarappa, *Why the Village Movement?*

a plea for a village-centred economic order in India. The latter is especially significant considering the fact that in this work Kumarappa gives a complete overview of the Gandhian model of development. Many of the ideas expressed in this work were later developed and further elaborated by Kumarappa through his activities at the AIVIA as well as through his contribution to various committees.

In order to reorganize the educational system, Gandhi had called a conference in Wardha in October 1937. The Education Reorganization Committee was constituted with Dr Zakir Hussain as its chairman and E. W. Aryanayakam as its secretary. Kumarappa was appointed as a member of this Education Reorganization Committee. The committee developed the Gandhian notion of education popularly known as *Nai Talim*. Kumarappa's contributions to this committee are published under the title *The Philosophy of Work and Other Essays*.[122] In these essays Kumarappa has tried to establish 'work as a medium of education'. He points out that every work has two aspects: physical labour and pleasure of the outcome. Western civilizations do not try to bridge the gap between these two aspects. In fact, they consider physical labour as the destiny of the weak, while the mightier section of the society takes pride in enjoying the fruits without doing any physical labour. Kumarappa rejects this approach and insists that physical labour is essential not merely for moral growth but also for the development of personality. He insists that no creation is possible without hard labour.

> No one can become a great musician, just by listening to good music; hours and hours of practice, is necessary. Similarly, a scientist cannot become a scientist unless he spends hours in laboratory, labouring hard with new experiments and bearing the odour of sulphureted hydrogen.[123]

[122] Kumarappa, *The Philosophy of Work and Other Essays*.
[123] Ibid., 2–3.

Kumarappa insists that basic education links the creative and educative aspects of work with the process of learning;[124] hence, he insists that learning should not be bifurcated from work (that is, physical labour). While designing the curriculum of the training programmes for the Gram Sevak Vidyalaya, Kumarappa gave utmost importance to these aspects. The course in oil pressing, for instance, introduced students not only to the technique of oil pressing but also to the mechanical aspects of the oil press, carpentry and smithy of oil pressing, economics of oil seed production, geographical aspects of oil seeds production, nutritional details, marketing techniques and so on.[125]

During this period Kumarappa made significant contributions to two important committees. The first one was the National Planning Committee appointed by the Indian National Congress, while the other one was Industrial Survey Committee constituted by the Government of Central Provinces (CP) and Berar. On the National Planning Committee, Kumarappa worked for a very short period as he resigned from the committee within months on a note of dissent. However, he played a significant role in presenting an alternate view of the relationship between the large-scale industries and the rural industries than what the National Planning Committee had assumed. In the Industrial Survey Committee, Kumarappa got more space and liberty to develop his ideas. In this report, he has given a blueprint for the revival of numerous village industries. The issues raised in both these committees are discussed at length later in this work. The experience of working on both these committees helped Kumarappa in consolidating his views on development and social justice.

With the breaking out of the Second World War in 1939 the Congress ministries in the provinces resigned and the entire context changed. The War had its own economic implications. Inflation had risen to an all-time high. Agriculture was badly affected from many of the governmental ordinances.

[124] Ibid., 20.
[125] Vinaik, *The Gandhian Crusader*, 93–96.

Kumarappa strongly protested against such ordinances and wrote critically about them in *Harijan* as well as in the *Gram Udyog Patrika*. One of the characteristic features of his writings of this period is that he propounded the 'barter system' as a solution to inflation. In one of his articles, he wrote:

> Money exchange is indispensable mainly for the extension of markets. Money in itself satisfies no want except that of a miser who delights in counting his coins [...]. Under modern imperialism when one country is kept down to produce raw materials for another distant country which produces manufactured articles, money economy has become the life breath of commerce [...]. Money and credit have their place in commerce and trade [...]. (But) where the standard of living of people is near the subsistence level, their purchasing power is spent mostly on food and other necessities. At such a stage, if money is largely used, then it would divert that purchasing power to some extent into luxuries, which often come from distant countries, and thus lower the true wealth computed in terms of human values [...]. A barter system would have helped to make it impossible for Government to perpetrate the injustice by using India's reserves to the tune of crores in London money market while our industries were striving for funds.[126]

AISA had already begun to promote yarn currency,[127] and Gandhians were debating over usefulness of yarn currency over grain currency.[128] The British government took serious note of such writings and practices. Kumarappa was charged for violating the Defence of India Act for his article in *Gram Udyog Patrika* entitled 'A Stone for Bread'.[129] In this article, he exposed the British tactics of inflation and the loot of the masses made possible thereby. He pointed out that the British policy of promoting

[126] Kumarappa, 'Exchange and Human Values', 143–144.
[127] *Harijan* 11, no. 9, 78.
[128] Mashruwala, 'Some Danger-Spots of Yarn Currency', 118–119.
[129] Kumarappa, 'A Stone for Bread'. *Gram Udyog Patrika*, 6, no. 12, 53–54.

the United Kingdom Commercial Corporation (UKCC) almost as a department of the government has affected Indian business badly. More seriously, 'It's being used as a medium for exchanging British "paper" for sweat of the brow of the masses of India'. He reiterated that the villagers should not be made to part with their commodities for paper money, but to exchange them against goods only. Due to this article and the solution given therein a warrant of arrest was issued against Kumarappa. He was produced before a session's judge. Kumarappa was sentenced to three terms of two and half years' rigorous imprisonment. While giving the judgement, the judge congratulated the public prosecutor for the ability with which he had handled a difficult and highly technical case and helped the court to understand its implications. At this stage, the public prosecutor interrupted and informed the court that he was working under the instructions of the prisoner himself, as he could not get any other professor of economics to help him.[130] A part of Kumarappa's statement in the court has been published under a title 'Currency Inflation: Its Causes and Cure'.

After spending two years in jail Kumarappa's health started deteriorating. Hence he was released in 1945. During this imprisonment Kumarappa produced two texts. The first was *Practice and Precepts of Jesus* and the other was *The Economy of Permanence*. In the *Practice and Precepts of Jesus* Kumarappa gives a revolutionary view of Jesus as a man. Kumarappa interprets the message of Christ in a hermeneutical vein. Kumarappa's approach towards religion in general and about Christianity in particular is discussed in Chapter 5. The other book *The Economy of Permanence* is cherished by many as a text of environmental thought. It has also been the most popular work of Kumarappa. This book comprehensively explains Kumarappa's ideal of 'mother economy' which enables one to transcend the evils of money economy. Kumarappa considers mother economy as the only economy of permanence.

Once released from jail, Kumarappa gave some time for improving his health, but very soon he was back to work.

---

[130] Ibid., 120.

During the inter-war period, the AIVIA work had suffered badly. The publication of *Gram Udyog Patrika* had been suspended after Kumarappa's arrest in March 1943; the publication resumed from April 1945. Independence was just round the corner. In 1946 in order to review the work of AIVIA, Kumarappa travelled 'over 20,000 miles from Colombo to Kabul and Kathiawar to Cuttack'.[131] His letter to Gandhi shows that he was not very happy with the progress of the work. If absence of coordination was one problem, lack of holistic understanding on part of the activists was a more serious issue. The debate over the role of large-scale industries was still hanging. This debate had encompassed within itself various other issues such as the export–import policy, agricultural policy and the entire domain of public finance. The differences over the nature of economic development started coming to the forefront around this time. In fact, the differences between Gandhi and Nehru on the matters of economic development had also become clearer by now. The correspondence between the two (Gandhi and Nehru) throws sufficient light on the differences. On 5 October 1945 Gandhi wrote to Nehru that he found 'sharp difference' between him and Nehru. Gandhi insisted that he still stood by his vision presented in *Hind Swaraj* and wanted to bring villages at the centre of the plans for rebuilding India.[132] Nehru in his reply submitted that the differences between the two were not fundamental in nature and hence need not be brought before the public.[133] Gandhi in his reply of 13 November 1945 insisted that the gist of their discussion was:

[...] There should be equality between town-dwellers and villagers in the standard of food, drink and clothing and other living conditions. In order to realize this equality, today people should be able to produce their own necessaries of life, i.e. clothing, foodstuffs, dwellings and lighting and water [...].[134]

[131] Kumarappa's letter to Gandhi dated 1 February 1947. Kumarappa Papers, NMML, Subject File No. 5, 52.
[132] CWMG Vol. 88, 118–120.
[133] Pyarelal, *Towards New Horizons*, 5–6.
[134] CWMG Vol. 88, 329.

The policies of the interim government that came in 1946, however, did not seem like confirming Gandhi's expectations. Kumarappa regularly wrote in the columns of *Gram Udyog Patrika* against the interim government's attitude towards village industries. He insisted for appointing a rural development committee of Congress to advise the various congress ministries.[135] Kumarappa's idea of a village development committee did not materialize; the Congress Working Committee in its meeting held on 7 March 1947, however, did appoint a constructive programme committee to guide and advise Congress committees.[136] Kumarappa was appointed as its member. Later, in November 1947, Kumarappa was also appointed on the Economic Programme Committee of the Congress.[137] Kumarappa was chosen on both these committees to represent AIVIA. The difference in the nomenclature (Village Development Committee for Kumarappa, Constructive Programme Committee and Economic Programme Committee for Congress) also implies the differences in approach. While Kumarappa was thinking from a point of view of non-capitalist development of villages, for the Congress it was an ancillary activity of its front organization and at its best one of the aspects of public policy! Such differences in approach had come to the forefront since the days of the National Planning Committee, now on the eve of Independence they became still clearer and sharper.

Throughout 1947 the number of articles that Kumarappa wrote in *Harijan* and in *Gram Udyog Patrika*[138] scrutinized the economic decisions of the newly formed interim government at the centre as well as at the provinces, and displayed the ways in which these governments were facilitating the growth

[135] Kumarappa's letter to Gandhi dated 1 February 1947. Kumarappa Papers, NMML, Subject File No. 5, 52.
[136] 'Resolution of the Constructive Programme', *Harijan* 11, no. 8 (23 March 1947), 77.
[137] Kumarappa Papers, NMML, Subject File No. 13, 2.
[138] Most of the articles were simultaneously published in *Harijan* and *Gram Udyog Patrika*.

of mechanized, large-scale capitalist industrialization at the cost of the village industries. In February 1947, for instance, he scrutinized Orissa government's textile policy of allowing the import of plant and machinery for textile mills.[139] In April 1947, he criticized the Advisory Planning Board for recommending the raise in the production of vanaspati ghee.[140] In the same month, he also wrote critically about the UP government's industrial policy of promoting sugar industries and thereby giving a deathblow to *khandasari* sugar and *desi chini* production.[141] In July 1947 he criticized the Government of India's agricultural policy of promoting cotton cultivation over foodcrops.[142] He had also expressed dissent over the way in which the Government of India was settling the issue of sterling balances. Earlier, throughout the late 1930s and early 1940s, Kumarappa had written about the colonial government's monetary policy. He had constantly insisted that the value of rupee should be de-linked from the pound sterling and while calculating the public debt of India, Britain should be made to own its due share.[143] In 1947 when the colonizers were leaving India, Kumarappa wanted India to firmly assert its claim for the credits which were generated from its own contribution of material goods. He wrote to Gandhi, 'I expect you will not let such material wealth slip through your *Bania*[144] fingers.'[145] Kumarappa also spoke to Pandit Nehru, but Nehru maintained that 'it was a political decision than an economic one'.[146] Kumarappa's suggestions regarding the account settlement with the colonizers thus went unheard.

---

[139] Kumarappa, 'Orissa's Suicide', 23.
[140] Kumarappa, 'Blindness at a Price', 96.
[141] Kumarappa, 'Science Runs Amuck', 96.
[142] Kumarappa, 'Let Us Learn', 239.
[143] Kumarappa's letters to Gandhi dated 9 June and 5 July 1947. Kumarappa Papers, NMML, Subject File No. 5, 53–54.
[144] To this Gandhi had replied, 'The *Bania* fingers seem to have paralysed.' CWMG Vol. 95, 256.
[145] Ibid.
[146] Ibid.

Meanwhile, an All India Shipping Delegation was visiting London under the leadership of Seth Walchand Hirachand to discuss and finalize the terms of transfer of shipping rights with the British counterparts, and eventually to contribute to the foreign trade policy of the Government of India. Shoorji Shapurjee, one of the members of this committee, requested Kumarappa to join this delegation with a hope that 'his very presence will deter vested interests from entering into selfish agreement'.[147] Kumarappa joined the delegation. The conference, however, broke down on the very presentation of credentials and terms of reference. On his return, Kumarappa wrote an article in *Harijan* entitled 'An Abortive Conference'.[148] In this article, in addition to reporting the developments at the conference, Kumarappa could be seen insisting for nationalizing the shipping industry. He maintained that since shipping influences foreign trade it should be owned by the State and private interests should not be allowed to predominate.[149]

In December 1947 Kumarappa was assigned with one more significant responsibility. He was appointed as the chairperson of the Agrarian Reforms Committee (ARC) constituted by the Congress. In the Revenue Ministers' Conference, held in December 1947, a decision was taken unanimously to constitute this committee. Accordingly, Dr Rajendra Prasad, the then Congress President, appointed ARC under the chairmanship of Kumarappa. Meanwhile with Gandhi's assassination in January 1948 the entire dynamics of constructive work activities and that of politics changed drastically. The Gandhian movement was shaken badly. In addition to the emotional loss, the absence of the guide, integrator, arbitrator and the task master changed the dynamics of the Gandhian movement significantly.

Kumarappa had already begun his work for the ARC. The ARC circulated a questionnaire in February 1948 to the provincial governments, provincial Congress committees, public men,

[147] Ibid., 53.
[148] Kumarappa, 'An Abortive Conference', 347–349.
[149] Ibid., 348.

kisan organizations, universities and experts regarding the status of prevailing agrarian relations at the provincial level.[150] After considering the responses the committee started touring the provinces from 15 June 1948. The itinerary of the tour shows that in a period of about 9 months the committee[151] travelled 14,037 miles, visiting 61 centres, interviewing 254 persons.[152] The ARC submitted its report in 1949. The recommendations of the committee are discussed in Chapter 4. The government or Congress did not accept any of the recommendations.

The differences over agrarian reforms was not the only issue over which Congress and Kumarappa parted their ways. The functioning of the Gandhi Memorial Fund contributed equally in highlighting the differences. Kumarappa was working for the Gandhi Memorial Fund simultaneously with his work at the ARC. He had certain reservations about the functioning of the fund. First, he wanted that the headquarters of Gandhi Memorial Fund should be situated in a village rather than in the capital city of Delhi. Second, he believed that instead of raising money, efforts should be made to mobilize devoted human beings for building a non-violent social order through constructive work. He maintained that since the government is a popular democratic government, it is not difficult to raise money; but to undertake various Gandhian programmes, committed workers will be required. Hence mobilizing devoted and renunciated human beings would be a truly Gandhian way of erecting a Gandhi Memorial Fund. For this purpose, he appealed to Pandit Nehru, Sardar Patel and Rajkumari Amrit Kaur to leave their positions and donate their own selves to the Gandhi Memorial Fund.[153] Kumarappa's suggestions

---

[150] *Report of the Congress Agrarian Reforms Committee*, 4.

[151] The entire distance was travelled only by Kumarappa and the Secretary of the Committee K. Mitra. Other members were present only in their respective province.

[152] *Report of the Congress Agrarian Reforms Committee*. See the Appendices to the report.

[153] Vinaik, *The Gandhian Crusader*, 147.

were supported by Vinoba,[154] but they were not acceptable to the other members. Hence the Gandhi Memorial Fund concentrated on collecting money. Kumarappa was asked to take charge of the work. He along with two clerks hesitantly looked after the work for some time from Delhi. But when the industrialists and financers joined the trust as its trustees, Kumarappa took a back seat and started involving himself in other activities.

In 1950, Kumarappa was appointed on the Planning Commission Advisory Board as a representative of the Sarva Seva Sangh. In the same year, he was also requested by the Government of the North West Frontier Province to conduct an industrial survey of its province. The then chief minister, Dr Gopichand Bhargava, was especially keen to develop the rural industries in the province through the mode of Gandhian planning. Accordingly, Kumarappa conducted this survey and also visited the rural development centres run by the Government of the North West Frontier Province and came up with his recommendations.

In 1951 Kumarappa set up an ashram named 'Pannai Ashram' at Seldoh (around 10 miles from Wardha). He migrated there from Maganwadi (Wardha). In this ashram he concentrated on agricultural research and experimentation. He however could not continue these experiments for a long time, as he shortly shifted to the Gandhi Niketan Ashram at T. Kalupatti near Madurai. It is believed that he decided to retire from public life due to his health problems and hence shifted to Madurai. Kumarappa's growing association with the communists during this period seems to have generated some stir in the Gandhian circles. Kumarappa had been a member of the cultural delegation to China in September 1951. On his return he published a report 'What I Saw and Learnt in China'.[155] The report was

---

[154] Bhave, 'No Money Donations', 389.
[155] Kumarappa, *A Peep Behind the Iron Curtain*. This report was reviewed by Margaret W. Fisher and Joan V. Bondurant for *The Far Eastern Quarterly*. See *The Far Eastern Quarterly* 15, no. 2, 249–265.

liberally appreciative of the Chinese model. Of course, in the conclusion of this report, Kumarappa had reiterated that India requires a village-centric model and not communism; but his growing association with the communists, especially on the issue of world peace, seems to have generated stirs. On his return from China, Kumarappa attended the All-India Peace Conferences organized by the communists. Later, he was also appointed as one of the Vice-Presidents of the pro-Soviet 'All India Peace Council' between 1952 and 1957.[156] He occupied this position along with Mulk Raj Anand, D. D. Kosambi and others. In this capacity, Kumarappa also became a member of the World Peace Council[157] and visited England, Germany (East & West), Bulgaria and Russia delivering speeches on the Gandhian approach to world peace.[158] Kumarappa's disposition about the Gandhian approach to world peace was an extension of his economic ideas (discussed in detail in Chapter 3), but its political fallout was his marginalization within the Gandhian circles. His differences with Congress and with other Gandhians on other issues were simultaneously coming to the forefront. As it is, Kumarappa was controversy's favourite child. Since the beginning of his association with the Gandhian movement, he had had difference of opinion/clash/conflict (with differing intensity) with practically every Gandhian/ Congressman—with Mira Behn over the issue of violence and non-violence,[159] with Shrikrishnadas Jaju over the organization

[156] Overstreet and Windmiller, *Communism in India*, 428.

[157] The origins of the World Peace Council could be traced to the World Congress of Intellectuals held in Breslau (Wroclaw), Poland in August 1948, which created the World Peace Committee in April 1949 at Paris with a 12-member permanent bureau and French scientist Frederic Joliot-Curie as the president. D. D. Kosambi was a member of the permanent bureau. The same year the journal *Cominform* had referred to the peace movement as the 'pivot of the entire activity of the Communist Party'. See Overstreet and Windmiller, *Communism in India*.

[158] Kumarappa, *A Peep Behind the Iron Curtain*, 4.

[159] The differences over maintaining secrecy in publishing *Young India* during the Civil Disobedience Movement as discussed earlier in this chapter.

of AIVIA,[160] with Gandhi himself over the allocation of daily allowance to earthquake rehabilitation workers in Bihar,[161] with Nehru in the National Planning Committee,[162] with Shankarrao Deo over the role of constructive workers,[163] with Kishorelal Mashruwala over the constitution of the Gandhi Memorial Fund,[164] with G. V. Mavlankar over the difference between Gandhian discipline and military discipline,[165] and so on. His harsh critique of Nehru's economic policies was another source of the discontent, and apprehensions about taking American aid for community projects were also received with annoyance. His insistence on nationalizing large-scale industries was seen by many as the result of his increasing inclination towards socialism. In this background, his praise for the Soviet Bloc and critical comments on Nehru's foreign policy in the preface to L. Natarajan's *American Shadow over India*[166] and an article in *Gram Udyog Patrika* entitled 'Chinese Sarvodaya'[167] must have added fuel to the existing misconceptions, thereby leading to Kumarappa's near-seclusion from the mainstream Gandhian movement.[168] Kumarappa did try to give material shape to his

[160] The controversy was regarding the methods of maintaining accounts. The exact nature of controversy is unknown, but as a result Shrikrishnadas Jaju resigned from AIVIA. Gandhi's letter to Amrit Kaur dated 3 April 1937. CWMG Vol. 7, 100.

[161] Kumarappa had first refused to allot any daily allowance to Gandhi during his visit to Bihar to inspect the rehabilitation work and later asked Gandhi to manage his daily expenses in the amount allotted to common workers. Gandhi, of course, agreed. Kumarappa also refused to meet Gandhi, since he was busy in his work and Gandhi had not taken his prior appointment. See Vinaik, *The Gandhian Crusader.*

[162] Controversy over the role of village industries vis-à-vis large-scale industries discussed in Chapters 3 and 4.

[163] See Deo, 'Congress and the Constructive Workers'.

[164] Mashruwalla, 'Controls for Sarvodaya', 320–321.

[165] Kumarappa, 'Non-violence and the Cult of the Rifle Club'

[166] Natarajan, *American Shadow over India.*

[167] Kumarappa, 'Chinese Sarvodaya', 12.

[168] In 1956 Kumarappa published a report of his tour to Russia, Germany and Bulgaria. Kaka Kalelkar in a preface to this collection

economic ideas by founding Arthik Samata Mandal along with G. Ramchandra Rao (the famous Gandhian atheist popular as Gora) in 1952,[169] but no longer continued to operate from Maganwadi, Wardha. He took semi-retirement from active public life in 1953 and shifted to Gandhi Niketan Ashram at T. Kalupatti near Madurai. His role in the Arthik Samata Mandal remained of an advisor. He continued writing in *Gram Udyog Patrika*, of course less frequently than before, reflecting upon the burning issues before the country and before the Gandhian movement.

Kumarappa's sudden disappearance from Wardha and from the Gandhian circles is normally explained by his ill health. His complete seclusion from the Gandhian discourses almost till his centennial birth anniversary could be understood from the controversies about his ideological location towards the very end of his stay in Wardha. Dissociated from the Gandhian mainstream, a diseased Kumarappa continued his stay at T. Kalupatti. With his health declining constantly, J. C. Kumarappa passed away on 30 January 1960.

of essays admitted that in the minds of 'some people' Kumarappa's views had created (in 1952) misgivings of him becoming a communist.

[169] Gora's eldest son Lavanam told this to Mark Lindley in an interview. Lindley, *J. C. Kumarappa: Mahatma Gandhi's Economist*, 53.

3

Locating the Problem
Money, Market and Machine

Kumarappa locates the root cause of inequality, poverty and unemployment in money economy and mechanized industrialism. He maintains that with the advent of colonialism in India, money economy entered this land and changed the socio-economic structure of the Indian society. It paved the way for mechanized industrialism. Kumarappa visualizes a symbiotic relation between money economy and imperialism. The advent of mechanized industrialism accentuates the growth of the money economy as well as imperialism. This he believes resulted in unemployment, poverty and acute disparity. The economic degeneration went hand in hand with moral degeneration of this society. As against Kumarappa's position, a prominent group of Gandhians held, 'the main problem of human race is moral and not economic or political'.[1] The faith in the primacy of moral over material resulted in locating different solutions for its resolution. As against this, Kumarappa, though equally concerned with moral degeneration, identified the material dimensions of the immediate problems India was facing during his period. In the course of this analysis

---

[1] Deo, *Planning for Sarvodaya*, 12.

Kumarappa's writings present the Gandhian critique of capitalism. This critique has three dimensions. First, it scrutinizes colonialism and develops it critique. Second, it equates capitalism with money economy and presents evils of money. Third, it presents the pitfalls of mechanized industrialism as an aspect of capitalism. Most of these themes are recurrent in the writings of some other Gandhians as well; however, Kumarappa's approach to these issues brings out a sharper critique of the capital and certain definite implications for the reorganization of political economy in an alternate way. This also expands the Gandhian economic discourse which has generally revolved around the idea of trusteeship, opposition to machines, pragmatism behind the advocacy of charkha and Khadi, Swadeshi and boycott of foreign goods, glorification of poverty and scarcity, etc. Normally, the analysis of the Gandhian critique of colonialism revolves around the symbolic significance of charkha vis-à-vis Manchester cloth, while Gandhi's critique of colonial modernity is seen more as moral and political rather than economic and political. Similarly, for many, Gandhi's friendly relations with the 'bourgeoisie' provide sufficient ground to believe that he merely attempted to ameliorate capitalism. Very few studies have seriously engaged themselves with exploring Gandhi's economic ideas systematically and thereby challenging this image.[2] The systematic and critical analysis of the dominant economic systems done by Kumarappa, therefore, has its own significance. Kumarappa's critique of colonialism, money economy and mechanized industrialism provides an alternate perspective to understand Gandhian engagement with capital.

While analysing Kumarappa's critique of colonialism, it is necessary to mention at the very outset that in Kumarappa's writings the term 'imperialism' is used more often than the term 'colonialism'. This, however, does not mean that Kumarappa was unaware of the cultural processes underneath

[2] Some of these studies have been discussed in the previous chapter. See also Mathur, *Essays on Gandhian Economics*. Diwan and Lutz, eds., *Essays in Gandhian Economics*.

imperialism–colonialism. Hence, his preference seems to be corresponding more with the usage of his time than a thoughtful choice. The present work has used both the terms corresponding with the context of usage.

Kumarappa's views on colonialism show a steady evolution. His critique of colonialism begins with the critique of British rule in India. This critique primarily confirms the 'drain theory'[3] and locates the roots of India's agony in the irresponsive and inefficient colonial administration. Kumarappa's postgraduate research report 'Public Finance and India's Poverty' is a classic example of this disposition.[4] In this work he points out how the unproductive, exorbitant and wasteful expenditure by the British colonial administration was leading to the impoverishment of India and how the revenue obtained from the poor was utilized in keeping up the prestige of the foreign rule. He proves with facts and figures that capital expenditure glaringly exceeded development expenditure in order to serve the colonial interests. Tariff system favoured British goods over indigenously produced commodities.[5] In the currency policy, the government was not concerned with the stability of the purchasing power of rupee which affects the welfare of the people, but with the maintenance of stability in the interest of those involved in trade.[6] Foreign merchants and landlords were exempted from income tax, while over-assessment of land was a remarkable feature of the land revenue policy.[7] In the concluding remarks to this report, Kumarappa asserts that India can be expected to progress economically only when it

---

[3] The drain theory was earlier propounded by Dadabhai Naoroji in a series of speeches and writings. They were later published in a volume *Poverty and Un-British Rule in India* (1901). Naoroji considered capital payments and defence expenses as the principal causes of the drain. Kumarappa, in addition, as could be seen, is talking about the ways in which colonialism affected the very structure of the Indian economy.

[4] Kumarappa, *Public Finance and Our Poverty*, 1.

[5] Ibid., 23–24.

[6] Ibid., 27.

[7] Ibid., 32–39.

wins fiscal autonomy. Like the earlier exponents of the drain theory, Kumarappa doesn't show any naivety about the intentions of the British and doesn't really find such policies 'un-British'. Rather he presses for fiscal autonomy, whatever that may mean politically! This critique doesn't merely remain the critique of the foreign rule; it also shows awareness about the colonial design. This awareness increases as Kumarappa comes into direct contact with the Indian masses.

Another early example of Kumarappa's critique of colonialism could be found in the report of the survey of Matar taluka,[8] which Kumarappa conducted in the early 1930s under the auspices of the Gujarat Vidyapeeth. In this report, he criticizes the British administration for over-assessment of land, indifference towards the conditions of the farmers and virtually non-existent agricultural department. But more importantly he locates the root cause of impoverishment of people and under-utilization of land in the faulty revenue code itself: 'The land revenue code as it stands today is an ordinance of the worst type giving unlimited power into the hands of the executive. It makes the administrative officer a tyrant even when he acts within law.'[9] Here he seems to be aware of the colonial design which created the economic structures to perpetuate underdevelopment. He warns the Indian masses about these deliberate ill designs:

Not content with themselves fleecing the people they have also introduced another quasi Government Department under the pretentious title Co-operative movement. It may be the reference to cooperation to the Government rather than to the people, as the result seems to indicate that the co-operative societies have conspired with the Government to heartlessly extract 'the pound of flesh' from people who have practically no knowledge of the management of such societies and their officers and organizers care more for government favour than for welfare of the people.[10]

[8] Kumarappa, *A Survey of Matar Taluka*.
[9] Ibid., 95.
[10] Ibid., 142.

Kumarappa insists on scrutinizing every single economic structure created by the colonial rule with sufficient care and thus cautions against colonial developmentalism.

In another article, written around the same time, Kumarappa expresses stern dissent about the way the foreign rule was eulogizing the interests of urban middle classes of Indian society. In this article, while scrutinizing the revenue account of the Government of India for the year 1928–1929, Kumarappa remarks, '[...] The whole system is a most wonderfully whited sepulchre calculated to hoodwink the few who are educated and who play up to the game of exploitation of the dumb masses. Money is drawn from villages and some of it spent on towns?'[11]

The early writings of Kumarappa make it evident that he was sufficiently aware that colonialism was not merely exploiting the Indian society in the interests of the metropolis but was also causing underdevelopment, dependency of the rural areas on the urban centres and sharp economic divisions within the Indian masses. However, at this hour, he doesn't indulge much in reflecting upon the structural foundation of colonialism or on the possible relationship between colonialism and capitalism. Instead, by following his teacher E. R. A. Seligman, Kumarappa merely pleads for progressive taxation.[12] He insists that this kind of a change is impossible in the presence of a foreign rule, and hence stresses for financial autonomy. The awareness of the prevalence of an economic system that necessitates the underdevelopment of a colony doesn't really come to the centre of the entire argument. The only time where this awareness becomes fleetingly visible is in the address given by Kumarappa before the National Christian Party in Bombay in July 1930. In this address, Kumarappa classifies nationalism into two types: 'Sheep-Flock or Herd-Type

---

[11] Kumarappa, 'Who Pays the Piper?', 66.
[12] E. R. A. Seligman was one of the chief exponents of progressive taxation. He had devised this system to remove the lacuna and weaknesses in capitalism. For details, see Chapter 2 of this work.

Nationalism' and 'Wolf-Pack Nationalism'.[13] He points out that the wolf-pack nationalism is a result of capitalist greed and consequent piracy.[14] Thereby Kumarappa recognizes the symbiotic relationship between the nation state and capital, and equates colonialism with capitalist expansionism. It is interesting to note that Kumarappa does not discard nationalism per se, but differentiates between hegemonic nationalism and anti-colonial nationalistic assertions. He maintains that the herd-type nationalism emerges in response to imperialism, and nationhood is claimed to provide the necessary structural context for facilitating the materialization of the pleas of justice for and equality of the exploited masses. The herd is together to protect itself from external threat, not to attack others. Besides a herd is not as tied together as a pack would be.[15] People come together in response to a peculiar historical moment and claim nationhood in the context of the existing world system. The policy measures recommended by Kumarappa attempt to delink nation-building from capital accumulation and colonial expansion. He insists that the processes of capital accumulation and colonial expansionism cannot be halted with socialism as it will only substitute the capitalist greed and piracy with a proletarian variety. Interestingly, in this address Kumarappa could be seen criticizing Marx for subscribing to the 'superior civilization' syndrome and considering the tropical countries as legitimate booty for European states.[16] This could be regarded as Kumarappa's awareness about 'the other history of Capital'. Since the 1970s, Marxists such as Arghiri Emmanuel and Samir Amin have criticized Western Marxism

[13] Kumarappa, *Nationalism*, 3.

[14] Ibid., 14–15.

[15] Generally, all groups of mammals are termed as herd, but large groups of carnivores are referred to as pack. In nature, a herd is subject to predation by pack hunters. After a certain limit, however, the etymological difference between the two terms loses its significance as both the terms are also at times considered synonymous. What is important here is the spirit in which Kumarappa uses these terms.

[16] Ibid.

for ignoring the 'unequal exchange' between the First and the Third Worlds in international trade, while scholars like Andre Günter Frank have written on the effects of the 'First' World industrialization on the 'Third' World and the consequent dependency of the latter, asserting that the history of capitalism is not similar all over the world. 'Two Histories of Capital' is a phrase popularized by the postcolonialist critic Dipesh Chakrabarty to interrogate the 'global' history of capital. It is interesting to see that Kumarappa's criticism of capitalism shares some of these concerns. In his concluding remarks in the address, Kumarappa talks about the need to reorganize international trade in order to facilitate mutual coexistence of nations.[17] The concern for the reorganization of international trade in the post-Independence period led Kumarappa to join the World Peace Conference.

Kumarappa developed and extended his argument about colonialism and nationalism further after he actively involved himself with the organization of the AIVIA. In the 1936 publication *Why the Village Movement?*[18] Kumarappa classifies human economic organizations into two types—the individualistic type and the social type. Using animal prototypes he names them the 'pack type' and the 'herd type', respectively. This description also indicated, albeit in a slightly chauvinistic way, Kumarappa's awareness of the cultural content of colonialism. He characterizes 'pack-type' economic organizations with the following features:

1. Short-term outlook on life
2. Central control and concentration of power in the hands of individuals or small groups in a personal way
3. Rigorous discipline
4. Disregard for the welfare of the actual workers or the contributors to the success of the organization

[17] Ibid., 36.
[18] Kumarappa, *Why the Village Movement?*

5. Suppression of the individuality of the worker and the spirit of intolerance either in competition or in rivalry
6. The prospects of obtaining gains being the motive force for all activities
7. Concentration of the benefits obtained and the sharing of them amongst a limited few
8. To gather as much as one can without reference to the altruistic value of service rendered, the object being predatory

Whereas the 'herd type' economic organizations are characterized with following features:

1. Long-term outlook in life
2. Social control, decentralization and distribution of power, the working and regulation being impersonal
3. Activity steered into desired channels by rules of conduct and social regulatory machinery
4. Attempts made to safeguard the weak and helpless
5. Encouragement given to individual growth and expressed by a considerable amount of tolerance
6. Activities directed by a consideration of certain set ideals and social movements
7. Distribution of gains as wide as possible according to the needs of the individual
8. The objective to satisfy needs judged from an altruistic point of view[19]

Kumarappa maintains that the Western economic organizations are pack-type organizations, while the Eastern economic organizations are herd type in nature. He classifies the pack-type Western economic organizations into five subtypes:

1. The dynasty of might (represented by feudalism)
2. The dynasty of finance (represented by imperialism)
3. The dynasty of machine (represented by American Industrial Society)

[19] Ibid., 4–5.

4. The dynasty of labour (represented by communism)
5. The dynasty of the middle classes (represented by Fascism/Nazism)

This typology is interesting in numerous ways. The usage of the two terms—dynasty of finance and dynasty of machine—is especially significant considering the fact that it enabled Kumarappa to address the issues of pre-capitalist economy along with the issues inherently linked with industrial capitalism, its different forms and phases without engaging himself into Marxist polemics. It also allowed Kumarappa to address both his concerns, that is, money economy and mechanized industrialism. Similarly, by describing communism as the dynasty of labour, Kumarappa was able to point out the hegemonic character of the working class rule in the communist regimes. The description of the class character of fascism/Nazism on the one hand demystified its economic content, while on the other exposed the myth of middle-class morality. These types are neither purely economic nor essentially cultural. The recurring theme of East versus West in Kumarappa's writings at times makes him appear as a cultural essentialist if not chauvinist. But the classification of pack-type systems into five types of dynasties and their respective descriptions make it evident that his typology addresses the politico-economic ethos of various social systems as it evolved over the period and is not as essentialist or chauvinistic as it may appear. Hence, his rejection of these models and his attempt to develop a new model that would avoid the evils of money and machine, establish the dignity of labour without making it hegemonic and reconstitute the middle class on ethical foundations exhibit his creativity in making moral choices.

Kumarappa's critique of colonialism was more or less acceptable to the Gandhians, as at least during the lifetime of Gandhi, no one seems to have taken any objection to any of the arguments mentioned above. In the post-Gandhi period, however, the Sarvodaya Plan developed by Shankarrao Deo and others rejected the use of animal prototypes to describe human societies without naming Kumarappa.

[...] Herds, packs, colonies, hives have a pattern of life in which each lives for all and all for each. The high social 'morality' there is worked out by instinct and organic laws. Human society is super organic, and what instinct and organic laws have left undone has to be achieved under culture, i.e. the moral effect of man.[20]

The material dimension and the politico-economic ethos of Gandhian economics thus gets underplayed by overarching morality, as if in Gandhi moral and material are binaries.

In Kumarappa's thinking, money economy is not to be equated with the economy that uses coinage and currency. Kumarappa was well aware that in India the use of currency and coinage dates back to the period of Kautilya's *Arthashastra*. At the same time he maintained that the domestic economic activities here were never linked to the flow of money and credit. First, because the export trade was mainly based on the surplus production, luxury items and curios;[21] and second, because the presence of money was balanced by the system of partial payment in kind known as *Dan, Baluta* or *Jamini*. Kumarappa insists that as a result the changes in the international trade never affected the lives of the common citizens and their socio-economic life continued peacefully, independent of the upheavals that may take place in the trading cycles. In the Report of the C. P. & Berar Industrial Survey Committee of 1939,[22] Kumarappa has dealt with this issue extensively. He writes:

[20] Deo, *Planning for Sarvodaya*, 16.

[21] This point is further illustrated in Kumarappa, 'Handicrafts and Cottage Industries', 106–112.

[22] This report was written primarily by Kumarappa. Three members of the committee submitted dissenting notes to the report. The common factor of their dissent was the apprehension about Kumarappa's recommendation for avoiding mechanized large-scale industries for the growth of village industries. They wanted to promote village industry only as an ancillary activity for the farmers during slack period and not at the cost of large-scale industrialization. See *Report of the Industrial Survey Committee*, 32–38.

Money economy has its own strong points but too great emphasis on the use of money has been necessitated by the economic organizations of the West where articles from very great distances become primary need for their industries. The farther we go for raw materials or markets, the greater is the need for a money economy.[23]

Kumarappa insists that emphasizing on money economy in villages has placed the villager at the mercy of a foreign salesman. Kumarappa makes certain pertinent observations regarding money economy. First, money represents the power to control other people's lives because the owner of money is on a foundation that differs from that of the possessor of the exchangeable article. It is not possible for exchange in commodities to take place equitably when one person is in possession of a stronger bargaining power. In case of perishable goods, such exchange becomes still more unequal since the seller of the commodity is in a hurry to sell off her products. Thus money operates as an unequal medium of exchange.

Second, in money economy public expenditure of the government loses the connection with the source of money. Money is drawn from villages and is used to maintain towns and cities. National wealth thus loses human value.

Third, the labour spent on article near the consumption stage pays much better returns than the one which is nearer the raw material stage because the principle of the ability to bear the charges operates. In a system of mechanized industrialism, where the gap between the raw material producers and finished goods manufacturers is wide, the former group is destined to perpetual underpayment.

Fourth, an increase in raw material production in agriculture amounts to an increase in the incidence of poverty as with the cash crop the farmer gets tied up either with the industry or with the fluctuations in the import–exports. Kumarappa

[23] *Report of the Industrial Survey Committee* Part I: Vol. 1, 3.

therefore insists that a farmer who cultivates money crop for factories is no better than a factory labourer.[24]

Fifth, money economy does not report true values. The values are changed as money passes from one individual to another. There is a difference in value between the rupee in the hands of a poor man and that in the hands of a rich man. A rupee in the hands of a poor man may represent the value of 4–5 day's food provision while a rupee in the hands of a rich man would represent the value of a cigar. Kumarappa thus writes, '[…] we have got to see that in our economy we prevent money going into the hands where it will lose its value.'[25]

Kumarappa insists that since money is not a commodity which satisfies any primary need and man cannot live by money alone, the usage of money has to be and can be minimized. In the Central Provinces Industrial Survey Committee Report, Kumarappa has recommended that villagers should be allowed to pay the taxes partially in kind. He writes:

> […] if revenues can be collected to some extent in kind, there will be some check in the fall of utility because the use of paddy or wheat collected by the Government will be restricted to payment to officers locally and the difficulties of marketing these products will create a certain amount of friction in bringing the purchasing power from the villages to the cities […].[26]

Later, in his best known work *Economy of Permanence*, Kumarappa came up with the idea of a multipurpose cooperative society which

> will collect the produce from the villager and will pay the government revenue in wheat or other commodities. It will pay government officials on government account in articles of food which will provide a balanced diet and when all this

24 Ibid., 4.
25 Kumarappa, *Economy of Permanence*, 136.
26 *Report of the Industrial Survey Committee* Part I: Vol. 1.

is carried out, ultimately there will be a very small adjustment to be made between government and the multipurpose societies and that can also be done by transfer of surplus between different regions.[27]

Kumarappa maintained that with the advent of imperialism monetary activities came to the centre stage of economy. He maintains that imperialism made the domestic economy dependent on the world economy. The dynamics of money, credit and banking started affecting the indigenous economy. Market economy replaced the indigenous economic modalities and the Indian social life was trodden under money economy. With the advent of the machine in the European economies, this invasion became more intense and deeper, necessitating the loot of the natural environment in the colonies for the survival of the predatory economies of the metropolis.

There are at least three dimensions of Kumarappa's analysis of money that are debateable and need to be problematized in wider contexts. First, the phases of imperialism as identified by him (pre-Industrial Revolution and post-Industrial Revolution) need be interrogated and analysed. Second, his view that the precolonial Indian economy was not a money economy needs to be corroborated with historical accounts of that period. And third, his insistence on reducing the incidence of money in economic activities needs to be analysed in the context of the modern economies.

As for the first dimension, that is, Kumarappa's views concerning the emergence and phases of imperialism, scholars by and large agree that empire-building, territorial expansion and domination of weaker by stronger powers, all features associated with imperialism, have a long history that dates back to the pre-industrial period.[28] Harry Magdoff has raised two pertinent questions about the rise and development of imperialism. First, are there any analytically significant differences between such drives in the pre-capitalist and capitalist

---

[27] Kumarappa, *Economy of Permanence.*
[28] Magdoff, *Imperialism: From the Colonial Age to the Present,* 2.

times? And second, what is the explanation for the almost simultaneous outburst of a renewed wave of expansion by a number of leading nations in the late nineteenth century, accompanied by a marked intensification of the power struggle among these states?[29] Explanations to both these questions could be found in Kumarappa's analysis. As could be seen in his typology of dynasties, Kumarappa locates the difference between pre-capitalist and capitalist imperialism in their respective approaches towards nature; while the outburst of the renewed wave of expansion is located in the advent of machine. These explanations of course are not exhaustive but are sufficient to bring out Kumarappa's awareness about the complexity of the phenomenon of imperialism.

As for the second dimension, that is, the role of money and market in India's precolonial economy, scholars are found to be divided over this issue. Scholars like Karl Polanyi[30] maintain that market economy characterizes a specific and very particular historic moment of Western society. In non-Western societies economic relationships were 'embedded' in social fabric. This view is challenged by scholars like Sanjay Subrahmanyam,[31] who have shown the evidence of market and monetary transactions in medieval India. *The Cambridge Economic History of India* by Raychaudhuri and Habib[32] has also shown the prevalence of networks in medieval India which linked the periodic markets with urban bazaars and long-distance trade, in a way refuting Kumarappa's arguments that internal trades were never linked with international trade. More recent studies of regional markets (market in Bihar by Anand Yang,[33] markets in Bengal by Tilottama Mukherjee,[34] for instance) do testify to the fact that

[29] Ibid.
[30] See Polanyi, *The Great Transformation*.
[31] Subrahmanyam, *Money and the Market in India 1100–1700*.
[32] Raychaudhuri and Habib, eds., *The Cambridge Economic History of India 1200–1750*, Vol. 1.
[33] Yang, *Bazaar India*.
[34] Mukherjee, 'Markets in Eighteenth Century Bengal Economy', 143–176.

the markets in India were not mere replicas of the European markets.

Eric H. Mielants in his concise and analytical account of the origin of capitalism cites numerous studies that identify the differences between the political economies of South Asia in the precolonial period with that of Europe. These studies provide for both supportive as well as contradictory incidences to Kumarappa's position. For instance it provides that around the eleventh century the impact of maritime trade was not limited to the coastal area and it had permeated to the hinterlands.[35] There are studies which maintain that around this period the incidence of forced labour decreased as more of it commuted into money payments, while the sophistication of credit and banking increased.[36] The flourishing urban economy in the period between 1200 and 1400 was characterized by widespread use of bills of exchange and joint trading as well as concurrent increase in craft production through the use of spinning wheels and treadle looms.[37] However, historians unanimously agree that even with the remarkable increase in overseas trade, capitalism did not spontaneously emerge in South Asia. While rejecting the sociological explanations of how the cultural values of caste system prevented modernization in the South Asian subcontinent and also rejecting that South Asian peasants were not market oriented or were fundamentally risk averse,[38] Mielants points out that the absence of capitalist system could be located in the fundamentally different political structure in the subcontinent. The polity in South Asia wasn't weak;[39] however, the mercantile class in South Asia was never institutionalized. Merchants were excluded from the political order. The merchant guilds rarely controlled production or defined

---

[35] Mielants, *The Origin of Capitalism*, 88.
[36] Ibid.
[37] Ibid., 89.
[38] Ibid., 99.
[39] Ibid., 95–96.

and defended regions of mercantile activity against rivals.[40] In the absence of such nexus, the synergy was never created for capitalist territorial expansion.

Such studies and emanating explanations facilitate to understand Kumarappa's arguments about money in a wider perspective and relieve his typologies from getting branded as mere cultural essentialism. However, his arguments about the phases of imperialism and his views on precolonial economies, when corroborated with each other, raise some crucial questions. Does Kumarappa equate imperialism with the very presence of European traders on Indian subcontinent? Can commercial expansion without definite political motives or support be considered as imperialism? In what way does Kumarappa define the incidence of pre-Industrial Revolution imperialism in India? Does he consider the Indian economy static before the advent of European merchandise on the Indian land, as no phases are identified by him for this period? Of course, Kumarappa was not a historian, to have explored these nuances. What is interesting is that though Kumarappa's analysis about the advent of money and ensuing perception about the economic history of the 'East' and 'West' at a number of places confirms the same processes that Marx had anticipated while writing about the Asiatic Mode of Production and Lenin had visualized while putting forth his thesis about imperialism; Kumarappa could be seen reversing the very logic of economic historicism. He comes up with an alternate interpretation of the economic unfolding of the West. While Marx and the Marxists looked at this process (Asian societies coming into the contact with the advanced mode of production through imperialism) as a sign of advancement, for Kumarappa this process meant not only economic subordination of the East but also of its own way of organizing the economic activities. Kumarappa's view that in the precolonial economies the local trades were delinked from the international trade thus provides an interesting insight for historical explorations.

[40] Ibid., 100–120.

Regarding the third dimension of Kumarappa's critique of money, that is, his plea to reduce the incidence of money in economic activities, it is necessary to note that Kumarappa is not the only Gandhian who considered money an evil. Even Vinoba had advocated for reducing money. Congress had advocated the use of yarn currency[41] as an alternative to imperial paper currency during the times of the Second World War in order to deal with currency inflation. This of course was a temporary measure. In the later period, however, other than Kumarappa, it was Vinoba who could be seen making frequent pleas to avoid the use of money. On the eve of Independence, Vinoba in *Harijan* wrote an article entitled 'Wanted Corn, Not Currency'. He argues:

> Businessmen say that agriculture is not a profitable vocation in India. But, since life depends upon agriculture, where agriculture is not profitable, life itself cannot be profitable. The result is not, cannot be, natural; it is the result of an artificial civilization. Currency is the symbol of this artificiality. The false prestige given to the possession of currency has become the cause of destruction of so much of life.[42]

In 1950 AISA passed a resolution to use yarn as currency rather than using the printed currency.[43] Later in his speeches during the Bhoodan Yatra, Vinoba advocated organizing village economy on labour by eliminating money; he named this experiment Kanchan Mukti, that is, liberation from money. He insisted that villagers should use their own currency rather than 'the one printed at Nasik at the behest of some ruler'. In this currency there would be no question of credit.[44] He also refused to take money in donation and appealed to build up

---

[41] *Harijan* 11, no. 9 (15 March 1942): 78.

[42] Bhave, 'Wanted Corn, Not Currency', 24.

[43] Bhave, *Vinoba Sahitya* Vol. 18, 146.

[44] Bhave, 'Freedom from Money', 373. Indian mints being located at Nasik (Maharashtra), Vinoba makes reference to Nasik currency.

labour for the sake of Gandhi.[45] In a speech delivered at Barahar, Vinoba says:

> ... I am often asked Gandhiji used to accept money, then why you are not accepting it? I answer, I don't accept because Gandhiji used to accept. He has sufficiently experimented with money. The river never flows in the same way as it flows at its origin. I don't want to give any respect to money. I want the poor to realise that they have the real riches while I want to make rich realise their poverty.... I want to liberate you from the enchantment of money.[46]

Vinoba considers money responsible for the moral degeneration of human race. In another speech at Pakkanarpur in 1956 he reiterates that if we want the truth to prevail we must constitute society on the principle of labour than on money.[47]

Vinoba makes no reference to Kumarappa's analysis of money and its economy. He doesn't even show any awareness about the existence of such an argument. Both these Gandhians arrive at similar positions from their respective paths and concerns, albeit, Vinoba concerned more with the moral degeneration of human race while Kumarappa's apprehensions emerge from the limitations of money in representing the true value of a commodity.

None of the modern-day economists would accept on moral or any other grounds the proposal of replacing money with a system that advocates barter or semi-barter. The very existence of traditional markets and parallel or informal credit and finance are considered as antithetical to the interests of national economies. The integration of informal markets into the formal markets has always remained one of the biggest concerns of the developing economies. The arguments to

[45] Bhave, 'No Money Donations', 389. Such references could be found in his later Bhoodan speeches as well.
[46] *Vinoba Sahitya* Vol. 18, 150.
[47] Ibid., 155.

reduce the use of paper money emanate basically from the concerns of integrating informal money markets into the formal mainstream economy rather than for reducing the incidence of money per se. When the emphasis has always been on integration of markets, the plea for reducing money and programmes for transactions through barter would look ridiculous and outdated. Besides when national economies are so much connected with each other, if at all such measures are to be implemented they would be necessitating complete seclusion of national economy from the international system. Having said this, a faithful reading of Kumarappa expects to approach his idea of reducing money the same way Gandhi approached non-violence. He believed that absolute non-violence is impossible as long as we have physical existence and yet non-violence should be the guiding principle. There can be no alternative to non-violence. Thus the practice of non-violence would be a matter of human beings' creative abilities and potentials in making moral choices. In a similar vein, one may approach the arguments about money. While considering the practical difficulties that such an approach would entail, the issues raised by Kumarappa about the limitations of money in representing the true value as well as in ensuring the dignity of labour cannot be just ignored. Bringing this idea into practice will taste an economist's creative abilities and also her faith in the limitations of the existing economic models, both liberal and that of the Marxist variety.

While insisting for the reduction of money, Kumarappa did have apprehensions with the Marxist model as well for the similar reasons. As early as in 1934, when Kumarappa was touring the country as a part of the propaganda and extension activity of the AIVIA, in one of his interviews, Kumarappa criticized capitalism and communism in acknowledging the dignity of human labour. '... Just as in peace time machinery that produced bicycles can at a moment's notice be converted into producing armaments, so can change of personnel at the helm of affairs convert a Soviet Russia of today into a Rockefeller organisation tomorrow....'[48] In 1938, while criticizing the centralized process of production Kumarappa wrote:

> Russia itself started off with the idea of banishing the evils
> of capitalism, but retained centralised production as its chief
> feature, with the result that though the profit motives have
> been socialised, yet admittedly many of the evils are left
> behind, i.e. in other words Soviet Communism has failed to
> achieve, what it had set forth to. Once this is granted, the
> situation challenges us to produce a system which is neither
> State Capitalism nor Private Capitalism.[49]

After his visit to Russia, China and other communist countries
in 1952, Kumarappa did start appreciating the organized and
focused efforts made in these countries to do away with poverty
and unemployment; however, he never subscribed to communism as an economic system. In his classificatory scheme, the
communist systems represented the Economy of Gregation that
necessitated submission to the will of group leading, perhaps
to even self-abnegation and sacrifice of personal interests and
carried the possibility of violence to those outside the group.[50]

It is interesting to note that while writing for the Indian readers Kumarappa has brought out the political and economic processes underlying the existing systems, his writings addressed
specifically to the Western audience emphasize the cultural
dimension more. While writing for the special volume on India
brought out by the Annals of the American Academy of Political
and Social Science in May, 1944 Kumarappa could be seen
emphasizing the cultural dimension more. Here he juxtaposes

[48] Prasad, ed., *Selected Works of Jayaprakash Narayan*, Vol. 1 (1929–
1935), 290–292 (Appendix 14). JP responded critically to this interview
and came out with a small pamphlet named 'Socialism versus All India
Village Industries Association'.

[49] Kumarappa, 'Is it Economic Anarchism?' in *Cent Per Cent Swadeshi*,
164.

[50] Kumarappa, *Economy of Permanence*, 21–22.

the Western economic organizations with the Eastern economic organizations and highlights the difference in their nature.[51] An attempt to recognize the difference in history and geography of both the systems could also be seen but in this particular classificatory scheme the way Kumarappa goes on articulating this difference, at times it appears as if he is resorting to what Partha Chatterjee calls 'orientalism in reverse'.[52] While discussing the nature of Eastern economic organizations, for instance, Kumarappa writes:

> It is in old countries like India, China and Japan (as she was) that we find agricultural civilization influencing economic organization. Such civilizations are the result of philosophy and conscious social planning. The western systems are haphazard growths without any thought behind them. In this sense *the West can hardly be said to have a civilization at all. It is a more refined barbarism.*[53] (Emphasis added)

Such statements move Kumarappa's perception of the world economic history from the domain of alternate historicism to reverse orientalism. No doubt his interpretation helps to

---

[51] It could be seen that Gandhi also has consistently taken the same position. In 1929 he asks a straight question in *Young India*: Why must India become industrialized in the Western sense? (*Young India*, 25 July 1929). He also insists India need not copy the Western model. Later in another article in 1931, he writes, '...the laws of economics vary in their application to different conditions. Their (European) advice cannot therefore guide us beyond a certain point. What is true of Europe is not necessarily true of India' (*Young India*, 2 July 1931).

[52] Partha Chatterjee argues that the problematic in the nationalist thought is exactly the reverse of orientalism. That is, the 'object' in the nationalist thought is still the oriental, who retains the essentialist character depicted in orientalist discourse. See Chatterjee, *Nationalist Thought and the Colonial World*, 36–38. In recent times Peter Heehs has come up with a taxonomy of orientalism depicting the different shades as they appeared in Indian historical writings. See Heehs, 'Shades of Orientalism'. Kumarappa's arguments would come under the category of 'nationalist orientalism' under his scheme.

[53] Kumarappa, *Why the Village Movement?*, 14.

interrogate and challenge the notions of historical progression (both the liberal and the Marxist) and European claim for the leadership of this progression, but cultural essentialism brings his analysis to the dangerous edge of Eastern chauvinism.

A year later while writing his much acclaimed work *Economy of Permanence* Kumarappa could be found revising his classificatory scheme. This new system draws heavily from the earlier one but doesn't resort to essentialism or to branding different stages as Eastern or Western. He presents this classificatory scheme as 'Stages of Human Development' identifying five stages, namely:

1. Parasitic economy (destroys the very source of benefit)
2. Predatory economy (benefit without contribution)
3. Economy of enterprise (benefit and contribution correlated, with a readiness to take risk)
4. Economy of Gregation (benefit to group rather than to individual member)
5. Economy of service (contribution without regard to any benefit received by the worker)

He also mentions about the three stages of civilizational growth, namely:

1. Parasitic or animal stage
2. Modern or human stage
3. Advanced spiritual stage

Kumarappa illustrates these stages with different examples but this time rather than branding a nation or a civilization with an essentialist stereotype he more reasonably cites specific episodes in history. As examples of parasitic civilization, Kumarappa identifies British opium trade in China, slave traffic with Southern States of America, King Leopold's exploitation of West African estates and the dependence of British manufacturers on Indian markets.[54] As an example of the modern human

---

[54] Kumarappa, *Economy of Permanence*, 27.

stage, Kumarappa cites agricultural civilizations of India and China supported by artisans pursuing their vocations for profit. Islamic culture is also seen by him standing for solidarity and group identity.[55] Though not in *Economy of Permanence*, but elsewhere he has considered the present-day economies of Japan and China as Gregarious economies, that is, the economies protecting merely the group interests.[56] In this background, he presents the Gandhian ideal of non-violent economy of permanence as an advanced and desired stage, a Gandhian utopia. Kumarappa is very clear that such a society doesn't exist anywhere at present. He maintains AISA and AIVIA are committed to translate this utopia into reality. In this stage, Kumarappa insists that the sense of duty not only towards those of the group but to all the creatures pervades the whole atmosphere.[57] Kumarappa thus presents the idea of mother economy as an alternative to the money-centric liberal and Marxist systems. Kumarappa's mother economy necessitates village-centric and non-mechanistic model of industrialization.

Kumarappa agreed with his contemporaries that India's economic regeneration necessitates intense industrialization on a priority basis. However, he also insisted that for industrializing the country, one need not follow the Western model of heavy industrialization. Kumarappa argued for non-mechanized, non-capitalist industrialization in India. Kumarappa's critique of the Western mechanized industrialism could be discerned from his analysis of the policy measures adopted by free India as well as from the number of pamphlets he wrote for the AIVIA. One of the chief concerns of Kumarappa was that of the survival of traditional craftsmen in the competition with mechanized industries. The process of mechanized industrialization deprived various craftsmen of their source of income. They were not provided with any other alternative occupation while

[55] Ibid., 28.
[56] See Kumarappa, *Report on Agriculture and Cottage and Small Scale Industries of Japan*. Also Kumarappa, *A Peep Behind the Iron Curtain*.
[57] Ibid.

the consumers were made to accept a lesser quality product. The traditional occupation of paddy-husking was, for instance, taken over by rice-mills. Thousands of villagers lost jobs and consumers were made to satisfy themselves with less-nutrient rice. Oil-pressing was taken over by oil-mills. Traditional oil-pressers lost their jobs, carpenters making the *ghanis* received a setback. Oil-cakes became unavailable as cattle fodder and consumers also lost the better-nutrient variety of oil. Similar trends were seen in other village industries also. In the Report of the Industrial Survey Committee for C. P. & Berar, Kumarappa has identified around forty village industries in the province that suffered due to mechanized industrialization.[58] Kumarappa tries to identify the social location of the sections that lost their livelihood. When *tongas* were replaced by automated vehicles, women and children who used to take care of horses lost their jobs. With the standardization in shoe industry, consumers were forced to adjust with the shoe sizes that were available in the market, while the cobblers lost their jobs. Marginalized in the process of mechanized industrialization, they became one of the most depressed communities in India.[59] In this background Kumarappa poses a pertinent question: When the beneficiaries of the mechanized industrialization were not the same as its victims, then how can one celebrate industrialization? In order to save the victims of mechanized industrialization from its evil effects, the AIVIA came up with the idea of reviving village industries; but certainly not as a caste-based occupation! The attempts to revive the oil-pressing industry best represent this point. AIVIA introduced *ghani* scheme in the year 1943 whereby *ghanis* were supplied at a concessional rate to anyone irrespective of caste interested in this work, and people were encouraged to use *ghani* oil instead of mill-pressed oil and vanaspati ghee. When it was realized that persons who take *ghani* from AIVIA do not start work themselves, AIVIA gave it a legal shape and started providing *ghanis* on loan after

[58] *Report of the Industrial Survey Committee* Part I: Vol. 1, 14–31.
[59] Ibid., 25.

ensuring that the worker has received training for oil-pressing.[60] Similar examples could also be found in various other village industries including tanning and leather industry. AIVIA set up a tanning centre at Nalwadi and tanning was included as one of the subjects in Gram Sevak Vidyalaya's curriculum. Irrespective of the caste background every student was required to do the work of cleaning dead cattle and that of tanning leather as part of their course. Extraction of alcohol from mahua flowers was another such occupation which Kumarappa had recommended for village industry, albeit for power generation. He insisted that though the cost of production for manufacturing alcohol from mahua flowers was higher, in ultimate analysis the amount of employment generated through such approach will be socially more beneficial.[61] Thus one of the major arguments that Kumarappa levels against mechanized industrialism is about the unemployment and displacement that it causes.

In the post-Independence period, when the effects of planning started becoming visible, some of the fears expressed by Kumarappa proved to be true. The letter given below, published in *Harijan* in 1954, is self-explanatory. The secretary of the Bombay State Kutch and Saurashtra Mochi Conference, Baroda, had written to the editors of *Harijan*:

Village mochi work and leather goods industry are a century-old important industry of India. In point of importance it ranks next only to the cottage industries of weaving and tanning. Those who earn their bread and butter from this vocation are quite large in numbers, amounting to millions.... But foreign firms like Bata and Flax have been dealing a death-blow to this cottage industry by their gigantic mass production. They have begun to bring wreck and ruin to our community. We strongly believe that if the government do not act in time to stop even at this stage the worsening condition of our industry, it will soon die out. And millions

[60] *Minutes of the Meeting of Board of Management of the All India Village Industries Association.*
[61] *Report of the Industrial Survey Committee* Part II: Vol. 1, 14–15.

of artisans whose only means of livelihood is this industry and who know no other vocation will be hurried into jaws of unemployment and starving.

The letter also lamented the fact that the First Five Year Plan had not included their industry in the list of the cottage industry.[62]

Kumarappa's second apprehension with the mechanized industries is its centralized process of production. Kumarappa insists that centralized production has two implications. First, centralization and consequent standardization kills originality thus obstructing the progress of humanity. Second, since the production is centralized in nature, the issue of distribution and redistribution emerges as a burning issue. In village industries since the process of production is decentralized, profit gets distributed through the very process of production itself.[63] Thus the role of the third party, that is, the distributive agency gets minimized.

Kumarappa is equally critical of the way in which mechanized industrialism colonizes agriculture at the cost of food security. Kumarappa's argument against the sugar industries best represents this viewpoint. In the Report of the Industrial Survey Committee, Kumarappa takes specific note of gur-making and sugar manufacture. He writes:

… Sugarcane cultivation requires good land in which wheat can be grown and it also requires intensive cultivation. On the other hand … there are jungles of *sindhi* trees all along the *nalas* and the banks of rivers, and Palmyra trees in the forest areas. These trees require hardly any cultivation and they grow in lands which cannot be used for anything else. If the sweet juice from these trees can be utilized for preparing *gur*, valuable lands on which sugarcane is now being cultivated can be released for other food crops. Of course, preparing

[62] Quoted in Editor's note, Desai, 'Village Shoe-Maker vs. Shoe-Making Factories', 40.
[63] Kumarappa, 'Is It Economic Anarchism?', 164–166.

gur from the juice of *sindhi* and palm trees cannot be carried out in mills [...].[64]

AIVIA later promoted palm-gur, classifying it as one of the village industries. At the dawn of Independence, Kumarappa linked this issue with the export–import policy as well. In 1947, Kumarappa wrote critically about the central government's decision to promote mill-made white sugar over *khandsari* sugar and gur.

> Before the advent of sugar-cane cultivation Biharis used their lands for rice cultivation and consumed hand pounded wholesome rice; but now the crops have been shifted with the result that they cultivate sugarcane and are dependant on Burma for their rice. And Burmese rice comes polished that means all the nutrition is removed as in pure starch. However much the sugarcane crop may have been increasing the bank balance of the mill owners, can we by any stretch of our imagination, lay claim of having increased production when we drive the masses of people from the nutritive rice of their own cultivation to devitalised polished rice imported from outside? This shifting of crops from food to raw material is not only a disservice to the country but is injurious to the health of the people [...].[65]

The fourth argument against mechanized industrialism levelled by Kumarappa is based on the implications it has for world economy and world peace. Kumarappa insists that mechanized industrialization necessitates cutthroat competition in the domain of international trade. Hence, mechanized industrialization proves detrimental to the cause of world peace. In the International Conference of Economists held in Moscow in April 1952, Kumarappa moved two resolutions. The first resolution pleaded for reorganization of international trade on more humane terms while the second one pressed for the promotion

[64] *Report of the Industrial Survey Committee* Part I: Vol. 1, 15.
[65] Kumarappa, 'Increasing Production', 137.

of cottage industries.[66] In another article written by Kumarappa in April 1953, he connects the issue of world peace with economic issues more aggressively. In this article he has classified the approaches to world peace into seven types:[67] Grave Yard Peace (experienced by Japan under American occupation), Volcano Peace (imposed by Germany on its allies), Hypnotic Peace (claimed by the British for the colonized India), Strategic Peace (European balance of power after the First World War), Sugar-coated Peace (second cousin of Hypnotic Peace, claimed by capitalist countries to keep the underdeveloped countries eternally under their wings), Peace propounded by Weed Top Method (propounded by the pacifists and the War Resisters International) and Gandhian peace.[68] Kumarappa insists that the seventh approach, that is, the Gandhian approach to world peace is different from all these approaches. He writes:

> Gandhiji has shown us the real road to peace. We must have courage to root out the basic cause of International conflict. This is primarily in our economic life. Each one of us becomes responsible for exploitation which leads to war. When we purchase or sell articles that are products of or raw materials for industries based on exploitation we become parties to the war that is occasioned. Hence prevention of war depends on our being self-sufficient on a decentralised basis....[69]

In Kumarappa's moral and economic critiques of the dominant economic systems are so much entwined with each other that it is actually not possible to separate them. In case of other Gandhians, however, the critique appears more moral than economic. While writing on the Vanaspati ghee issue, for instance (mentioned earlier in this chapter), Kishorelal Mashruwala argues:

[66] Kumarappa, *A Peep Behind the Iron Curtain*, 13–15.
[67] Descriptions in the bracket are from Kumarappa's original article.
[68] Kumarappa, *The Non-Violent Economy and World Peace*, 5–8.
[69] Ibid., 8–9.

[...] We must face the moral realities. More than even the food shortage and lack of industrial development is the moral shortage, and in devising controls or encouraging industries, greatest importance should be attached and place of honour should be given to the moral effects on the nation, and even while they are maintained, means and methods should be explored of ending them as quickly as possible.[70]

Having explored Kumarappa's critique of colonialism, money economy and mechanized industrialism, it becomes clear that his rejection of these 'modern' systems was not on merely moral premises; it encompassed a definite economic content. This economic content interrogates and rejects the premises of not only colonialism and capitalism but also communism. Thus, Kumarappa as an exponent of Gandhian economic ideas does not restrict himself merely to transform capitalism radically; he rejects capitalism and mechanized industrialism outrightly in favour of village-centred 'economy of permanence'. The political economy that he anticipates to realize this utopia of village-centred economy therefore necessitates a polity that will facilitate this decentralization of economy.

[70] Mashruwala, 'Facing Realities', 336.

4

Political Economy of Permanence

J. C. Kumarappa's idea of economy of permanence presents his interpretation of the Gandhian utopia of Sarvodaya. Gandhi had borrowed the term 'Sarvodaya' from Jainism to translate Ruskin's 'Unto This Last'. In his autobiography, Gandhi has narrated the influence that Ruskin's work had on him in defining the three crucial principles of Sarvodaya. First, that the good of the individual is contained in the good of all. Second, that a lawyer's work has the same value as the barber's inasmuch as all have the same right of earning their livelihood from their work. Third, that a life of labour, that is, the life of the tiller of the soil and the handicraftsman, is the life worth living.[1] In these principles, the 'moral' was intertwined with the 'material'. The economic order that Gandhi propounded and endeavoured to attain ensured that the moral and the material do not get bifurcated. Gandhi firmly asserted that man must be the focal point of every economic order. The attempts to generate wealth should not endanger the existence of the real wealth, that is, the mankind. At the same time, Gandhi also endeavoured to make the 'moral' economically viable. In 1921 Gandhi wrote

[1] Gandhi, *The Story of My Experiments with Truth.*

in *Young India*, 'Economics that hurt the moral well-being of an individual or a nation are immoral and, therefore, sinful.'[2] In 1937 he added, 'True economics never mitigates against the highest ethical standards, *just as all true ethics to be worth its name must at the same time be also good economics*'[3] (emphasis added). Economic viability of programmes was a matter of concern for Gandhi. But does he also support the organization of economic activity so as to generate surplus? Gandhian economics has always been equated with economics of scarcity by ignoring pertinent questions raised in the writings of Gandhi about the definition of surplus, abundance and economic progress. In 1938 when asked to respond to Pandit Nehru's support for the economics of abundance, Gandhi writes:

> [...] What is abundance? Not the capacities to destroy the millions of ton of wheat as you do in America? [...] If by abundance you mean having plenty to eat and drink and to clothe himself with, enough to keep his mind trained and educated, I should be satisfied. But I should not like to pack more stuff in my belly than I can ever usefully use. But neither do I want poverty, penury, misery, dirt and dust in India.[4]

The idea of village industries therefore neither necessitated glorification of poverty nor did it resort to justification of scarcity. The very reference to India's share in international trade in the pre-British era presumed that village industries do generate surplus so as to facilitate international trade but not to the extent of necessitating the plundering of foreign markets with excessive production. With this presumption Kumarappa reflected on the economic plans and policies of Congress in the pre-Independence and post-Independence India. These

---

[2] Gandhi, 'The Great Sentinel', 325.

[3] Gandhi, 'Primary Education in Bombay', 292.

[4] Dr John De Boer, an educationist from South India, visited Wardha. The report of his discussion with Gandhi, Kaka Kalelkar and Shri Aryanayakam compiled by Mahadev Desai was published in *Harijan*. Desai, 'Interpretation of the Wardha Education Scheme'.

reflections bring out the political economy that Kumarappa anticipated to realize economy of permanence.

The early sources of Kumarappa's views on the Gandhian political economy could be located in his reflections and comments on the proposals of National Planning Committee.[5] The decision to appoint the National Planning Committee was taken by the nine provincial Congress ministries in their meeting held in Bombay in 1937. Pandit Jawaharlal Nehru was selected as its chairperson, while Professor K. T. Shah was its honorary secretary. The committee comprised of industrialists such as Purushottamdas Thakurdas, Ambalal Sarabhai and Walchand Hirachand, as well as economists such as M. Visvesvaraya, J. C. Kumarappa and Radhakamal Mukherjee. It is interesting to see that around this time various other stakeholders also came up with their own economic plans for independent India. Though the industrialists were part of the National Planning Committee, they had also started conducting parallel sessions. This parallel committee comprised of J. R. D. Tata, Ghanashyam Birla, Sir Ardeshir Dalal, Lala Sriram, Kasturbhai Lalbhai, A. D. Shroff, John Mathai and Purushottamdas Thakurdas. They came up with their ideas of industrialization and capitalist development through what is known as Bombay Plan.[6] The third plan was developed by the Left wing. Their committee included B. N. Bannerjee, G. D. Parikh, V. M. Tarkunde and others. M. N. Roy wrote the foreword to this plan. This plan was popular as Peoples' Plan.[7] Shriman Narayan Agarwal came up with a Gandhian Plan[8] in 1944, while the Akhil Bharat Sarva Seva Sangh came up with the Sarvodaya Plan[9] in 1957 when the planning process had already begun in India after Independence. As far as Agarwal's Gandhian Plan is concerned, it came with a foreword from Gandhi that the latter had not

[5] Shah, *Report: National Planning Committee.*
[6] Thakurdas, *A Brief Memorandum Outline.*
[7] Bannerjee et al., *People's Plan for Economic Development of India.*
[8] Agarwal, *The Gandhian Plan of Economic Development for India.*
[9] *Report of the Sarvodaya Plan Committee: Planning for Sarvodaya.*

gone through the treatise with the attention it deserved, though he had read it enough to say that the author had not misinterpreted him at any place.[10] The other plan, that is, the Sarvodaya Plan, came on the eve of the Second Five Year Plan. This plan gave a disclaimer from its planners themselves that no one should look for a blueprint in this document. 'It is a draft, and its main purpose is only to help in promoting a clearer understanding of the meaning of Sarvodaya, the principles that should guide a Sarvodaya Plan and the methods and pro-grammes of the transition to a Sarvodaya social order.'[11] Thus, Gandhians who developed the Sarvodaya Plan were very clear that they were not producing any document as an alternative to the Nehruvian Plan. Though Kumarappa did not produce any such independent plan document, he wrote extensively in *Gram Udyog Patrika* and in the *Harijan* about the Bombay Plan as well as about the Nehruvian Plan. He had worked on the planning bodies for some time after Independence, represent-ing the village industries. A collection of Kumarappa's speeches on planning is available under the title *An Overall Plan for Rural Development*,[12] while a collection of his articles on planning is available under the title *Planning by the People, for the People.*[13] The recommendations of the Agrarian Reforms Committee[14] constituted under Kumarappa's chairmanship also deal with some of the critical issues regarding India's economic develop-ment and planning. And the 'Memorandum to the Second Five Year Plan'[15] submitted by Kumarappa is also a significant docu-ment in this regard. The exploration of the debate on planning facilitates the construction of certain critical issues in Gandhian political economy like the relationship between industry and

[10] Gandhi, Foreword to Agarwal, *The Gandhian Plan of Economic Development for India*, 1.

[11] Deo, Preface to *Planning for Sarvodaya*, 4.

[12] Kumarappa, *An Overall Plan for Rural Development.*

[13] Kumarappa, *Planning by the People, for the People.*

[14] *Report of the Congress Agrarian Reforms Committee.*

[15] Kumarappa, *Suggestions and Remarks on the Draft Memorandum of the Second Five Year Plan*, NMML, Subject File No. 34.

agriculture, between large-scale industries and village industries, the role of State in organizing the economy as well as the
implications of different economic models for various castes and
classes in the society. An attempt is also made here to explore
the normative content of this debate.

The first major context in which Kumarappa put forth his
ideas about planning was that of the plan proposed by the
National Planning Committee. The Conference of Ministers
of the Provincial Governments held at Bombay in 1937 had
constituted the National Planning Committee under the chairpersonship of Jawaharlal Nehru. The Conference of Ministers
was of the view that

> The problem of poverty and unemployment, of National
> Defence and of economic regeneration in general cannot
> be solved without industrialization. As a step towards such
> industrialization, a comprehensive scheme of National
> Planning should be formulated. This scheme should pro-
> vide for the establishment of heavy key industries, medium
> scale industries and cottage industries, keeping in view our
> national requirements, the resources of the country, as
> also the peculiar circumstances prevailing in the country.
> The scheme should provide for the establishment of new
> industries of all classes and also for the development of the
> existing ones.[16]

Thus, the term of references of the committee had demanded
recommendations regarding the pattern of industrialization in
India. The committee from its very inception was tilted towards
large-scale industrialization with the presence of industrialists
such as Ambalal Sarabhai, Purushottamdas Thakurdas and
others. In the chairman's note, written in 1938, Jawaharlal
Nehru had claimed, '... There appears nothing in the Congress
resolution against the starting or encouragement of large-scale
industries, provided this does not conflict with the natural

[16] Shah, *Report: National Planning Committee*, 5.

development of village industries.'[17] In 1939, when the Second World War had already broken out, Nehru declared in a memorandum, 'A large number of industries, which are essential for the independence and well-being of the country, must inevitably be on a large-scale.'[18]

Initially, Kumarappa was hesitant to be a part of the National Planning Committee. He believed that the members of the committee represented diverse interests; hence working with a committee of such a composition would be no less than dashing one's head against stonewalls.[19] He expressed his presentiment to Gandhi, to which Gandhi replied that such an approach is not the one of a Satyagrahi. He therefore insisted that Kumarappa should attend the meetings of the committee until he finds them futile and then with a clean conscience, he may resign. Kumarappa accordingly attended the meetings of the committee and kept on sending periodical reports to Gandhi. Between 21 June 1938 and 17 June 1939,[20] he attended almost all the sessions of the National Planning Committee.[21] However, in 1939 with Gandhi's permission, he resigned from the committee. In an article in *Gram Udyog Patrika*, he explained why he 'felt like fish out of water' in this committee and why he had to 'get out of the committee for the sake of his very existence'. He wrote:

Whatever the merits of a plan may be, if it fails to give employment and thereby direct a due share [of] the wealth produced towards the villager, it will stand condemned. The result or end of economic activity is wealth production for the purpose of consumption by producers. Wealth is usually produced by intelligent use of the means of production and the application or employment of human talent or power. Planning, in the

[17] Ibid., 35.
[18] Ibid., 41.
[19] Vinaik, *The Gandhian Crusader*, 106–107.
[20] During this period, the committee met in two sessions for 19 times. Kumarappa attended 17 meetings of the committee.
[21] Shah, *Report: National Planning Committee*, 23.

first instance, consists in rational coordination of these three factors. We may express this mathematically thus: $W = E + M$; where W stands for wealth, E for employment of human talent and M for means in the shape of tools, equipment or capital. In this equation, keeping W constant, if M is large, E will have to be small and vice versa, that E and M vary inversely. Therefore, in planning, our first step will have to be the ascertaining of the availability of E and M.[22]

Kumarappa's position is interesting, considering the 'growth versus employment' debate, which dominated the planning process in India after Independence. The entire debate approached the goals of growth and employment as mutually exclusive categories. As against this, Kumarappa did not approach growth and employment in a dichotomous way. For him, the creation of wealth was not likely to get affected due to the adherence to a labour-intensive model of growth. Rather, preferring large-scale industrialization over rural and small-scale industries was for him a sure road to perpetuate unemployment and consequently poverty. More importantly, denying work meant for him denial of humanity. Earlier, he had written: [...] Work is even more consequential than ceremonial religion. We may almost say that work is the practical side of religion. To deny man this opportunity is therefore to deny him the privilege of being a full-fledged human being [...] economically, the unemployed are like the untouchables.[23]

Kumarappa therefore gave primacy to employment generation without halting growth. He insisted that the National Planning Committee did not clearly understand the function of large-scale industry.

The method of large-scale production can only be employed as a handmaiden of the village or cotton industries, the

[22] Kumarappa, 'Out of One's Element', reprinted in *A J. C. Kumarappa Reader*, 124.
[23] Kumarappa, *Why the Village Movement?*, 59.

former supplying the basic needs of the latter on a service basis [...]. The decentralised units may work for profit but not so the centralised units [...]. The centralised units should not be allowed to enter the field of production of decentralised industries. If this line of demarcation is not kept clearly in view it will spell disaster.[24]

Kumarappa had also raised some serious objections regarding the organizational structure of the National Planning Committee.

The Planning Committee has proceeded to form subcommittees vertically, i.e., emphasizing the functions and thus making them into separate industries, e.g. Banking, Insurance etc., which is the way of capitalism. The other way would have been to take the industries horizontally, study the processes and apply functional aid at suitable points. Taking for instance, the textile industry, they would have arranged for buying of cotton instead of financing the cotton buyers, and they would sell the goods instead of arranging markets.[25]

In lieu of these two factors, Kumarappa warned 'we shall only be substituting brown capitalism for the white variety'.

Gandhi appreciated Kumarappa's position. In the 18 November 1939 issue of *Harijan* he reproduced the excerpt of the 'thought-provoking article' by Kumarappa.[26] Despite Gandhi's appreciation, Kumarappa's warnings went unheard in the National Planning Committee. Neither the rural and cottage industries came to the centre-stage of the entire planning process, nor did the organizational structure of the National Planning Committee change. In fact, the subcommittee of the National Planning Committee on Rural and Cottage Industries didn't even prepare a formal report. A collection of notes and

[24] Ibid., 125.
[25] Ibid.
[26] Gandhi, 'Horizontal v. Vertical', 346.

comments of individual members was submitted in lieu of a formal report.[27]

Kumarappa was working on the Industrial Survey Committee for CP and Berar almost simultaneously. This committee was constituted by the Government of the Central Provinces in 1938 to review the work done by the Ministry of Industries since its inception. Kumarappa was appointed as the chairperson of this committee. The committee was expected to examine the possibilities of reviving cottage industries and give a report on the measures which the government can undertake to promote industrial development within the province, especially of cottage industries in the villages. The committee was also expected to suggest the methods of financing the same or otherwise promoting them.[28] A team of 20 professors and 200 students joined Kumarappa for fieldwork. The team surveyed 600 villages covering a population of 15 lakh paying annual revenue of over 11 lakh. Kumarappa called this survey a diagnostic survey; a survey done in a short time with the set purpose of saving the patient's life by a suitable prescription. By juxtaposing the recommendations of the Industrial Survey Committee vis-à-vis the report (rather notes) of the National Planning Committee's sub-committee on rural and cottage industries, the focal point of Kumarappa's approach becomes clearer. While National Planning Committee considered large-scale industries inevitable for economic development and treated small-scale industries only as of strategic significance in the age of ceaseless international tensions,[29] Kumarappa's Industrial Survey Committee treated large-scale industry as a terrain of capital accumulation and concentration of wealth in the hands of few. Hence, the Industrial Survey Committee insisted, 'In the matter of Key Industries, Public Utilities and in the exploitation of

---

[27] Shah, *Rural and Cottage Industries: Report of the Sub-committee*, 17.

[28] *Report of the Industrial Survey Committee*, 1. Excerpts from the report were published in *Harijan* (20 May–17 June 1939) with Gandhi's comments. Gandhi, 'An Original Report', 131.

[29] Shah, *Rural and Cottage Industries: Report of the Sub-committee*, 30.

natural resources where large capital is required, the State must undertake such enterprise on behalf of the people.'[30] National Planning Committee treated the Rural and Cottage Industry as a source of supplementary employment, generally carried out in off-seasons when the principal occupation of agriculture is not available,[31] while Kumarappa's Industrial Survey Committee endeavoured to re-define the entire economic activities around the rural and cottage industries.

Whether it is the export-import policy or the fiscal and monetary policy, Kumarappa attempted to redefine the entire system in such a way that it will facilitate the growth of the small-scale and cottage industries.[32] Kumarappa in this way was in synch with Gandhi's vision of evolving a non-capitalist form of industrialization. His position about nationalizing the large-scale industries was, however, not supported by Gandhi. Kumarappa had consistently taken a position that the responsibility of erecting large-scale industries should lay with the State. In the National Planning Committee he had admitted that some large-scale industries are bound to remain inevitable and had to be undertaken. But he had pointed out that such industries were in the nature of key industries and should be controlled by the State.[33] He had taken the same position in the Industrial Survey Committee which is very much evident from the quotation cited above. In August 1941, he wrote an article in *Gram Udyog Patrika* entitled 'Public Costs of Centralised Production', where he showed that the actual cost of production of the large-scale industries is much higher than what is generally calculated considering the facilities of transport, security etc. provided to such industries by the State. Here, he reiterated that large-scale industries should be run in public sector and not in the private sector.[34] On this, Gandhi wrote to Kumarappa:

[30] Gandhi, 'An Original Report', 162.
[31] Ibid., 33.
[32] Gandhi, 'An Original Report', 162–164.
[33] Kumarappa Papers, NMML, Subject File No. 11, 81.
[34] Kumarappa, 'Public Cost of Centralised Production', in *A J. C. Kumarappa Reader*, 272–274.

Your article on industrialisation I consider weak. What we have to combat is socialisation of industrialism. They instance the Soviet exploits in proof of their proposition. You have to show, if you can, by working out figures that handicrafts are better than power-driven machinery products. You have almost allowed in the concluding paragraphs the validity of that claim.[35]

Gandhi thus seems to be cautioning Kumarappa that in the vein of rejecting capitalism he would end up subscribing to the Soviet model at the cost of the cause of village industrialization. Here, the issue was not about the use of machines in a qualified or enlightened manner;[36] the issue was that of supporting large-scale industrialization as a public enterprise. Was capitalism a greater evil than mechanized industrialism? And will the socialization of the means of production be sufficient to overcome these evils? These were the crucial questions. For Gandhi, rejection of mechanized industrialism in itself encompassed the potential to eradicate the evils in capitalism. Though Kumarappa supported this position, he found large-scale industrialization inevitable in certain sectors. In one of his articles in *Harijan*, Kumarappa wrote:

[35] Gandhi's letter to Kumarappa dated 12 August 1941, CWMG Vol. 80, 456.

[36] As far as the approach towards the use of machine is concerned, both Gandhi and Kumarappa held the same position. An interesting example in this regard appears in minutes of the proceedings of AIVIA Board of Management meetings. The manager of the handmade paper Mill in Pune, Mr K. B. Joshi, had written to AIVIA to allow the use of power-driven machine for making paper pulp since the extraction of raw material is better in quantity and quality with machines than with hands. The rest of the activities involved in paper-making, it assured, would be done manually. The AIVIA discussed the issue in the absence of Gandhi when he was interned during the Quit India Movement and allowed the use of power for pulp-making (1–2 February 1942). On Gandhi's return the entire issue was placed before him. Gandhi approved and confirmed the decision to allow the use of machine for paper pulp-making (14 August 1942). See 'Minutes of the Proceedings of the AIVIA Board of Management'.

In extremely rare cases where the life and expansion of an industry calls for aid from machines in one or the other process which cannot be performed by hand, where the fullest advantage of the raw material available can be taken over by the use of machinery, where processes involved are so heavy that it would be cruel to use manpower, where the capital and equipment needed for the due carrying out of the process is beyond the means available to the artisans, where it is possible to render the needed help by resorting to the use of machinery under safeguards to make sure that no exploitation is possible and the aid given on service basis, there can be no objection to machine power being used.[37]

At the same time he has categorically stated that centralized industries under private ownership were a form of internal imperialism.[38] In view of the inevitability of large-scale industrialization, in whatever small proportion, he considered nationalization a viable option to avoid the growth of capitalist enterprise. As against both these positions, Nehru was firm on adhering to the model of large-scale industrialization for attaining the growth of the economy. In response to Kumarappa's note on large-scale industries submitted to the National Planning Committee, Nehru made it a point to minute his own position that though Congress favoured cottage industries, it was not against the development of large-scale industries.[39] A dominant section within the Congress had also stood by large-scale industrialization firmly. The Committee for the Promotion of Village Industries appointed by the Government of Bombay, for instance, recommended in 1946:

[…] We do not believe that the task before us is to replace factory production by hand production throughout the country. We do not advise the country to accept this as their objective. We conceive it to be the function of the Government at the present moment rather to demarcate and to apportion

[37] Kumarappa, 'When the Machine Power', 76.
[38] Kumarappa, 'Imperialism within Us', 135–136.
[39] Kumarappa Papers, NMML, Subject File No. 11, 97.

sphere between machine production and hand production, putting down what Government thinks proper as the limits of machine production under the existing circumstances in India.[40]

The committee had also recommended supplying to the village artisans, models and samples from abroad for copying. It proposed to assign the entire organization of village industries—from purchase of raw-material to sales and marketing to the State. Kumarappa, in his correspondence with Gandhi, lamented the recommendations of the committee. He writes:

> [...] They are spending lakhs of rupees to no end but to show. We should have expected best results in Bombay but as Vaikunth Bhai himself says he has made a great blunder in choosing Manu Subedar as advisor. He throws the blame partly on you because you had given him a good chit in *Harijan*. Unfortunately our members on the committee, including Dhotre and Laxmidas have not been able to resist the powerful arguments of Manu Subedar. The result is that Bombay finds itself supplying mill yarn to handloom weavers and such like items disfigure their rural development plan [...]. You will remember pressing for a Rural Development Committee of the Congress to advise the various Governments. It is to avoid such gross blunders as have come about in Bombay [...].[41]

Kumarappa firmly maintained that promoting village industries as an appendage to large-scale industries will never result in the regeneration of village life. Kumarappa's models for rural economic regeneration as well as views on overall economic development placed village industries at the centre of the economic affairs.

[40] Manu Subhedar, Member of the Legislative Assembly of Central province was its chairperson, while Gandhians such as R. S. Dhotre of Gandhi Seva Sangh and Laxmidas Asher were its members. *Report of the Committee for the Promotion of Village Industries*, 2–3.
[41] Kumarappa's letter to Gandhi dated 1 February 1947, NMML, Subject File No. 5, 51.

Kumarappa had a different plan of economic reorganization of rural India. In a speech delivered at the Conference of Ministers in Pune in 1946, Kumarappa explained the meaning of planning. 'Planning means getting together of certain things to serve an end.'[42] How to identify the end? Kumarappa insisted that the end can be identified by knowing well the conditions that surround the people of that country. 'The plans must be rooted in the conditions that prevail in the country.' In case of India, Kumarappa pointed out that the severest problem of all was that of poverty. With repeated famines the people of the country were impoverished to such an extent that they hardly had any food to eat. Hence, Kumarappa emphatically stated that the primary factor in the plan must be food and prevention of famines. He also insisted that when human labour as a factor of production is available in abundance, it must be utilized fully for producing commodities to satisfy hunger. Planning must encourage such economic activities which will make maximum utilization of the human labour.

On the foundation of these assumptions, Kumarappa prepared a plan for rural development.[43] This plan identified five main areas around which rural development was to be organized. They were:

1. Agriculture and village industries
2. Sanitation, health and housing
3. Village education
4. Village organization
5. Village culture

Agriculture

Agricultural production will be regulated on the basis of two main considerations. First, the locality will try to produce all its own food requirements and raw materials for the primary

[42] Kumarappa, *Planning by the People, for the People*, 9.
[43] Kumarappa, *An Overall Plan for Rural Development*, 41–85.

necessities of life. Naturally, the production of commercial crops will be minimized and food crop will be encouraged. This will ensure food security for villages. The villagers will have access to nutritional food. Similarly, the primary needs of the villagers will be fulfilled. Second, it will try to produce raw materials suitable for village industries than for factories. It will facilitate employment generation through villages industries and consequently reducing the dependence of the village on the urban centres for employment. Naturally, migrations to urban centres will stop. The farmers will not depend on the industries for the payment of raw material. Thus, the flow and prevalence of money will be altered.

Kumarappa has also paid specific attention on the necessity of providing sufficient irrigation facilities to the farmers. In his scheme, the State will launch a drive for digging sinking wells, enlarging and dredging tanks, building canals and thus ensuring regular supply of water for farming. As far as supply of fertilizers is concerned, he insists on the use of compost manure and on forbidding chemical manure all together. This, Kumarappa believes, will on the one hand improve productivity of agriculture without affecting the quality of the soil, while on the other it will lessen the economic dependence of the farmers on the chemical industry for supplying fertilizers. He also thought of encouraging animal husbandry as a supplementary occupation, which will also facilitate the use of compost manure.

In order to make the farmers adopt this policy, in Kumarappa's plan, State in co-operation with farmers will play a crucial role in supervising the agricultural activities through the multi-functional cooperative societies. Such societies will regulate the utilization of land by issuing licences authorizing the farmers to grow certain kinds of crops. The societies will also look after the maintenance of the quality of soil, seed supply, etc. Similarly, district demonstration centres and provincial training centres will aid, assist and train the farmer as well as the village artisan. Kumarappa also visualized the need for agricultural research, which he insists will concentrate on improving the food crop rather than the cash crop.

Village Industries

Kumarappa identified following village industries which need to be encouraged and protected from competition from the mechanized large-scale industries.

1. Paddy-husking
2. Flour-grinding
3. Gur-making
4. Bee-keeping
5. Cotton and wool
6. Leather and tanning
7. Soap-making and lighting
8. Paper-making
9. Pottery
10. Mat and basket-making
11. Bell-metal work
12. Toy-making
13. Tool and equipment
14. Improved carpentry
15. Improved blacksmithy

The first four industries (paddy-husking, flour grinding, gur-making and bee-keeping) are the food industries. By proposing them to develop as decentralized village industries, Kumarappa has ensured a number of factors. First, these industries will facilitate a constant and regular generation of employment. Hand-pounded rice, manually grinded flour or palm-gur, none of these items can be stored for a long time. They are more perishable than those produced with the use of machines. Naturally, it will generate a regular flow of income. Second, these items being perishable, they will automatically arrest the tendency to hoard thereby facilitating the practice of *aparigraha*. Third and most important, it will supply the villagers with nutritious food. As discussed in the last chapter, Kumarappa had categorically opposed the mill-pressed rice for its low-nutritional value. AIVIA had also conducted research on the qualities of palm gur. By planning to make these food items available to villagers,

Kumarappa ensured that the most significant component of the basic necessities is accessible to them. Similarly, by protecting the cotton and village industry as a village industry, Kumarappa took care of another basis necessity, that is clothing, besides its advantages in employment generation.

In case of the village industries, it can be noticed, they are concerning the occupations of artisan castes. Nowhere does Kumarappa plead to confine these castes into their traditional occupations; he, however, suggests preserving the skills. He also proposes to introduce the artisans in these industries to the advancements in their respective area to make their occupations more useful, artistic and productive.

Sanitation, Health and Housing

Kumarappa proposes to improve the sanitation facilities in villages in a number of ways, such as educating the villagers to improve personal habits of cleanliness and hygiene, and training them to maintain habits of group cleanliness. He also advocates recycling drainage water for kitchen gardens and converting rubbish, waste into manure.

As far as the improvement in the health of the villagers is concerned, Kumarappa proposes to educate villagers about the nutritional value of the food they consume and encourage them to consume nutritious food. He has also proposed in this plan to display everywhere in villages, boards with information about the nutritive values of different articles of foods produced in the village. He has also proposed to train villagers about the basic preventive measures and cheap remedies for ordinary ailments.

Kumarappa has proposed that the model houses with better sanitation facilities will be exhibited by the Public Works Department of the government. Villagers will built such houses for their own usage on cooperative basis. Kumarappa has categorically insisted that while planning in villages for building such houses it needs to be ensured that the segregation of Harijans does not take place.

Village Education

Kumarappa proposes to undertake two types of schooling simultaneously and on urgent basis: first, basic education (*Nai Talim*), and second, adult education. The scheme for basic education will link education with the programme of rural development and will try to establish work as a medium of instruction. Adult education, on the other hand, will educate the villagers on the intelligent operation of village communities. It will try to create a more committed, responsible and efficient work-culture. Training the trainer programmes will be organized by the Hindustani Talimi Sangh. The persons trained at the Hindustani Talimi Sangh will conduct training centres in the villages. Each villager will spend at least six months at the adult education centre. With this proposal, Kumarappa put forth the necessity of citizenship training. Merely by virtue of being a citizen, every individual is not likely to realize his responsibilities towards society. Nor will he know automatically, the philosophy behind the village-centred model of development. Kumarappa believed that such training will introduce a villager to the purpose behind different policy measures. Thereby, it will equip him/her for a more learned response as a citizen and as a consumer.

Organizational Requirements for Implementing the Plan

In this plan, Kumarappa has also referred to the political organization that will be necessary for the implementation of such a plan. At the central level, he recommended a seven-member standing committee to coordinate the activities of village development. This committee will consist of one member each of the departments of rural development, agriculture, veterinary, forest, industries, public health and medicine, and local self-government.

At the village level, the organizational structure proposed by Kumarappa included three institutions:

1. Village panchayat for village administration on the basis of village self-government
2. Multipurpose cooperative society for the economic organization of the village
3. Gram Seva Sangh to mobilize non-official support and act as a backup to the whole scheme of rural development on the basis of voluntary support

Village Culture

Kumarappa expected the village self-government to make efforts to preserve village culture. He, however, wanted this to happen in a studied way and not in a chauvinistic way. He, therefore, proposed that village self-governments should arrange for studying village traditions, habits, institutions and history. Similarly, he also expected the government to encourage the study of folk songs, folk tales and folk art, and village handicrafts in the villages.

Kumarappa suggested that local folk arts as well as the village traditions of bhajans, kirtans and dramatics can be innovatively used for village education. He also wanted government to provide for the organization of libraries, village museums and village study circles. Kumarappa thereby attempts to develop a vibrant public sphere facilitating the growth of a deliberative democracy.

In late 1950, Kumarappa got an opportunity to implement this plan in the State of Punjab. The Punjab government had appointed a committee for rural development earlier in 1946. Kumarappa was asked to review the report of this committee, which he had found to be 'superficial'.[44] Punjab government invited Kumarappa to guide the implementation of the rural development plan in the state. In his meetings with the administrative heads of the concerned departments,

[44] Kumarappa's letter to Gandhi dated 1 February 1947. Kumarappa Papers, NMML, Subject File No. 5, 51.

however, Kumarappa was repeatedly questioned about the impracticability of the self-sufficiency programmes. The idea of reducing raw-material production in agriculture was difficult to fathom. The idea of State marketing the products of village industries and thus competing with private enterprises was not considered 'proper'. Serious apprehensions were expressed regarding reviving barter system in villages. The bureaucrats also expressed a fear that such scheme will isolate their region from the national economy. One industrial development officer submitted a note advocating the expansion of cottage industries on the lines of Japan.[45] Such objections and suggestions convinced Kumarappa that the implementation of the village self-sufficiency schemes needs to be entrusted only to those who have faith in its principles.[46] Bureaucratization of the plans is bound to result in deadlock, since the Gandhian schemes of village regeneration were no mere policies; they were matters of faith and of urge to search for an alternative to the capitalist model of development. The Japanese model, Kumarappa pointed out, did not challenge the logic of capitalist development. Though dispersal of industry reduces the cost of production and thus creates a semblance of protecting consumer rights; however, in reality it merely relieves the capitalist from providing congenial and healthy working conditions to the worker. Later in the Report on Agriculture and Cottage and Small Scale Industries in Japan, Kumarappa has discussed the limitations of the Japanese model in details. He writes:

[...] Under conditions of dispersal the worker is thrown on his resources. This results in a strain on his living conditions as he uses his own over-crowded house in slums for his workshop. This makes an inroad into the space, ventilation and light available to his family and children. It introduces factory conditions of din, dust and dirt into his very home. He submits himself to overwork as he is beyond the provisions

[45] Tour notes of Kumarappa's Punjab visit. Kumarappa Papers, NMML, Subject File No. 21, 57–58.
[46] Ibid., 62.

of the requirements of factory Legislation. This may surely reduce costs. But is this the only desideratum? Are the social and human considerations to be thrown overboard? Material production is not the only goal of economic activity. This is forgotten in the present competitive rush for markets.[47]

Kumarappa also elaborated the historical and social conditions that promoted the particular type of cottage industries in Japan and insisted that every society must search for an economic model which will be conducive to its sociohistorical conditions. Kumarappa's faith in applying a society-specific model of development in India got deepened after his visit to China. He has minutely elaborated the difference between the Chinese model of communism and the Russian model. He appreciates the Chinese model in prioritizing agrarian reform to rebuild its peasantry. As against this, the Russian model based its nation-building on proletarian reform. Hence, the Russians emphasized large-scale standardized production, while the Chinese committed themselves to place the peasantry on its feet.[48] Kumarappa insists that India can learn a lot from China while developing its model of development within the Gandhian framework.[49]

While considering the historical and social specificity in India, Kumarappa wanted Indian planners to give priority to the issue of unemployment over growth and labour-intensive model over a capital-intensive one. He had warned Indian planners that the policy to encourage the capital-intensive industrialization will ultimately promote imperialism and not a socialistic pattern of society.[50]

Kumarappa's Gandhian model could be characterized by the following features:

[47] Kumarappa, *Report on the Agriculture and Cottage and Small Scale Industries in Japan*, 7–8.

[48] Kumarappa, *A Peep Behind the Iron Curtain*, 108–110.

[49] Ibid., 111.

[50] Kumarappa, *Suggestions and Remarks on the Draft Memorandum of the Second Five Year Plan*. Kumarappa Papers, NMML, Subject File No. 34, 24.

1. Kumarappa held that the model for economic development needs to be society-specific. It must be in conformity with the historical and sociocultural set-up of the region. Kumarappa interrogated the domination of the Eurocentric models of development and insisted on recognizing the diversity of needs emerging from different regional contexts. It is interesting to find that Kumarappa's emphasis on the context-specific model of development shows an affinity with the Hungarian scholar Karl Polanyi who around the same period had advocated cultural approach to economics.[51] With the thrust on context-specific model of development, Kumarappa insisted that for India, a model of non-capitalist, non-mechanized industrialization was the most suitable model considering its huge population and agricultural economy. This model propagated the idea of a village-centred economy that aimed at reviving local skills and using locally available raw material.

2. Kumarappa's Gandhian model of development questioned the very propriety of large-scale production for any society for that matter. In the resolutions presented by Kumarappa in the World Peace Council meeting, he had insisted on encouraging the small-scale production units that use locally available raw material to avoid, among other things, the unnecessary competition in international markets leading to wars.[52]

This Gandhian model considered large-scale production permissible only in the key industries with two preconditions. First, that the large-scale industries will play a supplementary role to the village industries and that they will not compete with the village industries. Second, that the large-scale industries will not be under private ownership, they will be under public ownership.

Kumarappa maintained that large-scale industries thrive on centralization. He pointed out that centralization

---

[51] Polanyi, *The Great Transformation.*
[52] Kumarappa, *A Peep Behind the Iron Curtain*, 13–15.

originates from the accumulation of capital and leads to concentration of wealth in few hands. He, therefore, considered centralization as a 'hot-bed of class difference'.[53] Kumarappa had identified another very dangerous evil, inherent in centralized process of production. He insisted that centralization of production leads to regimentation of labour, which, in turn leads to concentration of power. Kumarappa regarded concentration of power even more dangerous than concentration of wealth.[54]

3. In agriculture, subletting of land except in case of widows, minors and disabled persons, will be completely prohibited. Only those who put in a minimum amount of physical labour and participate in the actual agricultural operations will be considered to be cultivating land personally.

   This provision in Kumarappa's Gandhian model of development reflects his strong commitment and determination to eliminate the unproductive class of zamindars from agriculture. Second, it attempts to reinstate the dignity of labour in the society. Third, it attempts to arrest the growth and development of commercial interests in agriculture. Fourth, this provision also reflects Kumarappa's approach towards the disabled and dependents in the society.

4. The production of food crops will be encouraged and that of commercial crops will be minimized. As discussed elsewhere in this work, Kumarappa's insistence on encouraging food crop production touched a number of issues from food security and commercialization of agriculture to reducing its dependence on industry. Food security at societal level was likely to reduce India's dependence on foreign lands for food imports, while at the individual level it would have ensured availability of food for the peasant and his family. Similarly, by arresting commercialization of agriculture it was likely to save the farmer from the interference of non-agricultural classes in the agricultural processes.

[53] Kumarappa, *The Gandhian Economy and Other Essays*, 15.
[54] Ibid.

5. Kumarappa's Gandhian model of development allowed international trade only of the surplus production in agriculture as well as in industry. He did not want the production targets to be set in view of the commercial interests of exporting goods in the foreign land, since he strongly believed that such an organization of international trade generates heavy competition, ultimately culminating in wars.[55] As a mechanism to facilitate and ensure world peace, Kumarappa suggested restricting international trade only for surplus production.

6. This Gandhian model also insisted that the domestic market will not be linked to the upheavals in the international trade. Kumarappa was well aware of the implications of competitive international trade for the domestic markets. He maintained that the linking of domestic markets with the upheavals in the international markets on the one hand increases the prevalence of money in an alarming way, while on the other it takes away the autonomy of producers and consumers in the local markets. International markets dictate to the producer what he is supposed to produce, while the price-mechanism of international markets determines the availability and non-availability of commodities for the local consumer. Thus, international trade takes away the autonomy of the local economy and places it in perennial uncertainty. To avoid all these evils, Kumarappa proposed to restrict international trade only to surpluses and also to avoid connecting it with the domestic markets.

7. Attempts will be made to reduce the evil-effects of Money on agriculture. Accordingly, taxes will be collected partially in kind. As discussed earlier in the third chapter of this work, Kumarappa had maintained that money had always played a mischief with the use value of the commodity by putting high premium on its exchange value.[56] To avoid

---

[55] This theme had occurred regularly in Kumarappa's writings. Its emphatic assertion could be found in *The Non-violent Economy and World Peace*.

[56] Kumarappa, *Vicarious Living*, 17.

the subordination of use value to the exchange value, Kumarappa proposed for partial payment of taxes in kind.

Besides, the rural surveys that he had conducted, had introduced him to the reality of rural India that peasants many a times do not have cash at their disposal, but they have food grains. They are willing to contribute their share to the society. Kumarappa's provision of partial payment of taxes in kind, ensured for the peasants a dignified way to contribute their share.

8. Kumarappa's Gandhian model of development assigned a crucial role to the State and expected it to ensure through taxation that large-scale industries do not compete with the village industries. Second, it also wanted the State to ensure that the export-import policy is not antithetical to the growth of village industries. Third, it wanted the State to facilitate the adequate marketing avenues to the village industries. Fourth, this model had put crucial responsibility of environmental protection on the State. Kumarappa maintained that the private interests, in view of their short-term interests, are likely to ignore the implications of their activities for nature and thereby may encroach upon the natural environment.[57] It is the responsibility of the State to prevent such instances.

9. Multipurpose economic society will play a crucial role in organizing rural economic activities. Economic activities will be organized and implemented through voluntary work, than through the State bureaucracy. The voluntary organizations and constructive workers will be organized through the Lok Seva Sangh which will function as the opposition to the government. By providing for multi-purpose co-operative societies as well as by assigning the role of opposition to the Lok Seva Sangh, Kumarappa tried to ensure that the powers of the post-colonial Indian State are regulated by a dynamic civil society.

[57] Kumarappa, *Economy of Permanence*, 2–4.

Kumarappa's Gandhian model of economic development reflects on certain crucial aspects of the political economy dimension of Gandhian political ideas. First and the foremost, Gandhian scheme of village-centric economy does not attempt to revive the village system in its existing form. It visualizes an improved village system reorganized on the principles of Sarvodaya. For such a village system, it also puts forth the necessity of citizenship training. Second, the scheme for the revival of traditional occupations does not deny occupational mobility to anybody. Nor does it differentiate between or create hierarchy in different occupations. Third, Gandhian scheme proposes to revive only those occupations that were associated with the artisan castes and not those of the service castes. In fact, the learning of skills associated with the service castes (tanning, sanitation, etc.) was considered as a pre-condition, essential to de-caste oneself. In case of artisan castes, the emphasis was on the preservation of skills developed through the expertise of centuries and not on the preservation of caste-based occupations. Fourth, it aims to reduce the dependence of agriculture on industry and make agriculture a more viable occupation. Fifth, the prevalence and dominance of non-productive class in agriculture is prohibited by putting the precondition of physical labour in agriculture for landownership.

Thus, the plea for village industrialism and for preservation of traditional crafts is meant to prevent the evils of centralized, mechanized capitalistic industrialism as discussed in Chapter 3 of this work. Interestingly, different Gandhian models that came around this period had more or less the same features. However, indicates that on many crucial issues of political economy they differed notably and visualized completely different role for the State.

The Gandhians, by and large, visualized an ideal society which would increasingly reduce its dependence on the State and be self-governed. However, it was a distant goal. In the meanwhile what approach was to be adopted towards the State vis-à-vis the Sarvodaya utopia, was certainly an issue where the

Gandhian stalwarts differed from each other and reflected on the role of the State in their own ways. On this background, it is interesting to see how Kumarappa viewed the role of the State in the process of development and reflected on the State–society relations.

As the debates about what should be the priorities and content of economic planning became intense at the time of the formation of the National Planning Committee, Gandhian stalwarts including Kumarappa engaged themselves with this debate and put forward their respective views on and agenda of economic development that would suit India's requirement as a nation state on the one hand and reorganization of an ideal society in the light of Sarvodaya on the other. In this process, various perspectives on the role of the State emerged within Gandhian circles. Shriman Narayan Agarwal, Vaikunthbhai Mehta, Shankarrao Deo and Vinoba contributed to this debate. Kumarappa's perspective on the issue of the role of state emerged both as a critique and response to his contemporaries and hence needs to be understood from this point of view.

As mentioned earlier when debates about the National Planning Committee were taking place, Shriman Narayan Agarwal had come up with a Gandhian Plan of economic development. This Gandhian Plan was widely circulated and debated.[58] It had more or less the same features as Kumarappa's model including the critique of heavy industrialism. At the dawn of independence also, Agarwal could be seen writing critically against large-scale industrialization.[59] The twist in the story came when, in the 1950s, Agarwal changed his position altogether and started rationalizing Nehru's mixed economy

[58] On the eve of Independence, Agarwal came up with another tract named *Gandhian Plan Reaffirmed* where he mentions that his plan was translated into many Indian languages and its abridged versions were published in Britain and Russia. See Agarwal, *Gandhian Plan Reaffirmed*, 8.

[59] See Agarwal, 'National Government's Industrial Policy', 86.

model as another incarnation of the Gandhian Plan.[60] He insisted on a regular basis in his articles in the *AICC Economic Review* that the Nehruvian Plan was an attempt to realize Sarvodaya. By legitimizing Nehruvian model as a Gandhian one, Agarwal played a crucial role in de-emphasizing the radical economic content in Kumarappa's Gandhian model. In his article 'Sarvodaya and Marxism', Agarwal charged Kumarappa 'for creating confusion in public mind about the twin ideologies of Gandhism and Communism'. He condemned such attempts as un-Gandhian.[61] It is necessary to note here that the entire debate was not only about the nature of industrialization or about the relationship the heavy industries should have with the rural industries. It was equally about the role the State was supposed to play in organizing the economic activities. In Kumarappa's scheme, though the role of the State in organizing economic activities was not denied altogether, the entire responsibility of implementation of the economic programmes was entrusted to the body of constructive workers, thereby deemphasizing the role of the State.

In this regard, Kumarappa's public debate with Shankarrao Deo, then one of the members of the Congress Working Committee, is worth noting. Kumarappa in a small note on the constitution of the *Akhil Bharat Sarva Seva Sangh* wrote in Harijan:

> ... Gandhiji had expressed a wish that the Congress should turn itself into a *Lok Seva Sangh* now that even the political activity of the past has resulted in a measure of independence and that it should now work in the Constructive field to bring *Swaraj* to the masses in terms of self-sufficiency of the villages. *Such a change of policy and constitution was not acceptable to Congress.*[62] (Emphasis added)

---

[60] See Agarwal, *A Plea for Ideological Clarity*.
[61] Ibid., 42–46.
[62] Kumarappa, 'Akhil Bharat Sarva Seva Sangh', 337–338.

This comment instigated the adherent Congressman Shankarrao Deo to come out openly against the constructive workers' indifference towards politics in general and that of Kumarappa in particular. In a series of articles written in *Harijan* during the early 1949, Deo claimed that Congress had never accepted Gandhian philosophy though it had looked up to Gandhi for his political leadership. The onus of carrying forward Gandhian philosophy always remained with the constructive workers. He, therefore, insisted that rather than criticizing the Congress, the constructive workers should join politics and put forth their ideas in policy formulation. Their indifference towards politics can never bring about qualitative change in the policy regime.[63]

In his response to Deo, Kumarappa questioned the very efficacy of politics in realizing Sarvodaya. He maintained that in the pre-Independence period, politics was inevitable due to the presence of the colonial power. The constructive workers participated in the political activities of the Indian National Congress whenever required, simply because the foreign power had to be thrown out. After attaining independence, however, there should not be any need for the constructive workers to participate in politics. Congress can increase the proportion of constructive workers in its constituent bodies if it really wants the constructive workers to contribute in realizing the Gandhian ideal. He also added:

> The Congress must adopt a plan of decentralised production which should form part of the permanent economy of the country. It must give special attention to the rapid development of cottage and small-scale industries and must aim at national and regional economic self-sufficiency at least in the essentials of life. When the Congress adopts such a policy and programme to implement it, we are certain the constructive workers will not wait for invitation.[64]

---

[63] Deo, 'Congress and the Constructive Workers'.
[64] Kumarappa, 'Politics Then and Politics Now', 34–35.

Kumarappa wanted the Lok Seva Sangh, the central unit of constructive organizations, to play the role of opposition to the government.[65] In the article written in response to Deo, Kumarappa expressed his discontent for not appointing a sufficient number of constructive workers on the Gandhi Memorial Trust. Kumarappa maintained that the symbolic presence of constructive workers in the government bodies is likely to end-up making them ineffective. So even when he was opposed to the constructive workers joining politics he want them in advisory role to the government. To make this advisory role effective he wanted them in sizeable number in government bodies. This would have made the government to recognize the constructive work bodies as a force to reckon with and would have stopped the bureaucratization of developmental projects. It would also have lessened the dependence of the constructive programmes on State funding or foreign funding. This, however, did not happen and the presence of constructive workers in government bodies remained symbolic.

As against this, by legitimizing the Nehruvian model (that had entrusted the responsibility implementing constructive programmes initially to the Khadi and Village Industries Board and later to the Khadi and Village Industries Commission [KVIC]), Agarwal facilitated the consolidation of State power in the domain of economic activities and indirectly gave approval to the bureaucratization at the cost of voluntary activism independent of State.[66] Moreover, he legitimized the entire idiom as Gandhian while the Gandhian ethos in Kumarappa's

[65] In the revised edition of *Economy of Permanence*, published on 4 January 1948, that is, just a few days before Gandhi's assassination, Kumarappa added 11 new chapters to the original work published in 1945. In this edition, he assigns the role of opposition to Lok Seva Sangh. See Chapter 11, 'A Pilot Plan of Economy of Permanence', *Economy of Permanence*, 194–200.

[66] The Khadi and Village Industries Board was constituted in February 1953, while the KVIC was constituted in 1956. The KVIC took up the charge from the Board in April 1957.

approach was challenged. Kumarappa's association with the communist world peace organizations around this time was received in the Gandhian circle with apprehensions and suspicion. On this background, denouncement of Kumarappa's critique of the Nehruvian economic policy as un-Gandhian and communist was an obvious fallout. The rise of Agarwal as an authority on Gandhian economics further enhanced the process of marginalization of Kumarappa's economic ideas. At a wider level, it resulted in the confinement of the constructive workers to the task of giving moralistic talks or blessings to the government. The Sarvodaya Plan developed by the Akhil Bharat Sarva Seva Sangh[67] was a classic example of this process. The Plan presented the utopia of Sarvodaya Samaj in all the minute details, but without a single word about the Nehruvian Plan. The simultaneity of silence on the government policies and a desire for a lesser State was a characteristic feature of this plan. This plan visualized the existence of self-restrained communities and hence maintained that they will not require any expenditure on administration. All wealth will be regarded as common property. There will be no distinction between capital and labour, while profit, rent, interest and wages will lose their meaning and thus disappear.[68] The decision will be taken by consensus and not by counting votes. There will be no room for a party system. There will be sharing rather than distribution, since distribution implies outward change while, sharing, inward change.[69] It will not be incorrect to assume that these idealistic, unrealistic overtones in the Sarvodaya Plan indirectly pleaded for the unconditional acceptance of the Nehruvian Plan.

[67] Akhil Bharat Sarva Seva Sangh constituted a committee with Shankarrao Deo as convenor and Dhirendra Mazumdar, JP, Annasaheb Sahasrabuddhe, R. S. Dhotre, Siddharaj Daddha, Achyutrao Patwardhan, Ravindra Verma and Narayan Desai as members. The committee submitted the report under the title *Planning for Sarvodaya*.

[68] Ibid., 19.

[69] Ibid., 23–25.

Pertaining to the role of the State, two more approaches could be found in the Gandhian circles around this period. The pro-State approach was developed by Vaikunthbhai Mehta, while the pro-community approach emanates from Vinoba's positions. This is not to say that both these approaches were mutually exclusive. Rather they confirmed each other while putting high premium on the different aspects of the same processes. Vaikunthbhai Mehta, the first chairperson of KVIC and a pioneering leader of India's cooperative movement, looked at the developmental role of State in a positive way. In an article written in *Khadi Gramodyog* in 1954, Mehta expresses his optimism about the State's role.

> [...] It is to promote the reorganization, on systematic lines, of khadi and allied village industries that Central Government established in 1953 the All India Khadi and Village Industries Board and *agreed to place adequate resources at its disposal for the orderly expansion of production on a nationwide scale.*[70] (Emphasis added)

Thus, Mehta considered the state support essential for the expansion of the Khadi and Village Industries. At the same time, he maintained that sole dependence on the State support was not desirable. At the end of this article he appealed to the community at large to contribute to the promotion of Khadi and village industries in order to generate wider employment. Interestingly Pandit Nehru could also be seen reminding the employees of Community Development Projects engaged in village development that their work should not affect the natural initiative and industriousness of people at large.[71]

The other side of this position could be found in Vinoba's address at the Sarvodaya Conference in Chandil, Bihar (1953).

[70] Mehta, 'Sources of Inspiration', 5. See also Mehta, *Decentralised Economic Development*.
[71] Nehru, *Jawaharlal Nehru on Community Development, Panchayati Raj and Cooperation*.

This address is popularly known as Sarvodaya Manifesto. About government's role in promoting Khadi, Vinoba says:

Khadi Board is being organised, government is willing to support [...]. It's our and Spinners' Association's duty to help the government; because the Spinners' Association has wider experience in this field and this work necessitates expertise. At the same time, I believe that our help to the government must be the help only of a wise citizen. If we consume ourselves in this entirely, we will not be able to serve Khadi in a true way [...]. While searching the ways of eradicating war if a war breaks out, we will make ourselves available to nurse the wounded soldier with the clarity in mind that this is not our real work. Similarly, we will never ignore that Khadi work is aimed at the establishment of Gram Swaraj.[72]

Constructive Work and State: Four Models

Shankarrao Deo	Constructive workers must join politics and support State
Vaikunthbhai mehta	Constructive workers facilitate the developmental role of the State and the State provides financial support to expand constructive work
J. C. Kumarappa	Constructive workers function independent of State and act as opposition to the government
Vinobā	Constructive workers function independent of State, help State when invited; let the State function in its domain

In Vaikunthbhai Mehta's position the vantage point lies with the State, while in Vinoba's position the vantage point rests with the community. Kumarappa's position is more tilted towards Vinoba, but he also wants to direct the state towards a particular goal. Like Vinoba he is not ready to let state have complete autonomy in its domain. Probably it is the economist in him who reminds him the role public finance, trade policies

[72] Bhave, *Sarvodayache Ghoshana Patra*, 10–11.

and monetary policies can play in promoting village industries. He wants to engage with the state critically to direct it for bringing about the macro level changes in the economy. He wants the state to organize economy in such way so as to facilitate the growth of village industries, not the way Nehru or Mehta had planned, that is, not as an ancillary activity in large-scale industrialization but as the key sector of the economy. While Nehru and Mehta were employing village industries to enhance the developmental role of the State, Kumarappa wanted to employ state to facilitate the growth of village industries. While Vinoba wanted the constructive workers to function mostly in their own domain, Kumarappa wanted them to act as a social force directing the state to impose regulatory tax regime on the big capitalist houses restraining large-scale industrialization. With this outlook even with pro-community approach Kumarappa ended up supporting a strong state and extra-constitutional authority of the body of constructive workers. With Kumarappa's marginalization his idea never got chance to get implemented, the fall-out of what was implemented also became visible soon.

Mehta's position of taking State support in the promotion of village industries ultimately resulted in making the constructive work organizations excessively dependent on State-funding and thus paralytic. From the very year of its inception, the columns of *Khadi Gramodyog* (mouthpiece of KVIC) are filled with discontent about the bureaucratic approach of the high officials that was resulting in delay in fund release allocated for village industries. In certain cases, the funds were not disbursed since the Gramodyog Sanghs at the State level were not statutory bodies and thus legally non-entities for funds-transfer.[73] In some cases, the money was disbursed as late as in February; that is, towards the end of the financial year, thus, making it difficult to utilize it within a short span of time. And since the fund sanctioned in the earlier year was not fully utilized, in the

[73] Kapadia, 'Relationship between Central and State Boards', 19.

next year's budget, the allocation was reduced.[74] There were complaints regarding the absence of uniform policy as well.[75] If the State-support was amounting to red-tapism, the position of distancing from the State had its own limitations.

It would be interesting and instructive to see what happened with pro-community approaches of Vinoba and Kumarappa. Kumarappa's criticism of government policy and plea for decisive role to state in economy amounted to his marginalization and seclusion. On the front of Gandhian organizations and their constructive work programmes, the leadership was bestowed upon Vinoba. Naturally, his position of functioning independent of State was followed. Vinoba at this juncture directed the constructive workers towards the goal of Bhoodan. The noble ideal of redistribution of land through Bhoodan, no doubt infused new energy in the Gandhian movement, it also shifted the focus from constructive work to land donation. This, intentionally or unintentionally, facilitated state's primacy in the organization of constructive work and village industries. Besides, Bhoodan as an additional or as alternate Gandhian programme was also not free from lacuna.

Kumarappa raised two sets of objections regarding Bhoodan. The first set of objections interrogated the very efficacy of Bhoodan as a Gandhian technique to realize Sarvodaya, while the second set of questions were related to the organization of the Bhoodan Movement. In an article

[74] 'Report of Board Activities', 33. The Statement of Account for 1954–1955 shows that the sanctioned amount was not disbursed. The amount of ₹45,000, for instance, was sanctioned to the T. Kallupatti Ashram (where Kumarappa had shifted from Wardha) for bee-keeping. Till 6 October 1954 only ₹1800 out of this was disbursed. Over the years, the dependence of the constructive work organizations on the State became so acute that in March 2013 the KVIC proposed to sell the Khadi production units to a multinational bank. See "Khadi udyog videshi udyogankade sopavinyacha ghat" (News) *Loksatta* Pune Edition, 16 March 2013, 4.

[75] Sundaram, 'Common Production Programme', 52–55.

named 'Underlying Principles' written in *Gram Udyog Patrika* Kumarappa argued:

> [...] The Bhoodan Movement started by collecting lands from Zamindars and giving it to the landless with the slogan, 'Land belongs to tillers.' This is not duty-based, but centred on rights. It amounted to: 'Bring me your property and I will give it to others.' A Dharma-centred call will be 'Use your own property in the service of the society.' This will be the proper application of the 'trusteeship' ideal advocated by Gandhiji [...].[76]

Kumarappa considered sharing and co-operation rather than distribution and re-distribution as essence of Sarvodaya economics and hence insisted for starting 'land-ownership demonstration centres' rather than merely collecting land donations.[77] Second, Kumarappa insisted that the ultimate ideal of Sarvodaya should be common ownership of land rather than private ownership. 'Land cannot be held in private ownership, whether in large or in small pieces. It is not the extent that is objectionable, but the ownership itself.'[78] As discussed earlier in this chapter as well as in the preceding chapter, in the report of the Agrarian Reforms Committee Kumarappa had recommended that the subletting of land should be completely prohibited. Here, he went a step further in denying the ownership rights in agricultural land altogether. He therefore suggested to Vinoba that the latter should attempt establishing collective ownership of land rather than redistributing it to a single owner.[79] To this Vinoba replied, since the entire village

[76] Kumarappa, 'The Underlying Principle', in *Vicarious Living*, 20–21.
[77] Ibid., 22.
[78] Ibid., 27.
[79] Kumarappa, 'After Bhoodan?', 1. It seems that Kumarappa had written about the issue of collective ownership of land to Vinoba earlier. The letter is not available. Vinoba responded to Kumarappa on 5 February 1953. Kumarappa's suggestions and objections to Bhoodan

land has not been acquired everywhere, collective-ownership of land was not possible.[80] Third, Kumarappa considered the act of collecting more land than one's capacity for redistribution as an act of stealing, antithetical to the Gandhian principle of *asteya*. He wrote to Vinoba:

> You have spared no pains in collecting lands for the landless. Lands have been gifted much faster than we can handle them—either distributing or utilizing them. I strongly hold that it is stealing when we hold more property than we need, even if it is gathered with the owner's full consent [...]. In so far as our possessions are far more extensive than we could handle, we stand guilty of stealing.[81]

Fourth, Kumarappa had argued that collecting land by setting targets of time and extent ultimately leads to violence[82] and hence was un-Gandhian. Before expressing this objection publicly, Kumarappa had written to Vinoba in April 1955 that the movement suffers from short-sightedness. He wrote:

> [...] This short-sightedness comes of fixing targets. These lead to violence. What is the hurry? Simply because we had fixed a certain time within which to get a certain quota, should we rush forward at all costs? The targets have emphasized the end and the means are very destructive. We have formed an attachment that is landing us in violence [...].[83]

along with Vinoba's letter have been published in the issue of *Gram Udyog Patrika* mentioned above.

[80] Vinoba's letter to Kumarappa dated 5 February 1953. Kumarappa Papers, NMML, Subject File No. 31, 2.

[81] Kumarappa's letter to Vinoba dated 27 April 1955. Kumarappa Papers, NMML, Subject File No. 31, 13.

[82] Kumarappa, 'Ends and Means of Bhoodan', reprinted in *Vicarious Living*, 32.

[83] Kumarappa's letter to Vinoba dated 27 April 1955. Kumarappa Papers, NMML, Subject File No. 31, 13.

Later in an article published in *Gram Udyog Patrika* in June 1955, Kumarappa classified the ends and means of Bhoodan in following manner:[84]

Ends and Means of Bhoodan

Economic	The End	Removal of poverty
	The Means	Proper production and utilization of land
Social	The End	To vest ownership in community
	The Means	Redistribution
Political	The End	Peaceful transfer of land
	The Means	Change of character and outlook through persuasion

Kumarappa held that Vinoba's Bhoodan Movement was focusing more towards the ends that it had aimed to achieve than towards the means that need to have accompanied the ends.[85]

The second set of objections that Kumarappa raised regarding the Bhoodan Movement were about its organization. Kumarappa held that the movement to collect donated land should have been accompanied with a body of constructive workers committed to educate people in appropriate use of land. He made a pertinent point regarding land usage by asking Vinoba about his position, whether after redistribution the land is to be used to grow crops such as tobacco and sugarcane. To this Vinoba responded, 'One must not put any condition while donating. But we can certainly recommend to the beneficiary of the donated land to avoid taking these crops. In case of sugarcane, we shall recommend, in case of tobacco we may put condition also [...].'[86] What worried Kumarappa more

[84] Kumarappa, 'Ends and Means of Bhoodan', in *Vicarious Living*, 30–31.

[85] Ibid., 32.

[86] Vinoba's letter to Kumarappa dated 5 February 1953. Kumarappa Papers, NMML, Subject File No. 31. Ibid., 3.

was the lack of planning on part of Vinoba and his colleagues in Bhoodan for redistributing the collected land. Instead of making efforts to build a new band of constructive workers for this purpose, Vinoba had relied entirely on the existing team of constructive workers, thereby practically shutting down the other constructive work activities in Gandhian organizations. Kumarappa wrote to Vinoba:

Bapu fostered many aspects of constructive work simultaneously. Each side supplemented and complemented the other and formed a whole. Can we not follow his example? When he wanted workers, he did not empty the existing institutions, but recruited new ones and trained them. Thus all work grew up together. We are living on capital and reserves when we draw on our old institutions [...].[87]

Kumarappa's objections about Bhoodan prompted a variety of responses from fellow Gandhians. Kaka Kalelkar responded:

Vinoba started his movement with Kanchan Mukti i.e. doing without the use of money, boycotting all money. Today his movement is releasing the Gandhi Smarak Nidhi of 10 or 12 lakhs of rupees. So the Nidhi is learning Kanchan-Mukti. This is one side of the picture. His movement is good in conception and although faulty in execution, deserves support.[88]

Mira Behn wrote an article entitled 'Some Reflections on the Bhoodan Movement', where she argues:

Now that land has been made the focal point, why do we not hear more about the problems connected with the utilisation of land? Should there not be an Akhil Bharat Hal Sangh or All-India Ploughmen's Association? Should not Bhoodanists become ploughmen, just as the followers of Bapu became

[87] Kumarappa's letter to Vinoba dated 27 April 1955. Kumarappa Papers, NMML, Subject File No. 31, 13.
[88] Kaka Kalelkar's letter to Kumarappa dated 20 May 1955, Kumarappa Papers, NMML, Subject File No. 31, 20.

spinners? [...] Bhoodanists should go deep into the problem not merely as moralists or propagandists, but as realists like Bapu [...] I think that we must concede that if Bapu had made the land his central activity we should have had an army of workers trained in the field, along with practical training in the practice, they would have been well-grounded in theory also. The whole India would have been worked up to the problems of shallow ploughing versus deep ploughing, of organic manure versus artificial manure, of crop rotation, harvesting methods and the like [...].[89]

Vinoba responded to the entire debate in a letter to Kumarappa dated 20 June 1955. He wrote:

Little do I like to enter into discussion. The chances of discussing matters together are rare these days. I wish to point out one thing to you. If you avoid the harsh language that you use in most of your writings, the letter is apt to create a better reaction [...].[90]

Dhirendra Mazumdar, on the other hand, suggested Kumarappa to 'understand each other's point of view before expressing in public'.[91] Kumarappa's response to Mazumdar makes it evident that Kumarappa wanted the constructive workers to focus on agriculture along with village industries and Bhoodan.[92]

[89] Mira Behn, 'Some Reflections on the Bhoodan Movement', in *Vicarious Living*, 55–59.

[90] Vinoba's letter to Kumarappa dated 20 June 1955. Kumarappa Papers, NMML, Subject File No. 31, 28.

[91] Dhirendra Mazumdar's letter to Kumarappa dated 4 July 1955. Kumarappa Papers, NMML, Subject File No. 31, 29.

[92] Kumarappa in his letter of 8 July 1955 wrote:

I was not satisfied with merely submitting the Agrarian Reforms Committee's report in 1949 as Chairman. I felt the need for something practical to guide us in distribution and utilisation of land. With this idea the Pannai Ashram at Seldoh was started. At that time Vinobaji came to me and discussed the whole problem.

Such differences over priority and strategy could be deemphasized as incidental but the main critical issue arises from the way the pro-community approaches of Vinoba and Kumarappa visualized organization of the political economy of Sarvodaya. In the pro-State approach to Sarvodaya there was at least a clear indication about its overwhelming support to the developmental state; the pro-community positions however indicated a substantial ambivalence about the role it wanted the State to play. Vinoba wanted a strong state though not a total state. He didn't want the constructive workers either to become State-dependent or to engage critically with the State. Despite this position, as the later developments reveal, Vinoba wanted the State to make laws in support of the issues raised by the Gandhian movement. The Bhoodan–Gramdan Acts as well as the Cow Protection Acts are testimony to Vinoba's engagement with the State. Kumarappa while emphasizing the role of a watchdog for the constructive workers also wanted the State to arrange public finance in such a way as to deemphasize

He expressed full agreement with my views but stated that land utilisation must be my part as he himself was unable to understand it. Later, I discussed this question of distribution with Sri Jajuji and Sri Vallabhswami, if I remember rightly, Shri Shankar Rao Deo was also present, and pointed out that distribution without utilisation had great dangers. They found it difficult then to agree to distribution with conditions of how to utilise land. I spoke on my views at the whole sessions at the Patna Sammelan and also addressed the Sarva Seva Sangh meetings emphasising the need for establishment of Agrarian Research Colleges to train workers on land utilisation. I think you were also present then as well as at the last occasion at Puri. Also while handling over the Pannai Ashram to the Sarva Seva Sangh, I explained my ideas on these matters at its meetings.... You will now see that for over five years I have been waiting patiently to see some change for the better utilisation of land and training workers of Bhoodan in vein. Now I felt the time was ripe for me to place my views before the public....

Ibid., 30.

large-scale industries and facilitate the growth of the village industries. Thereby Kumarappa could be said to have added another dimension to the already existing air of expectancy that surrounded the Indian state. Both Vinoba and Kumarappa could anticipate the culmination of the developmental state into a bureaucratic leviathan, but in the absence of any alternative to replace state, returned to state for facilitating lesser state. It is this ambivalence about the role of the State that makes the Gandhian critique of capital weak. At the level of ideas, Vinoba comes up with very interesting moral–political critique of the liberal democratic model, while Kumarappa provides for a politico-economic critique of capitalism. Both very creatively conceptualize an alternate model to organize polity and economy. At the same time, both expect the State to facilitate the making of a sphere independent of the State. The very expectation that an excessively expanding power centre will write its own death sentence and also perhaps an obituary was naïve, at the most, utopian.

5

Locating Kumarappa in Gandhism After Gandhi

Exploring political thought is not only about how the ideas of a particular thinker got shaped in a particular period; it is also to explore how and why the ideas of a particular thinker were recognized with prominence in the history of ideas and how certain ideas remained ignored for a long time; and when these ignored ideas surface, how are they perceived? In case of J. C. Kumarappa, as the preceding chapters show, the marginalization of his ideas seems to have resulted from the allegedly communist content in his writings and in the emanating positions. If Kumarappa was perceived as a latent supporter of communism during his lifetime, a recent study by Benjamin Zacharia finds Kumarappa's approach supporting the Hindu nationalist project.[1] As seen before, Ramachandra Guha refers Kumarappa as a Green Gandhian, giving impetus to numerous studies that found different shades of green in Kumarappa's writings.[2] The multiple studies and interpretations certainly

[1] Zacharia, *Developing an Intellectual and Social History of India*, 174.
[2] For instance, see Lindley *J. C. Kumarappa: Mahatma Gandhi's Economist*.

present Kumarappa as an interesting phenomenon for normative explorations. Despite the differences over the moral dimension of the norm in Kumarappa, there is, by and large, agreement that Kumarappa's economic ideas are essentially moral, and morality is embedded with the material. Moral and material are not binaries in Kumarappa. His engagement with religion enables Kumarappa to transcend this kind of dualism. Thereby, religion emerges as an aspect of Kumarappa's Gandhian political economy. This chapter analyses Kumarappa's interpretation of Christianity with a view to understand the moral foundation of his ideas.

One of the significant characteristics of the nineteenth- and the twentieth-century political thinking in India is that it engages itself with religion in a creative way. Interestingly, the political content of most of these religious engagements is not ecclesiastical but secular.[3] The same is true of Gandhi and Kumarappa. Gandhi engaged himself with religion, asserted the need to make religion a foundation not only of the personal life, but also of the social and political life. The sociopolitical content of Gandhi's religious discourse remained essentially secular and humanitarian. Gandhi explored the ceaseless endeavours made by the major religions in the world to seek the Truth and consequently drew heavily on them to discover new morality for reconstructing Indian society. In case of Kumarappa, Jesus' religion played this crucial role. As discussed earlier, Kumarappa hailed from a devout Tamil Protestant Christian family. Christianity played a very significant role in defining his world view. Kumarappa's association with Christianity was a life-long affair. He attempted to reinterpret the message of Christianity to contemporary times

[3] Yashwant Sumant presented a thought-provoking analysis of the religious discourse in the nineteenth and twentieth centuries problematizing the ideas of Phule, Agarkar, Ranade, Tilak, Vivekananda, Javdekar, Ambedkar, Gandhi and Vinoba. A collection of his essays is being published posthumously. See also Sumant, 'Situating Religion in Ambedkar's Political Discourse', in *Reconstructing the World: B.R. Ambedkar and Buddhism in India*.

and endeavoured to spread his interpretation to the different Christian conglomerations and conferences. He debated with Christian missionaries on the role that the Church needs to play in case of the non-violent struggle for India's liberation. The idea of mother economy through which Kumarappa attempted to build Sarvodaya economics was grounded in the Christian ethics and morality. Kumarappa was associated with Christianity in a number of ways. His understanding of the Christian faith is best represented in two of his works: *Christianity and Its Economy* and *Practice and Precepts of Jesus*. The first work is a collection of his addresses delivered at various occasions, mostly to the Christian audience. The second work was produced during Kumarappa's imprisonment owing to his participation in the Quit India Movement. Both these works present and emphasize Christianity as a faith propounded by Jesus, the man and not Christ, the Son of God. This chapter attempts to explain J. C. Kumarappa's understanding of religion in general and that of Christianity in particular, which inspired him to lay down the moral foundation of his economic ideas.

Kumarappa's anchorage in Christian faith is visible throughout his writings. The titles of his articles in *Young India*, *Harijan* and *Gram Udyog Patrika*, and the use of images and metaphors in his writings echo Christian ethos. Kumarappa was not a trained theologian, but he recognized and asserted the individual's need as well as capability to define and then practise his or her faith. Kumarappa has sufficiently clarified his idea of religion in the speech he delivered in December 1935 before the Council of the Federation of International Fellowships. To him, 'Religion is the relation that governs a man's personal attitude to God, to his ideals, to his fellow-man, to his society and to the world.'[4] His address at the Parliament of Religions held in Bombay in 1936 further clarified this approach. Kumarappa says:

[4] Kumarappa, 'Speech Delivered before the Council of the Federation of International Fellowships at Wardha on 29 December 1935', in *Christianity: Its Economy and Way of Life*, 54.

All pure religions are personal. For the sake of convenience we may group common experiences under common category, but individual religion knows no label.... As a pebble thrown upon the bosom of the ocean causes ripples on the mighty expanse of water, a man, however small he may be, causes his impression to be set on the Infinite.[5]

Kumarappa engaged himself in describing Christianity from the same viewpoint. In his inaugural address to the annual camp of the Student Christian Movement at Hoshangabad in 1941, he raised a basic question about the very definition of the term 'Christian'. He said:

What do we mean by Christian? [...] There are the professional Christians who say 'Lord, Lord' and live like lords. There are others who adhere to the Church—the mistress of the State—with the hope of preferment and so on; but I propose to confine myself to the Jesus' definition:

'Whosoever shall do the will of my Father which is in heaven the same is my brother, and sister and mother.' Jesus points out in a parable what the will of the father is when the invitation to heaven is given. 'Come ye blessed of my Father, inherit the kingdom prepared for you from the foundation of the world; for I was hungered, and ye gave me meat: I was thirsty and ye gave me drink: I was a stranger and ye took me in: naked and ye clothed me: I was in prison and ye came unto me.' 'Verily I say unto you, in as much as ye have done it unto one of the least of these my brethren ye have done it unto me.' These are the duties developing on youth who style themselves as 'Christians'.[6]

This definition clearly shows that for Kumarappa, adherence to the Christian faith indicated the extension of one's compassion

[5] Kumarappa, 'Address Delivered Before the Parliament of Religions, Bombay 1936', in *Christianity: Its Economy and Way of Life*, 59.

[6] Kumarappa, 'Inaugural Address at the Annual Camp of Student Christian Movement at Rasulia, Hoshangaba, C. P. in October 1941', in *Christianity: Its Economy and Way of Life*, 21.

to the needy and diseased in the society rather than following the ritualistic religion. Second, for him practising the faith did not necessarily mean submission to the authority of Church. Rather, he did not visualize any mediator or a middle-man in man's relationship with his God.

Kumarappa maintained that every religion performs a definite social function corresponding with the social system in which it operates. Accordingly, he classified religions into four phases/types. At the early stage of evolution of society, crude superstitions are bound together with inhibitions and prohibitions to regulate the primitive man and his dealings. It is believed that the failures would incur punishments and obedience would be awarded. Fear deters him in his selfish ventures while avarice and desire for pleasure makes him consider the welfare of others. The religion that emerges in such a primitive society performs the function of regulating social life through its norms and rituals. Kumarappa describes this type of religion as 'authoritarian religion'.[7] The second stage of evolution is that of 'Militant Religion'. Kumarappa explains:

In this stage, national codes of laws are bound together with social sanctions and religious colouring. Here too man is kept to the 'right path' by an external power invested with a jealous spirit to guard its rights, and with vengeance to visit the inquiry of the father of the third and fourth generations of them that hate it and doing good to thousands of them that fear it.[8]

Third, Kumarappa talks of the ethnic religion which man uses in an organized way to preserve, propagate and consolidate the culture evolved by him. In the fourth stage, religion plays the role of ascribing social status for observing certain recognized customs and rituals. Kumarappa names this religion as 'social

---

[7] Kumarappa, 'Address Delivered before the Parliament of Religions, Bombay 1936', in *Christianity: Its Economy and Way of Life*, 53.
[8] Ibid., 54.

religion'.[9] By highlighting the evolutionary aspect of religion, Kumarappa tries to assert that religion is not a static concept. It evolves with time and changes corresponding to the different social contexts. Kumarappa has described the prevalence of these four stages into the evolution of the Christian faith. As per the authoritarian religion norm, God is depicted in Christianity as 'a strict accountant keeping a record of all that we do in book of fate and visiting our lapses with uncompromising justice'. The second phase, that is, the phase of militancy is located by Kumarappa in the establishment and expansion of Church. He maintains that the institution of Church, which was established by Peter, has been used by the State as a means to control the people.

> Such churches are necessary adjuncts to Imperialism.... Christian mission in our land and all other 'heathen' lands fall into this group naturally. It is painful to see adherents of Christianity rushing to interview disgruntled members of other religions to recruit them to their fold. They sing a song of civilizing the savage, and end up by sapping his blood, exploiting his labour, and annexing his territory.[10]

Kumarappa's criticism of the institution of Church comes here sharply as ever. The ethnic phase of Christianity has also been identified by Kumarappa in the imperialistic and expansionist motives of the Church. He identifies this phase in the Dark Ages in Europe when Christianity was 'marshalling its forces on a crusade against Sarscenic hordes and pagan world'. Kumarappa maintains, 'The desire to bring light and learning to those who sit in darkness arises out of ethical religion, with an admixture of the imperialistic militant spirit.'[11] The phase of social religion has been identified by Kumarappa in the contemporary history of Christianity when the membership of the Church of England is considered as a way to enter the upper circle of the

[9] Ibid.
[10] Ibid., 56.
[11] Ibid.

British society. 'It is a sign of respectability. Even a Jew Viceroy has to be respectable by attending the Church of England services on State functions.'[12] After taking a historical overview of Christianity, Kumarappa finds it necessary to differentiate between Christianity and the religion propagated by Jesus. He narrates the true ethos of Jesus' religion through 10 principles. These 10 principles, he maintains, can be discerned from the practices and precepts of Jesus as against what is preached in the dictates of the Church. These principles are as follows:

1. *Jesus' religion as a non-institutional religion:* Jesus' religion emphasized man's right to explore and seek God through his own light. Kumarappa insists that Jesus condemned institutional religion when it was made a means of exploitation and 'in no uncertain words' denounced the stalwarts of institutional religion.[13] In doing so, he tried to establish man's right to express his religiosity in his own way. Kumarappa points out that Jesus' religion is a universal religion in as much as all religions have God as a common factor and each seeker as a variant. It is interesting to note that Kumarappa here refers to Ramakrishna Paramhansa while emphasizing the unity of religions. Paramhansa's experimentation with religion had a deep impact on the entire generation to which Kumarappa belonged. It was then but natural that Kumarappa believed in unity of religions.

2. *Jesus' religion as a non-ritualistic religion:* Kumarappa maintains that Jesus' religion does not restrain human beings into fixed customs and rituals. It is not a ritualistic religion. 'Spirit knows no rituals. Religion is a personal contact with God,' Kumarappa maintains. Jesus doesn't propound the exclusive idea of worship. In support of this proposition Kumarappa cites from the Gospel of Mathew:

> When thou prayest enter into thy closet and when thou hast shut thy door, pray to thy Father which is in secret....

[12] Ibid.
[13] Ibid., 60.

Ye shall neither in this mountain nor at Jerusalem, worship thy Father.... The true worshipper shall worship the Father ... in Spirit and in truth.... God is a Spirit and they that worship Him must worship Him in Spirit and in Truth.[14]

While advocating the need to follow the Spirit of Truth in one's personal endeavour to seek God, Kumarappa also expects man to connect with others in their journey to seek God.

We have to recognise that the experiences of others are helpful to us and there are several spirits quite close enough in their make-up to be able to fall into convenient groups. Such groups may get together for common worship, for mutual aid and help, but such common forms are definitely sinful when they assume an exclusive aspect.[15]

3. *The concept of brotherhood in Jesus' religion:* Jesus emphasized universal brotherhood. Kumarappa insists that in doing so he did not regard anyone as an outsider, nor did he ask to wait till the child was baptized. While interpreting the concept of universal brotherhood of man, Kumarappa criticized two types of practices prevalent in the Church. First, he criticized Church for discriminating among its members on racial grounds. He asked, 'Is it not blasphemy to call such churches Christian? Such may be "White Clubs" but not churches of God.'[16] Second, he criticized Church for not extending the warmth of brotherhood to the non-Christians and for reserving it till they convert themselves to Christianity. He wrote:

Will any Church dare deny entry to one whom Jesus claims as His brother? Where then is the foundation for conversion

[14] Ibid., 61. For a detailed and critical discussion on the meaning and content of prayer, also see Kumarappa, *Practices and Precepts of Jesus*, 39–57.
[15] Ibid., 62.
[16] Ibid.

or closing the doors of any church against non-Christians? ...
If we wish to trace the origin of the missionary spirit in what
is called as Christianity we shall find it goes to St. Paul, the
child of imperial Rome, and not to the Jesus of Nazareth.[17]

In Christianity, the Church is supposed to play an immensely
crucial role in directing and supervising the spiritual journey of
a seeker. In the absence of the Church how will the seeker know
that his worship is following the right direction? In answer,
Kumarappa cites from the Bible, 'By their fruits ye shall know
them.' If the seeker is on the right path, he is bound to yield
right results. Hence, even for spiritual guidance Kumarappa
does not find the necessity of Church.

4. *Jesus' attitude towards himself:* Kumarappa maintained that
   Jesus considered himself as a tool in the hands of God.
   His short life was one of intense active service. He wished
   to be known not as son of David, but by the service He
   was rendering. Similarly, he expected his followers to be
   known through their deeds. Kumarappa insists that Jesus'
   idea of mission was to serve the fellow being in need. The
   outward appearance did not matter to Him. In view of this,
   Kumarappa criticized the lifestyle and practices of Indian
   Christians for taking pride in the blind imitation of the
   Western mannerism in the name of Christianity and not
   incorporating either the Spirit of Truth or the Spirit of
   Service in their lives.
5. *Attitude towards elders in Jesus' religion:* According to
   Kumarappa, Jesus' religion gives no such special status to
   man's relationship with the elders, which would create hierarchy. This was done in view of the fact that Judaism had
   nurtured a tradition of obeying the elders in order to prove
   oneself a righteous person. Such an obedient person would
   then despise all others as 'publicans and sinners'. Under
   such a hierarchy, life became oppressive and burdensome
   and people were living in constant fear of priesthood. In

[17] Ibid.

this background, Jesus preached that no human authority can claim unconditional obedience. It is only to God that a man can submit unconditionally. Every other relationship has to be subordinated to the relationship with God. More importantly, Jesus also wanted human beings to replicate their respect for the elders in their all other relationships, including those with the subordinates. While explaining this aspect of Jesus' religion Kumarappa writes, 'If one is in close relationship with a personality like Gandhiji, that relationship is of no value, unless it is reflected in all one's other relations.'[18]

6. *Relationship with the neighbours and the equals:* Kumarappa insists that Jesus anticipated equal relationship between the followers of different religious practices. The commandment to 'Love thy neighbour' implied that man should consider all legitimate prejudices of our neighbours. Kumarappa asked:

> Is it so essential to the propagating of the religion of Jesus that among a vegetarian people who refrain from eating even roots that grow below the surface of the land, as such roots have more life, to practise a ritual in which the blood of the founder is symbolically drunk and his flesh is ceremonially eaten, nay, in some, they claim to consume actual blood and flesh? These gruesome practices would have no weight in the religion of Jesus.[19]

He further insisted, 'The religion of Jesus is not a measuring rod of the "Pagan" but a helpful ladder at the disposal of everyone who wishes to use it.'[20]

7. *Organization of State and role of society:* Kumarappa insists that the history of Church shows that since the Church entered into the 'unholy alliance' with the State, and became its handmaiden, it has enjoined unquestioning loyalty to the

[18] Ibid., 66. See also Kumarappa, *Practices and Precepts of Jesus*, 7.
[19] Ibid., 68–69.
[20] Ibid., 69. See also Kumarappa, *Practices and Precepts of Jesus*, 11–12.

State from its believers. As against this, Jesus stood for the supremacy of ideals and never pleaded unconditional and final obedience to the State and society. In so far as the State endeavours for the welfare of people, it is duty of the citizen to do his share. However, when the State or society became tyrannical, Jesus revolted against it and he expected the same from his followers. On this, Kumarappa made a very insightful comment, 'The Sabbath was made for man will be the motto of civil disobedience.'[21] Here the context is that of a debate between Kumarappa and the retired Reverend Dr F. Westcott (the Lord Bishop of Calcutta and the Metropolitan for India) over the sanction for civil disobedience in the Bible. The Bishop held that there is no sanction; on the contrary the Bible expected its followers to be law-abiding citizens. On this Kumarappa argued that Jesus expected the Scribes and Pharisees to act as the custodians of Mosaic Law only as long as they are part of the Roman bureaucracy, he never enjoined them to blind obedience. In support of his argument, Kumarappa cited from the Gospel of Mathew: 'Sabbath was made for Man.'

Kumarappa pointed out that attempts were made in history to formulate definite forms of governments from Jesus' words, but they resulted in gross blunders, since Jesus had laid down only principles and had expected everyone to decide his course of action for himself, led by the spirit of Truth. He further stated that Jesus left no comprehensive plan and did not claim to be the final revelation.[22]

8. *Jesus' views about material possessions:* In Kumarappa's opinion, Jesus valued material possession only as a means of achieving His (Jesus') ideals. At the same time, he was critical of property when it makes one lose all sense of proportion. Kumarappa pointed out that Jesus' religion expected human beings to do away with the hindrance of property as a swimmer casts away all unnecessary garments. Kumarappa, at this

[21] Ibid., 72.
[22] Ibid.

point, made a very interesting observation. He insisted that Jesus' religion does not preach mere asceticism, he expects human beings to use wealth positively for the use of the society.

9. *Primacy of human values:* Jesus' religion, according to Kumarappa, pays equal attention to the material side of human life as it does to the moral side. 'In dealing with the soul, the body is not forgotten,' he writes. While doing so Jesus does not deal with man in bulk but applies general principles in relation to each individual. The religion of Jesus is not an impersonal set form of conduct, but adjusts itself to the ability of the individual to see God. There are no absolute standards and no strict parameters to decide who will go to heaven and who will go to hell. The fulfilment of human values is the only consideration.

10. *Approach towards other religions:* Kumarappa insists that Jesus' religion is not exclusive. In this religion, there is no intolerance towards other religions. Jesus' religion gives equal respect to all the religions. For Jesus, individual's allegiance to a particular faith did not matter as much as the attitude of the individual towards his fellow men.[23]

Kumarappa thus presents Jesus' religion as the one founded on the principle of love and service, acknowledging the material and spiritual need of every human being, having equal respect for all the religions and committed to inter-religious dialogue. It is very evident that this kind of depiction of Christianity maintains a clear distance from the conventional Christian faith. It will be interesting to see what prompted Kumarappa to have such a critical understanding of Church.

Kumarappa in the Preface to his second major work on Christianity, *Practice and Precepts of Jesus*, has enumerated the factors that shaped his approach towards Christianity. He acknowledged the credit of his mother for 'all the drilling in Christian literature' as well as for making him aware about his responsibility towards the ailing and the diseased in the society.

---

[23] Ibid., 76.

As he grew up and observed the practices of the Church in different places, he increasingly became aware of the contradiction between Jesus' preaching and the practices followed by the Church. Kumarappa writes:

… When I came to the discerning age of 16 years, at my confirmation service, in spite of all the catechism and theory we were taught, I was frankly perplexed at the 'Communion Service'. A Bishop of the Church of England will freely partake 'Communion' with his chauffeur at the 'Lord's Table' but will abhor doing so with a Scotch Presbyterian Doctor of Divinity and perhaps a Chancellor of a university. While on the other hand, his Lordship, the Bishop, will be pleased to invite socially the Presbyterian Divine to his home to dinner but will not dream of sitting at the festive board with a driver![24]

Kumarappa further adds:

As a student in England during the World War I, when I attended war services at St. Paul's Cathedral or at Westminster Abbey, however imposing the service may have been, I failed to reconcile worship of a Universal Father and the Prince of Peace with tribal appeals to destroy enemy. Nor could I understand the use of pulpit by Bishops and other clergy for recruiting. The blood bespattered banners of many a battle and the tombs of noted generals in these places of worship seemed a desecration. These and similar contradictions between Jesus and the church shook my faith in the 'Christianity' of the churches.[25]

Later the positions taken by the missionaries and officials of Indian churches about India's freedom struggle confirmed his perception.

Kumarappa has raised certain interesting questions about the missionary approach towards the Civil Disobedience Movement. He raised these issues while contributing to the

[24] Kumarappa, *Practices and Precepts of Jesus*, viii.
[25] Ibid., ix.

ongoing debate that was taking place in the journal *Indian Social Reformer*[26] in the background of Gandhi's criticism of and opposition to conversions.[27] A variety of viewpoints were expressed in the readers' correspondence. The editors of the journal were also reproducing the relevant columns from different Christian newspapers such as *The Catholic Leader, The Indian Witness, The Guardian* and *The Examiner.* The general tone of the responses from lay Christians as well as the missionaries was that missionaries were not in India for educational, medical or social work alone. They were here on Christ's command 'Go ye into all the world' to disseminate the blessings of the Christian religion.[28] As far as the Civil Disobedience Movement was concerned, the readers and the reported Christian newspapers were doubtful whether the movement would remain non-violent till its desired culmination. They also debated whether breaking law could be considered Christian. In this gamut of positions, Kumarappa contributed a letter through which he appealed to the Christian world to condemn the violence resorted to by the colonial government to suppress the non-violent agitations.[29] This invited a number of responses. Most of the respondents held that it is no business of the missionaries to interfere in India's political matters. Another divisively diplomatic response insisted that missionaries cannot outrightly support the Gandhian movement as they also need to pay equal attention

[26] *Indian Social Reformer* was a weekly journal founded in Madras in 1890 by Kamakshi Natarajan. The journal publication was shifted from Madras to Bombay in 1897.

[27] On 7 July 1927 Gandhi wrote in *Young India*, '… This suggestion (a declaration from the Diwan of the State of Mysore) is a gentle warning both to Christian missionary and Muslim missionary not to try to wean these suppressed classes from Hinduism but, if at all wish to interfere, to act so that they become better Hindus….' He had consistently taken position against conversion. See Gandhi, *Christian Missions and Their Role in India.*

[28] See for instance 'Letter from C. Bradford of Dharchula, U. P.', 40–41.

[29] Kumarappa, 'Police Violence', 553.

to the 70 million Indian Muslims.[30] A support was extended to Gandhi's constructive work activities like prohibition as well as to the Sarda Bill, but on political issues the Christian missionaries as well as laymen preferred to remain silent.

Kumarappa had also written simultaneously to various missionaries in his private capacity. One such correspondence had taken place between Kumarappa and Dr F. Westcott.

Since the reverend had responded to Kumarappa in his official capacity, Kumarappa published the correspondence in the *Indian Social Reformer*. A part of it was also published in the *Young India*. Kumarappa differed with the Bishop over his interpretation of the Gospel and that of the New Testament that Christianity does not support disobedience and yet accepted the Bishop's decision not to support the Civil Disobedience Movement. He, however, vehemently criticized the clergy's indifference and silence over the violence employed by the British government against the non-violent Satyagrahis. Kumarappa writes:

[...] I fail to understand how you could stand aside calmly watching without a word of protest while such brutalities and torture is being used. This attitude of callousness is tantamount to a denial of our Lord, more culpable than that of Peter's and the only hope is that it may be followed by repentance and more ardent services as in the case of the rugged Apostle. My letter does not even refer to the present political situation but application of the principle of non-violence in settling all manner of dispute. Perhaps you do not wish to follow Christ to the extent of non-violence. You will forgive me if I say that most of our missionaries and other leaders of the Christian Church seem to be Britishers first and Christians afterwards if convenient. They are themselves products of the civilisation based on violence and so are not

---

[30] Edwards, 'India's Crisis: An Appeal to Men of Goodwill', 585–587.

able to fully appreciate Christianity's teaching on the subject. May God forgive them for the mischief they are doing.[31]

Kumarappa's interpretation of the Christian faith, his position about the churches and his criticism about the Indian Christians has invited scholarly attention in recent times. These scholars have critically analysed Kumarappa's religious thinking from different theological frameworks and have made some interesting observations about Kumarappa's theology. The discussion of these works is helpful to analyse Kumarappa's religious thinking and to understand the moral location of his Gandhian political economy. Hence, a critical overview of these works is taken here.

John Dilip Chakkanatt in his pioneering study of Kumarappa's religious thinking[32] found a counterpoint for critiquing the neo-liberal economic ideas. He describes Kumarappa's economic ideas as religious economics and finds in these ideas potential to interrogate and reject the religion of economics as established through globalization. Chakkanatt's main concern is to combat the evil effects of the General Agreement on Trade and Tariff (GATT) on Indian agriculture, for which he finds promising sources in the works of J. C. Kumarappa. He appreciates Kumarappa's economic ideas at two levels. First, he underlines the significance of Kumarappa's economic ideas in inducing morality in economics.[33] Second, he also finds these ideas interesting to refute the meta-economics advocated through globalization. He equates Kumarappa's ideas with E. F. Schumacher's ecofriendly economics.[34] It is necessary to note here that though Chakkanatt claims to deal with Kumarappa's religious ideas, the entire focus of his study remains Kumarappa's economic ideas. He doesn't sufficiently explore the religious dimension of Kumarappa's thinking beyond the biblical term 'mammon'. According to Chakkanatt, Kumarappa interpreted mammon as

---

[31] Kumarappa, 'Christianity and Civil Disobedience', 626.
[32] Chakkanatt, *Of God and Mammon*.
[33] Ibid., 26–27.
[34] Ibid., 7, 24, 30, 33.

the wealth entrusted for safekeeping. Chakkanatt insists that for Kumarappa in order to be close to God, renunciation from wealth is essential.[35] Chakkanatt's interpretation of Kumarappa doesn't really do sufficient justice either to Kumarappa's economic ideas or to his religious ideas. The significance of his study, however, lies in the fact that in the onslaught of globalized, neo-liberal economic ideas, he remembers Kumarappa's economics in support of the impoverished sections of Indian society.

A very interesting and profound study of Kumarappa's religious thinking could be found in Solomon Victus' two major works, namely *Religion and Eco-economics of J. C. Kumarappa: Gandhism Re-defined* and *Jesus and Mother Economy: An Introduction of the Theology of J. C. Kumarappa*. Victus, a trained theologian and a social analyst by profession, juxtaposes Kumarappa's religious ideas with the religious thinking of some of his contemporary South Indian Christians such as Vengal Chakkarai, P. Chenchia, A. J. Appasamy, P. D. Devanandan, K. T. Paul and S. K. George primarily with two intentions. First, to highlight the uniqueness of J. C. Kumarappa's theology in the galaxy of the twentieth-century South Indian Christian theologians/thinkers, and second, to trace the sources for building Indian Christian theology.

Victus has identified certain distinctive features of Kumarappa's interpretation of Christianity. The first and the foremost feature of Kumarappa's approach, according to Victus, is that Kumarappa uses the term 'Jesus' more often than the term 'Christ', thereby emphasizing historical Jesus over the dogmatic Christ of devotion.[36] For Kumarappa, Jesus stood for the principles of the person denoted. In Jesus, Kumarappa doesn't find any ambition to establish a new religion, he rather considers Jesus as a reformer committed to the removal of all the malpractices from Judaism. Kumarappa maintained that divinity was ascribed to Jesus by the Church for the sake of its vested interests. Jesus was a son of man, a fellow of his coworkers and

[35] Ibid., 10–11.
[36] Victus, *Religion and Eco-economics*, 15.

not a Son of God.[37] Second, Kumarappa prefers to highlight the Jew ethos of Christianity. This is evident from the fact that while Kumarappa's contemporaries confined themselves only to the New Testament, Kumarappa could be found accommodating some of the Old Testament themes, though he doesn't reject J. N. Farquhar[38] altogether.[39] Third, Victus maintains that while most of the Indian Christians engaged in interpreting salvation and grace, the creeds certainly equivalent to Sanskrit terminology, Kumarappa explained God and Jesus from an economic perspective … Kumarappa presented God as an economist.[40] Victus maintains that this implies that Kumarappa's approach to Christianity is less Brahmanical than his contemporaries. Fourth, according to Victus, Kumarappa has considered the 'Spirit of Truth' as the central concept of Christianity, thereby taking away from the Church its exclusive rights to guide in spiritual matters. Fifth, Victus also highlights Kumarappa's moral–secular interpretation of some of the Christian concepts such as sin, Kingdom of God, as well as Kumarappa's application of the biblical hermeneutics of certain texts. Sin, for Kumarappa, refers to exploitation of nature, creation of poverty, unemployment and famine as well as exporting of raw material. Kingdom of God for him is Sarvodaya.[41] Victus points out that Kumarappa engages himself in the biblical hermeneutics of the Gospels, the Old Testament as well as some of the Epistles. The Hebrew term 'Moloch' used in the Old Testament to refer to the sacrifice of children by fire is used by Kumarappa to describe the modern war machines. The idea of the 'Spiritual Eyes of the David'

[37] Kumarappa, *Practices and Precepts of Jesus*, 74, quoted by Victus, *Religion and Eco-Economics*, 32.

[38] J. N. Farquhar (1861–1929) was a Scottish educational missionary to Calcutta and an orientalist. He is one of the pioneers who popularized Fulfillment Theology in that which propounded that Christ is Crown of Hinduism as he best manifests Hindu ethos. In his book The *Crown* of India (1913) he presented Christ in consonance with the Hindu world view.

[39] Victus, *Jesus and Mother Economy*, 5.

[40] Ibid., 8.

[41] Victus, *Religion and Eco-Economics*, 40.

from the Old Testament is used by him to refer to the ability to recognize the social cost of production.[42] Jesus' order to Simon 'Feed my Lamb' is interpreted by Kumarappa as an order to alleviate poverty.[43] The hermeneutics applied by Kumarappa is thus essentially social and political hermeneutics.

Solomon Victus' study is very insightful in comprehending the Christian ethos of Kumarappa's thinking. It is interesting to see how he describes and categorizes Kumarappa's theological approach. In his first work on Kumarappa, Victus has placed Kumarappa in the framework of contextually developed theology of nationalism,[44] while in the second work he assesses Kumarappa's theology from two different theological frameworks, namely liberation theology and postcolonial theology.[45] The nationalist theology has placed nation before Christianity. Victus writes:

> He (Kumarappa) was not an armchair theologian who sits and writes in a room and conducts conferences for professional theological people. But as a lay economist and a communicant member of Indian Church, he responded spontaneously to the call of national struggle against oppression and tried to wake up the Christian community who were slumbering to the tunes of Western Christian music and urged them to fight for the cause of Jesus and their motherland....[46]

Within the framework of nationalist theology, Victus places Kumarappa in the framework of Gandhian theology. Gandhian theology, according to Victus was highly critical of Churchianity while the Indian Christian theology did not necessarily attack the Church per se. Second, Indian Christian

---

[42] Ibid., 42.

[43] Victus, *Jesus and Mother Economy*, 34.

[44] Victus, *Religion and Eco-economics*, 54.

[45] See Dietrich, 'Preface' to *Jesus and Mother Economy*, 2. Later in his work, Victus has stated that Kumarappa shows affinity with the concerns of the Asian theological framework.

[46] Victus, *Religion and Eco-economics*, 34.

theology did not recognize the equality of all religions.[47] A. J. Appasamy, Kumarappa's friend and a trained theologian, for instance, did not recognize equality of religions. Kumarappa, as against this, maintained that all religions are equal. He also went a step further and like Gandhi, stood for inter-religious dialogue. Victus maintains that Kumarappa provides an interesting model for Christians to have faith in Jesus while simultaneously accepting inter-faith relationship in a rational way.[48] Here he quotes one of the very profound unpublished essays of Kumarappa entitled 'Equality of Religions'. Kumarappa has written in this essay:

> Jesus reveals the God through love ... the Muslims see God as a Father and regard all co-worshippers as brethren ... the Hindus consider God as the Creator and so divine and sacred ... the Buddhists may even deny the existence of God, yet their moral sense regards killing as a sin, so all life becomes sacred. Thus though each may differ in its philosophy and application, they are all one fundamentally. The separatist tendencies arise out of human limitations only. Therefore, let us not emphasise these minor differences but recognise the fundamental brotherhood of humans and work together for unity.[49]

Thus Kumarappa's plea for the unity of religion and for primacy of Indianness over Christianity is described by Victus as his anchorage in the nationalist theology.

The placement of Kumarappa in the framework of nationalist theology and Gandhian theology is bound to have raised certain critical questions in view of the recent debates in nationalism[50] and the nationalist movement in India.[51] This debate sees nation as an imagined community and describes the Indian

---

[47] Ibid., 57–58.
[48] Victus, *Jesus and Mother Economy*, 27.
[49] Ibid., 30.
[50] Benedict Anderson.
[51] Chatterjee, *Nationalist Thought and the Colonial World*. Also see Chapter 1 of the present study.

nationalist project under Gandhi as a hegemonic exercise aimed at appropriating the subaltern masses. The description of Kumarappa's project as a 'nationalist' theology therefore implies that this theology aimed and facilitated, intentionally or innocently, the integration of the subaltern masses and the minority communities, particularly the Christians into the hegemonic Indian nation. In this regard, two recent works need serious attention. First, Chandra Mallampalli's *Christians and Public Life in Colonial South India, 1863–1937: Contending with Marginality*, and second, as mentioned earlier Benjamin Zacharia's *Developing India: An Intellectual and Social History* since the former has considered Gandhi's nationalist project as a project of Hinduization,[52] while the latter has described Kumarappa's theology as an attempt to Hinduize Christianity.[53] Mallampalli's work primarily traces the process of community formation of the South Indian Christians as well as the causes of their political and economic marginalization. This work shows that while the South Indian Christians preferred to maintain a distance from the nationalist movement, many Protestant Christians supported the nationalist movement. The Protestant Christians were highly critical of the non-Indian churches.[54] They pleaded for the transfer of administrative and financial responsibility into Indian hands, phasing out of missions and recognition of Indian churches. This they termed as 'missionary euthanasia'.[55] Politically, the Protestants stood by Gandhi and in order to overturn the perception of Christians being anti-national or colonial, identified themselves with national culture interpreted along Hindu or Sanskritik lines.[56] In their endeavour to prove themselves as nationalists and for the disavowal of communalism, the Protestant Christian leaders opposed the principle of separate electorates for Christians

[52] Mallampalli, *Christians and Public Life*, 112.

[53] Zacharia, *Developing India*, 174.

[54] Solomon Victus' study, however, shows that anti-Church position was not a feature of all the Protestant Christian theologians.

[55] Mallampalli, *Christians and Public Life*, 102.

[56] Ibid., 111.

during the Communal Accord of 1932.[57] This, among other things, Mallampalli maintains, amounted to the disempowerment of the Protestant Christian community. It is surprising that Mallampalli while discussing the nuances of the positions of the various Protestant Christian leaders, completely ignores Kumarappa. Despite this ignorance, Mallampalli's work is cited here to underline the way nationalism is perceived vis-à-vis community rights in general and that of Christians in particular and thereby to highlight the implications for locating Kumarappa within the framework of nationalist theology.

As long as nationalism is perceived as a high ideal or goal aimed at protecting the enlightened political aspirations of a society, the nationalist theology can claim some amount of progressiveness. The moment nationalism is perceived as a hegemonic ideology, nationalist theology becomes a regressive intellectual trap planted to appropriate the subaltern/marginalized masses. The same happens in the analysis of Kumarappa's approach to Christianity. While Solomon Victus finds in Kumarappa's nationalist theology potentials to indigenize Christian theology, Benjamin Zacharia finds Kumarappa's approach to Christianity as an attempt to Hinduize Christianity. Zacharia observes:

> Kumarappa adopted many of Gandhi's own ideas deriving from 'Hinduism' and Gandhi's debates with 'Hindu' tradition, especially regarding the alleged moral basis of caste categories, though he systematized them more than Gandhi himself did; but as a Christian, Kumarappa adapted these arguments to his interpretation of Christianity as well; and they fit. The moral colouring of Gandhian economic thought, it could, therefore, be argued, was compatible with a vision of God and religious belief, irrespective of particular faiths. Yet Kumarappa used the 'Hindu' version far more often than he used the Christian, unless he was specifically addressing Christians, in the knowledge that the Hindu appeal is likely to be wider. It is perhaps a pity that there was no one to

[57] Ibid., 121.

provide a version of 'Gandhian economics' compatible with Islam.[58]

As discussed earlier, Victus has shown that Kumarappa's theology was less Brahminical and Sanskritik than his contemporaries. Kumarappa endeavoured to make Christianity less hierarchical and thus more egalitarian. Instead of taking note of such uniqueness, Zacharia considers Kumarappa's attempts to Indianize Christianity as attempts of Hinduizing Christianity. This placement raises a variety of fundamental questions, such as how to demarcate the difference between Hinduization and Indianization? Isn't there any difference between Hinduization and Hindutvaization? Can Indianness be defined by completely ignoring and excluding Hinduism? Does the borrowing of a word (in this case 'nation') signify unconditional adherence to its paradigmatic ethos or its entire conceptual trajectory? Can Kumarappa's religious thinking be completely segregated from his plea for protecting the rights of livelihood and dignity of the artisan castes of Indian society? These questions, however, do not seem to bother Zacharia while labelling Kumarappa's theological endeavours as Hinduization of Christianity, subserviently employed in Gandhi's nationalist project. It seems that while undertaking such an assessment, Zacharia was either not sufficiently aware of Kumarappa's classification of nationalisms into herd-type nationalism and pack-type nationalism, as discussed in Chapter 3, or perhaps the project of rejecting the imperialism of categories did not allow such interpretations to recognize the entirely different trajectory in which Gandhi and Kumarappa anchored themselves even while they claimed the nation. The emergence of the nation in Western societies shared a symbiotic relationship with the development of capitalism. As discussed in Chapters 3 and 4 of this work, Kumarappa never encouraged similar processes for building the Indian nation. Instead, he proposed a model of development that would do away with the domination of capital and would place the toiling masses of Indian society at the centre

[58] Zacharia, *Developing India*, 174.

of the Indian polity. The very idea of claiming the nation was itself rooted in the experiences of the common people that were shaped by the economic implications of imperial power. In the spiritual domain, Kumarappa's theology was deeply concerned about the integration of the issues of alleviation of poverty and inequality with the spiritual quest of human beings. In the political domain, Kumarappa was equally careful, as discussed in Chapter 4, to direct the State towards regulating capitalism. Besides, the issues raised by Kumarappa about the political content of the missionary approach towards the Civil Disobedience Movement, as discussed earlier in this chapter, further justify his being a 'nationalist' theologian. The entire debate about the missionary positions regarding the civil disobedience shows that though the missionaries claimed a higher moral position of spreading Christ's message in India, most of them were governed by their own national interests. In this scenario can one really blame the 'nationalist' Christians like Kumarappa for their anti-Church position? If their theological approach was determined by their national interest, it was equally true of the colonial missionaries who claimed higher moral positions.

This entire debate about nationalist theology and about taking anti-Church position has another interesting dimension of Tamilization of Christianity. The issue of Tamilization of Christianity had come up in the early nineteenth century due to the controversy related to the works of the Tamil Protestant poet Vednayaka Pillai (1774–1864),[59] who also happens to be in relation to Kumarappa's mother.[60] Vednayaka Pillai authored more than 120 literary works and enjoys a deep impact on the protestant Tamils till today. By writing in Tamil and by translating certain works into Tamil, he is also considered to have contributed significantly to the construction of Tamil identity.[61] The range of his writings included prose tracts and

---

[59] Viswanathan Peterson, 'Between Print and Performance', in *India's Literary History: Essays on the Nineteenth Century*, 25–59.

[60] Vinaik, *The Gandhian Crusader*, 34.

[61] Mallampalli, *Christians and Public Life*, 116–117.

pamphlets in Tamil, doctrinal material for catechists, religious poetry for children to recite, poems for Tamil evangelical festivals and family occasions and more than 500 devotional hymns. Though these hymns were written mostly for personal worship, they were also sung in churches. These hymns showed deeper lineage with the Tamil *Shaiva Bhakti* ethos which was one of the reasons for them being so popular. The *Bethlehem Kuravanci*, written in musical–dramatic genre, was the most celebrated of them all. In 1809 Pillai was felicitated by the St Mathias' Church of Vepery in Madras with the title Sastri and with other ceremonial honours for contributing to Tamil Christianity. Almost till the end of first two decades of the nineteenth century, Vednayaka Pillai received a number of testimonials from different Christian congregations for his contributions. Soon he emerged as a senior leader of the Tanjore congregation when it was under German influence. With the appointment of an Anglican Bishop of India in 1814, however, things started changing drastically. The Anglican Bishop took serious objections to the observance of caste practices that had required people of high caste and low caste sit in separate areas in the church and had prohibited inter-dining and inter-marriage. Second, the Anglican Bishop also ordered proscription of the performance of Vedanayak Pillai's hymns in church.[62] Both these decisions were taken in order to do away with the 'heathen' elements in Indian Christian practices. Pillai was one of the strong supporters of caste practices in church. But Indira Viswanathan Peterson has shown that his proscription was not the result of his adherence to caste as the church had soon reconciled with others who had supported the caste practices and they were taken back in the church. In case of Pillai, however, such decision was not taken primarily due to his anchorage in the Tamil Bhakti tradition. The entire issue underlines the need for a subtler and nuanced understanding of the relationships between non-Indian religions, Indianness, regional cultures, Hinduism, caste and nationalism. None of these categories are monolithic nor do they have a fixed kind

[62] Viswanathan Peterson, 'Between Print and Performance', 34–35.

of relation with each other. Necessary precautions are therefore deeply warranted before branding a thought/thinker as Hinduized or Sanskritized.

In the background of all these factors, can one really charge Kumarappa for appropriating Gandhi's ideas for Hinduizing Christianity? Was it an attempt to Hinduize Christianity or Indianize Christianity or simply an attempt to reclaim the Tamilization of Christianity which was denied by colonial missionaries of European sensibilities? And can we then place Kumarappa in an orientalist framework as done by Zacharia?

Without being apologetic about nationalism, Kumarappa's religious discourse could be placed within the framework of nationalism since Kumarappa has endeavored to define alternate nation. This nation structurally may appear similar to a modern nation-state but does not replicate the processes inherent in its European avatar. However, at the same time, it is necessary to note that the theological compass of Kumarappa's thinking does not confine itself to nationalism, however enlightened or liberating it may be! Kumarappa's primary concern is to establish an egalitarian social order not only at the national level but in the entire world. It engages itself with colonialism and claims the nation to be a step towards this goal. His religious thinking does not confine itself to claiming and reclaiming the nation, but commits itself to respond to the pleas and claims of the deprived sections of the society for equality, dignity and harmonious living and for the establishment of an egalitarian society. It, therefore, becomes necessary to locate Kumarappa beyond the framework of nationalist theology. It is perhaps with the same outlook that Solomon Victus, in his second work, could be found placing Kumarappa in a broader framework of Third World theology instead of nationalist theology.[63] Third World theology is propounded by the Ecumenical Association of the Third World (EATWOT) and draws heavily from the framework of the postcolonial biblical studies as well as from liberation theology. While liberation

---

[63] Victus, *Jesus and Mother Economy*, 134.

theology emerged in Latin America in the mid-1970s in the works of scholars like Gustavo Gutiérrez,[64] postcolonial theology is comparatively a recent creed developed by Sri Lankan scholar R. S. Sugirtharaja.[65] The primary emphasis of the framework of the postcolonial theology is on exploring and exposing the discursive aspect of the power relations; liberation theology, on the other hand, has emphasized the need to explore the material dimension of power relations. While liberation theology acknowledges unity and certainty of truth, the postcolonial theology constantly puts certainty in question. While 'shutting back and forth in methodologies'[66] Victus has very ably shown how Kumarappa's theological approach to Christianity carries potentials for confirming both these frameworks simultaneously, thereby subscribing to the Asian ethos of synthesizing the pleas for liberation in material as well as ideological fields. According to Victus, the political ecology dimension of Kumarappa's theological thinking enables him to engage himself with both the discursive and the material analyses of power relations and simultaneously address the issues of acknowledgement, identity, dignity and equality. Victus therefore insists that Kumarappa's theological thinking carries potentials to develop into a Dalit theology.

Victus' placement of Kumarappa in the framework of postcolonial and liberation theology is intellectually very stimulating. However, there are a couple of issues that are missed out in such

---

[64] Gutiérrez, *A Theology of Liberation*. Also Rowland, ed., *The Cambridge Companion to Liberation Theology*. published in 1999, second Edition, 2007.

[65] See for instance Sugirtharajah, *Asian Biblical Hermeneutics and Postcolonialism*. Also *The Postcolonial Biblical Reader*.

[66] Some of the South African theologians, feminist theologians as well as scholars like Tat-Siong Benny Liew have insisted on the need to put hyphen between post-colonial theology and liberation theology instead of making them mutually exclusive. They have also advocated 'shutting back and forth in methodologies and starting points' while applying them. See Liew, *Postcolonial Interventions*. Quoted in the review of the work by Erin Runion, *Journal of Postcolonial Theory and Theology* (November 2010).

a placement. First, while liberation theology attempted to interpret Christinaity to accommodate the pleas of the exploited and marginalized sections of the society, it did not engage itself in interrogating and critiquing capitalism. Kumarappa, on the other hand, through his critique of money economy and mechanized industrialism, has engaged himself in the critique as well as rejection of capitalism. Second, though the liberation theology framework was developed by Latin American scholars, its origin remained in the resolution passed by the Vatican Council II which, on the background of Left activism, allowed and encouraged the reinterpretation of the Christian faith to suit the aspirations of the downtrodden thereby making the Church relevant. Kumarappa on the other hand has consistently interrogated the necessity of the church for the fulfilment of one's spiritual aspirations. Third, there is no doubt that Kumarappa's thinking stands for the livelihood rights of the artisan castes and responds positively to the right to dignity of the service castes. His critique of the middleman between man and his God carries potentials to do away with priesthood and Brahmanism. At the same time, one cannot ignore Kumarappa's glaring limitations in comprehending the nature of the caste system. While discussing the nature of Eastern economic organizations, for instance, Kumarappa points out that the Eastern economic organizations were based on the conception of work itself as a method of distribution. These organizations were free from over-production, personal greed and uncontrolled competition. In case of India, Kumarappa cites the caste system as the example of Eastern economic organizations. He considers the Brahmins as those who are idealistic; who are able to see far in the future. 'He will sacrifice his all to attain this ideal. He knows no compromises.'[67] The Kshatriyas are altruistic. 'He loses himself in seeking the welfare of the society. His glory is the service of his fellowmen and his reward is position and power.' The Vaishyas are for him the materialists. He amasses wealth but gets no social honour or position other than what he may secure by dedicating his possessions for the use of the

[67] Ibid., 15.

community. The Shudras, according to Kumarappa, are those who follow in a rut without much imagination. 'He prefers a well laid outline. He is happy with his salary, pension and provident fund.' In the final analysis Kumarappa adds:

Pruned of all extraneous growth, this is the core of the caste system. It curbs the devastating cut-throat competition as a factor in social alignment and emphasizes cooperation and obedience as the basis of law and order. It is graded on a cultural standard of values almost unknown to money economy.[68]

Kumarappa has also maintained elsewhere that caste system was incidental in ensuring equilibrium of occupations and this equilibrium was broken with the advent of the British. He writes:

The British traders set their minds on destroying their competitors by every means they could use. Military exploits, political intrigues and economic barriers were all pressed into service to gain their ends.... With the breakup of the economic order the caste system became a grading order of the high and the low by accident of birth, leading to meaningless snobbery.[69]

Kumarappa thus looks at the caste system as a non-competitive organization of the economic activities.

This newly created mythology of caste makes Kumarappa's ignorance about sociology of caste strikingly evident thereby limiting potentials of developing Dalit Theology from Kumarappa's thinking.

Where then can we place Kumarappa's religious thinking? And what significance does it carry in his entire body of thought?

[68] Ibid., 20.
[69] Kumarappa, 'Handicrafts and Cottage Industries', 108.

First, it is necessary to acknowledge that Kumarappa's engagement with religion is an engagement of such a seeker who conventionally doesn't enjoy the right to interpret or comment on the religious matters. Hence, the entire exercise itself remains outside the ecclesiastical domain and is secular in nature. Kumarappa, just like Gandhi, did not approach religion to make it relevant but searched in religion the spaces for transcendence and for integration. Both Gandhi and Kumarappa were deeply aware of the contextually determined existence and aspirations in human life, and hence insisted on the need to evolve society-specific models of economic development. At the same time, it is necessary to acknowledge that the ontological premise in which Gandhi and Kumarappa anchored themselves was that of holism. This premise recognized plurality and multidimensionality of reality but did not perceive these multiple dimensions as fragments. How to recognize this connectivity and integrity while simultaneously honouring plurality and multidimensionality was a challenge. Gandhi's and Kumarappa's anchorage in spirituality enabled them to connect unity with plurality. Kumarappa's insistence that religion is one's personal relationship with God speaks volumes of this unity–plurality dynamics. While Kumarappa advocated the observance of religion in one's own light, his faith in the unity of religions also prompted him to enter into a meaningful inter-religious dialogue. The search for the spaces of dialogue and communication between different experiences, in turn, halted the fragmentation of existence. In this entire process, Kumarappa also liberated religion from its historical and institutional lineages.

In the domain of economy also Kumarappa tries to simultaneously address unity and plurality. At the micro level of the economy he proposes to facilitate plurality through village industries, while at macro level he expects the State to coordinate these activities through public finance and other policies. His very emphasis on engaging with the State emanates from this need to balance between plurality and integration. This aspect of Kumarappa's ideas will be evident if it is understood in the light of the contemporary status of Gandhian constructive programmes. In contemporary times the Gandhian constructive programmes exist more or less as artefacts in museums. Whether it is organic farming, self-sufficient villages with participatory democracy, activity-based education or handicrafts, they exist as fragments. They do not form a force, a movement; neither do they challenge the mainstream model. They are either state-dependent or are so cut off from the domain of the State that they seem to have lost the element of critique with which they were conceived and impregnated. Kumarappa's emphasis on engaging with the State aimed at avoiding such fragmentation and seclusion. His idea to control money or regulate large-scale industry, however impractical it may sound, was a reminder that village-centric economy and participatory democracy is not possible if necessary changes are not introduced at the macro level. This was precisely the reason he criticized and rejected the developmental State that had reversed the logic of village industries for its own benefits. This was also the reason he wanted the body of constructive workers play the role of opposition to the government, and thereby direct it towards regulating large-scale industrialization.

Exploring J. C. Kumarappa through the intertextuality of narratives of the contemporary Gandhians brings out that though Kumarappa's ideas do provide interesting insights to build a model of sustainable development, his focus was to critique capitalism or the money economy. He visualizes a symbiotic relation between money economy, mechanized industrialism and imperialism. By the time Kumarappa was addressing the issues of India's colonial economy, capitalism in the West had gone through different stages. The talks about finance capitalism had already begun. In this context, Kumarappa's preference on the one hand of the term 'money economy' while on the other of the term 'mechanized industrialism' seems apt to denote the processes both intrinsic to and beyond industrial capitalism. This usage performed two primary functions. First, it enabled Kumarappa to address the issues of pre-capitalist economy along with the issues inherently linked with industrial capitalism and its different forms and phases without engaging himself into Marxist polemics. Second, it relieved Kumarappa of what Dipesh Chakrabarty would refer as the 'waiting room syndrome',[70] that is, the burden of waiting for the growth of capitalism in order to bring about revolutionary change in the Indian society. For many Indian Marxists, the evils of colonialism lay more in terms of its halting effects on the growth of capitalism than on its impoverishing effects on the Indian masses.[71] Kumarappa was concerned more about the drastic change that imperialism and its appendages—money economy and mechanized industrialism—brought about in the lives of Indian people. Imperialism not only exploited Indian people economically, but it violently disturbed and dismantled the indigenous ways of living. It systematically killed India's village industries, local skills and entrepreneurship, and forcefully implanted money economy on the Indian soil. Money economy placed high premium on the exchange value over use value. This drastically altered the lives of indigenous people ranging from their economic, social and political practices to their nutritional dietary habits. It also led to heavy commercialization in every walk life. Kumarappa has shown that the commercialization of agriculture resulted not only in its dependence on industry but also affected food security. The tying up of the domestic markets to the international economy not only caused intense rural unemployment but also generated a threat to world peace. Unemployment not only resulted in impoverishment of the masses but also demoralized them by denying them the right to work. Centralized–mechanized industrialism further squeezed their life-blood. In the name of growth, it took away from them the right to and pleasure of work and concentrated wealth in few hands.

[70] Chakrabarty has used this term more in the context of historicism and the liberal democratic notion of political development. See Chakrabarty, *Provincializing Europe*.

[71] Chandra, *Essays on Colonialism*. See also Thorner, 'Semi-Feudalism or Capitalism', 1961–1968, 1993–1999 and 2061–2065.

No doubt, many of the themes that Kumarappa dealt with and analysed had already appeared sharply in Marx. However, Kumarappa's critique of money addressed certain fundamental questions which were beyond the purview of industrial capitalism along with those inherently linked with it. In his times, though India had just newly started its journey towards industrialization, the way Kumarappa connected mechanized industrialism with money economy, a space was created to address simultaneously the concerns of both industrial capitalism and finance capitalism. His insistence on the idea that the evils of capitalism cannot be eliminated merely by socializing means of production along with the plea for decentralizing the entire process of production had significant implications for challenging industrial capitalism, though it was never taken seriously by his contemporaries. Now, in the age of global capital, when the money markets have become more dominant than ever before, his critique of money economy and his plea to avoid the money-centred organization of economic life calls for attention at least at ideational level. This critique warns us that elimination of capitalism is impossible without reducing the influence of money. The growing interest in Kumarappa's economic ideas in recent times, however, doesn't seem to take sufficient note of this aspect of his thinking. It is in this context that the celebration of Kumarappa either as a 'god of small things' or as a 'Green Gandhian' needs to be interrogated. There is no doubt that he propounded decentralized system of production and advocated village industries over large-scale industries, but for him the solution to these problems lay not merely in erecting small-scale industries but also in reducing the usage of money. The recent studies, however, do not seem to take sufficient note of Kumarappa's critique of money while presenting him as an advocate of Buddhist economics with a faith in 'small is beautiful' or as an ecological economist.

Glossary of Persons

Agarwal, Shriman Narayan (1912–1978). Was Founding Principal of Seksaria College of Commerce at Wardha. He married Jamanalal Bajaj's daughter Madalasa. In the pre-Independence period, he was against large-scale industrialization. However, changed his position later and started supporting Nehru's mixed economy model. Member of the Parliament during 1952–1957, and General Secretary of the Indian National Congress and the Chief Editor for the *AICC Economic Review* between 1952 and 1958. During Emergency, Indira Gandhi appointed him as Governor of Gujarat. Immediately after the Janata government came to power, he re-produced some of his essays on Gandhian Plan with a lamenting note that so far no one paid serious attention to Gandhi.

Amrit Kaur, Rajkumari (1889–1964). From the royal family of Kapurthala State. Joined All India Women's Congress in 1929, later became its Secretary, President and Chairperson. Played significant role in establishing the All India Women's Education Fund Association. Participated in Salt Satyagraha and the Quit India Movement. Independent India's first Health Minister.

Aryanayakam, E. W. (1889–1967). Sri Lankan Christian of Tamil origin from Jaffna. Studied Education at Edinburgh University. Worked for Young Men's Christian Association in England. Taught at Shantiniketan, and later at Wardha with his wife Ashadevi Aryanayakam, also an educationist.

Deo, Shankarrao (1871–1958). Member and later President of Maharashtra Congress Committee. General Secretary of Sarva Seva Sangh. Initiator of India–China Friendship Yatra of 1951.

Dharmadhikari, Dada (1899–1985). Participated in every movement launched by Gandhi. Imprisoned in 1930, 1932 and 1942. Taught at Rashtriya Shala at Nagpur. Co-edited the monthly *Sarvoday*. Founded Rashtriya Yuvak Sangh.

Dhotre, Raghunathrao (1897–1967). Second Secretary of Gandhi Smarak Nidhi. Secretary of Gandhi Seva Sangh since its inception until his death. Convenor of the Sevagram Conference in March 1948.

Jaju, Shrikrishnadas (1882–1955). Left his lucrative practice as an advocate and joined Gandhi in 1921 for the promotion of khadi. Actively involved with AISA, AIVIA and later in the Bhoodan Movement.

Kalelkar, Kaka (1888–1981). Worked with both Tagore and Gandhi. Authored a number of books in Gujarati and Marathi. Nominated Member of Rajya Sabha. Chairman of the First Backward Classes Commission.

Kumarappa, Bharatan (1896–1957). Younger brother of J. C. Kumarappa. Trained in theology. Joined J. C. Kumarappa along with his wife Sita to assist in the AIVIA work as well as in the basic education work.

Mazumdar, Dhirendra (1900–1978). Left education in 1921 to join Non-cooperation Movement. Committed to serving villages from 1923. Participated in freedom movement, imprisoned during the Civil Disobedience Movement and Quit India Movement. Established Ashrams at Raniva, Sevapuri, near Varanasi, and Shrama Bharati Khadigram in Bihar. Participated in the Bhoodan Movement. Did many experiments towards establishing a self-sufficient village founded on the principle of *shrama* (physical labour).

Mashruwala, Kishorelal (1890–1952). Was a close associate of Gandhi from 1917. Mashruwala, himself a follower of the Swaminrayan sect, had come to Gandhi to convert him to this sect, which never happened. He acted in the capacity of the first Registrar of Gujarat Vidyapeeth, President of Gandhi Seva Sangh (1934–1940) and Member of the Basic Education Committee (1937). He authored a number of books including *Gandhi and Marx*.

Mehta, Vaikunthbhai (1891–1964). Was a pioneer leader of the Indian Cooperative Movement. Vaikunthbhai was born at Bhavnagar in Gujarat and served the Bombay State Cooperative Bank (now Maharashtra State Cooperative Bank) as Chief Executive for an uninterrupted period of about 35 years. He was Minister of Finance and Cooperation of the then Bombay state and was first Chairman of Khadi and Village Industries Commission.

Nayyer, Pyarelal (1899–1982). Was among the 79 Dandi Satyagrahis in 1931, Secretary to Gandhi after Mahadev Desai's demise in 1942, principal biographer of Gandhi in the 'Last Phase' and the 'Early Phase' volumes. After Gandhi's demise, he requested to relieve him from the editorial responsibility of *Harijan* as he wanted to concentrate on writing Gandhi's biography.

Slade, Madeleine/Mira Behn (1892–1982). Daughter of British Rear Admiral Edmond Slade. Close associate of Gandhi from 1925, who named her Mira. Accompanied Gandhi at the Second Round Table Conference, held in London. Witness of the Simla Conference and the Cabinet Mission. After Gandhi's assassination, established Pashulok Ashram near Rishikesh and a settlement named Bapu Gram. Left India in 1956 and settled in Vienna. Recipient of Padma Bhushan in 1981.

Subedar, Manu (1889–1972). Industrialist from Mumbai. One of the board members of the Tatas. President of Indian Merchants' Chamber in 1935–1936. Member of Home Rule League. Worked on various committees of the Congress. Philanthropist—one of the founders of the Bapnu Ghar (old-age home in Mumbai) and the Lotus College, Mumbai. Translated *Dnyaneshwari* from Marathi to English. Wrote on Gandhian economics. Member of Legislative Assembly of the Central Province during the Provincial Government of 1937.

Bibliography

Primary Sources

Private Papers

Papers of J. C. Kumarappa. Nehru Memorial Museum and Library. New Delhi.

Papers of Organizations

Minutes of the Proceedings of the Board of Trustees of the All India Village Industries Association. Wardha: Gandhi Seva Sangh Office.

Minutes of the Proceedings of the Board of Management of the All India Village Industries Association. Wardha: Gandhi Seva Sangh Office.

Minutes of the Proceedings of the General Assembly of the All India Village Industries Association. Wardha: Gandhi Seva Sangh Office.

Minutes of the Proceedings of the Study Circle of the All India Village Industries Association. Wardha: Gandhi Seva Sangh Office.

Minutes of the Meeting of Board of Management of the All India Village Industries Association, 4 September 1944. Sevagram: Khadi Vidyalaya Hall.

Official Publications

The Imperial Gazetteer of India Vol. 23, 1908.

Report of the Industrial Survey Committee. Nagpur: Government of Central Provinces and Berar, 1939.

Report of the Committee for the Promotion of Village Industries. Bombay: Government of Bombay, 1946.

Report of the Conference of Representatives of State Boards and Constructive Workers. Bombay: All India Khadi and Village Industries Board, 1954.

Report of the Village and Small Scale Industries (Second Five Year Plan) Committee. New Delhi: Planning Commission, Government of India, 1955.

'Report of Board Activities'. *Khadi Gramodyog* 1, no. 3 (December 1954): 33.

Non-official Reports

Report of the Congress Select Committee on Financial Obligations between Britain and India. Allahabad: All India Congress Committee, 1931.

Shah, K. T., ed. *Manufacturing Industries: Report of the Sub-committee (National Planning Committee* Series). Bombay: Vora & Co. Publishers, 1947.

———. *Rural and Cottage Industries: Report of the Sub-committee (National Planning Committee* Series). Bombay: Vora & Co. Publishers, 1948.

———. *Report National Planning Committee.* Bombay: Vora & Co. Publishers, 1949.

Report of the Congress Agrarian Reforms Committee. New Delhi: All India Congress Committee, 1949.

Annual Reports of All India Village Industries Association. Wardha: All India Village Industries Association, 1936–1951.

Report of the Sarvodaya Plan Committee: Planning for Sarvodaya. Kashi: Akhil Bharat Sarva Seva Sangh, 1957.

In Memory of Mahatma Gandhi: 27 Years of Gandhi Smarak Nidhi. New Delhi: Gandhi Smarak Nidhi, 1976.

Newspapers/Periodicals

Young India (Reprint)

Harijan (Reprint)
Gram Udyog Patrika
Indian Social Reformer
Khadi Gramodyog

Published Works of J. C. Kumarappa

Public Finance and Our Poverty. Ahmedabad: Navjivan Publishing House, 1930.

'Christianity and Civil Disobedience'. *Indian Social Reformer* XL, no. 38 (24 May 1930): 619–620.

'The Price of Righteousness'. *Indian Social Reformer* XL, no. 47 (26 July 1930): 760.

'Gandhiji's Place in History'. *Indian Social Reformer* LXI, no. 27 (September 1930 and 4 October 1930): 59–60 and 76.

'Who Pays the Piper?', *Young India* 12, no. 9 (27 February 1930): 66.

'A Call and a Lead to Indian Officials'. *Young India* 12, no. 21 (22 May 1930): 193.

'Police Violence: An Appeal to All Christian Workers and Missionaries'. *Indian Social Reformer* 40, no. 34 (26 April 1930): 553.

A Survey of Matar Taluka (Khaira District). Ahmedabad: Gujarat Vidyapeeth, 1931.

'Great Possessions'. *Young India* 13, no. 37 (10 September 1931): 253–254.

'The Financial Crisis'. *Young India* 13, no. 41 (8 October 1931): 291.

'Exorcising Demon'. *Young India* 13, no. 49 (3 December 1931): 375.

Public Debts of India (Congress Golden Jubilee Brochure No. 5). Allahabad: All India Congress Committee, 1935.

The Philosophy of the Village Movement: Collection of Speeches and Articles of J. C. Kumarappa, edited by Sanivarapu Subba Rao. Wardha: All India Village Industries Association, 1935.

Why the Village Movement? Wardha: All India Village Industries Association, 1936.

Village Industries Association: Its Scope and Functions. Wardha: All India Village Industries Association, 1936.

Education for Life. Wardha: All India Village Industries Association, 1937.

Nationalism. Rajahmundry: Hindustan Publishing House, 1937.

Unemployment. Rajahmundry: Hindustan Publishing House, 1938.

War: A Factor of Production. Rajahmundry: Hindustan Publishing House, 1938.

'Is It Economic Anarchism?' In *Cent Per Cent Swadeshi or the Economics of Village Industries*. Ahmedabad: Navjivan Publishing House, 1938, 164–166.

'Out of One's Element'. *Gram Udyog Patrika*, September 1939. Reprinted in *A J. C. Kumarappa Reader*, edited by P. Bandhu. Udhagamandalam: Odyssey, 2011.

'Public Cost of Centralised Production'. *Gram Udyog Patrika* (August 1941). Reprinted in *A J. C. Kumarappa Reader*, edited by P. Bandu, 272–274. Udhagamandalam: Odyssey, 2011.

'Exchange and Human Values'. *Harijan* 11, no. 15 (3 May 1942): 143–144.

'A Stone for Bread'. *Gram Udyog Patrika* (December 1942). Reprinted in *J. C. Kumarappa Reader*, edited by P. Bandu, 69–70. Udhagamandalam: Odyssey, 2011.

'When the Machine Power', *Harijan* 9 no. 9 (15 March 1942): 76.

'Imperialism within Us', *Harijan* 9, no. 15 (26 April 1942), 135–136.

'Handicrafts and Cottage Industries'. *Annals of American Academy of Political and Social Science: India Speaking* 233 (May 1944): 106–112. http://www.jstor.org/stable/1025828 (accessed on 25 April 2009).

Economy of Permanence. Ahmedabad: Navjivan Publishing House, 1945.

Christianity: Its Economy and Way of Life. Ahmedabad: Navjivan Publishing House, 1945.

An Overall Plan for Rural Development. Nagpur: Government Printing Press, 1946.

Practices and Precepts of Jesus. Ahmedabad: Navjivan Publishing House, 1946.

'Increasing Production', *Harijan* 11, no. 14 (4 May 1947): 137.

'Orissa's Suicide'. *Harijan* 11, no. 3 (16 February 1947): 23.

'Blindness at a Price'. *Harijan* 11, no. 10 (6 April 1947): 96.

'Science Runs Amuck'. *Harijan* 11, no. 13 (27 April 1947): 96.

'Let Us Learn'. *Harijan* 11, no. 25 (10 July 1947): 239.

'An Abortive Conference'. *Harijan* 11, no. 35 (28 September 1947): 347–349.

Clive to Keynes: A Survey of the History of Our Public Debts and Credits. Ahmedabad: Navjivan Publishing House, 1947.

The Organisation and Accounts of Relief Work. Wardha: All India Village Industries Association, 1947.

'Akhil Bharat Sarva Seva Sangh'. *Harijan* 12, no. 40 (5 December 1948): 337–338.

Banishing War. Wardha: All India Village Industries Association, 1948.

Blood Money. Wardha: All India Village Industries Association, 1948.

Swaraj for Masses. Bombay: Hind Kitab, 1948.

Currency Inflation and Its Causes and Cure. Wardha: All India Village Industries Association, 1949.

Our Food Problem. Wardha: All India Village Industries Association, 1949.

Peace and Prosperity. Wardha: All India Village Industries Association, 1949.

Science and Progress. Wardha: All India Village Industries Association, 1949.

Stone Walls and Iron Bars. Wardha: All India Village Industries Association, 1949 (1st edition published in 1946).

Tad-gud. Wardha: All India Village Industries Association, 1949.

The Gandhian Economy and Other Essays. Wardha: All India Village Industries Association, 1949.

The Philosophy of Work and Other Essays. Wardha: All India Village Industries Association, 1949.

'Politics Then and Politics Now'. *Harijan* 13, no. 5 (3 April 1949), 34–35.

Gandhian Economic Thought. Bombay: Vora & Co. Publishers, 1951.

The Unitary Basis for a Non-violent Economy. Wardha: All India Village Industries Association, 1951.

A Plan for Economic Development of North West Frontier Province. Ahmedabad: Navjivan Publishing House, 1951.

Women and Village Industries. Wardha: All India Village Industries Association, 1951.

A Report on Agriculture and Cottage Industries in Japan. Poona: Deccan Book Stall, 1952.

'Chinese Sarvodaya'. *Gram Udyog Patrika* (February 1952): 12.

People's China: What I Saw and Learnt There. Wardha: All India Village Industries Association, 1952.

Hands across the Himalayas: Indians in Soviet Union. Wardha: Akhil Bharat Sarva Seva Sangh, 1953.

'After Bhoodan?', *Gram Udyog Patrika* 15, no. 3 (March 1953): 1.

Planning by the People for the People. Bombay: Vora & Co. Publishers, 1954.

Lessons from Europe. Wardha: Akhil Bharat Sarva Seva Sangh, 1954.

Sarvodaya and World Peace: Collection of Speeches Delivered at Paris. Wardha: Akhil Bharat Sarva Seva Sangh, 1955.

The Non-violent Economy and World Peace. Wardha: Akhil Bharat Sarva Seva Sangh, 1955.

A Peep Behind the Iron Curtain: Life in the Soviet Union and in People's China. T. Kallupatti: J. C. Kumarappa, 1956.

The Cow and Its Economy. Kashi: Akhil Bharat Sarva Seva Sangh, 1957.

Vicarious Living. Madras: Kumarappa Publications, 1959.

Back to Basics: A J. C. Kumarappa Reader, compiled and edited by P. Bandu. Udhagamandalam: Odyssey, 2011.

'Ends and Means of Bhoodan'. Reprinted in *Vicarious Living,* 32.

'The Underlying Principle'. Reprinted in *Vicarious Living,* 20–21.

Published Works of the Contemporaries Cited

Agarwal, Shriman Narayan. *Gandhian Planned Reaffirmed.* Bombay: Padma Publication House, 1948.

———. 'National Government's Industrial Policy'. *Harijan* 12, no. 9 (2 May 1948): 86.

———. *India's Current Problem.* New Delhi: All India Congress Committee, 1956.

———. *A Plea for Ideological Clarity: Collection of Articles from AICC Economic Review.* New Delhi: All India Congress Committee, 1958.

———, compiled and edited. *Co-operative Farming.* Ahmedabad: Navjivan Publishing House, 1957.

Bannerjee, B. N., G. D. Parikh, and V. M. Tarkunde. *People's Plan for Economic Development of India.* Delhi: Indian Federation of Labour, 1944.

Bhave, Vinoba. 'Wanted Corn, Not Currency'. *Harijan* 11, no. 3 (16 February 1947): 24.

———. 'Freedom from Money'. *Harijan* 15, no. 44 (29 December 1951), 373.

———. 'No Money Donations'. *Harijan* 15, no. 45 (5 January 1952): 389.

———. *Sarvodayache Ghoshana Patra* (2nd edition). Nalwadi-Wardha: Gram Seva Mandal, 1954.

Bhave, Vinoba. *Sarvodaya Vichar ani Swarajya Shastra*. Pavnar: Paramdham Vidyapeeth Prakashan, 1956. (Marathi)

———. *Bhudan Ganga* (7 Vols.). Pavnar: Paramdham Vidyapeeth Prakashan, 1957–1958. (Marathi)

———. *Vinoba Sahitya Vol. 16: Teesari Shakti*. Pavnar: Paramdham Prakashan, 1996. (Hindi)

———. *Vinoba Sahitya Vol. 18: Samyayogi Samaj: Khadi Vichar, Khadi Goseva Adi*. Pavnar: Paramdham Prakashan, 1998. (Hindi)

———. *Samyavad ki Samya-yoga*, edited by Parag Cholkar. Pavnar: Paramdham Prakashan, ND, 2000. (reprint, Marathi)

———. *Gandhi: Jase Pahile–Janile Vinobanni*, edited by Kantibhai Shah. Pavnar: Paramdham Prakashan, 2005. (reprint, Marathi)

Deshmukh, C. D. *Economic Developments in India, 1946–1956: Personal Retrospect*. Bombay: Asia Publishing House, 1957.

Deo, Shankarrao. 'Congress and the Constructive Workers—I, II, III'. *Harijan* XII, nos. 51–52 and 13, no. 1 (20–27 February and 6 March 1949), 2–3, 433–434, 441–442.

Dharmadhikari, Dada. *Sarvodaya Darshan*. Pavnar: Paramdham Prakashan, 1957 (2nd edition 1998).

———. *Manishichi Snehgatha*. Pavnar: Paramdham Prakashan, 1996.

———. *Samagra Sarvodaya Darshan*, Vols. I–IV. Varanasi: Sarva Seva Sangh, 2000–2005. (Hindi)

Dhebar, U. N. *Creation of Workers in the Post-Gandhian Period* (Vaikunth L. Mehta Memorial Lecture). Bombay: Mani Bhavan, 1968.

Edwards, J. F. (Rev.). 'India's Crisis: An Appeal to Men of Goodwill'. *Indian Social Reformer* 40, no. 36 (10 May 1930): 585–587.

Fifty Years of Co-operation: Golden Jubilee Souvenir 1904–54. Bombay: The Bombay Provincial Co-operative Institute, 1954.

Gandhi, Gopalkrishna, ed. *Gandhi Is Gone. Who Will Guide Us Now?— Nehru, Prasad, Azad, Vinoba, Kriplani, JP and Others Introspect*. Ranikhet: Permanent Black, 2007.

Gandhi, M. K. *The Story of My Experiments with Truth*. Ahmedabad: Navjivan Publishing House, 1927.

———. 'An Original Report'. *Harijan* 7, no. 15 (20 May 1939): 131.

———. 'Horizontal v. Vertical'. *Harijan* 7, no. 41 (18 November 1939): 346.

———. 'The Great Sentinel'. *Young India* 3, no. 45 (13 October 1921): 325.

———. 'Primary Education in Bombay'. *Harijan* 3, no. 35 (9 October 1937): 292.

Gandhi, M. K. *The Nation's Voice: Collection of Speeches of Gandhiji at the Round Table Conference*, edited by C. Rajagopalachari and J. C. Kumarappa. Ahmedabad: Navjivan Publishing House, 1947.

———. *Christian Missions and Their Role in India*, edited by Bharatan Kumarappa. Ahmedabad: Navjivan Publishing House, 1941.

———. *Economic and Industrial Relations*, Vols. I–III, compiled and edited by V. B. Kher. Ahmedabad: Navjivan Publishing House, 1957.

———. *Collected Works of Mahatma Gandhi*, 90 volumes. Delhi: Government of India, 1958–1984.

Javdekar, S. D. *Adhunik Bharat*. Pune: Continental Prakashan, 1938. (reprint Marathi 2001)

———. *Gandhivad*. Pune: Continental Prakashan, 1949. (Marathi)

———. *Satyagrahi Samajwad* (selected by Suhas Palshikar). Bombay: Maharashtra Rajya Sahitya Sanskriti Mandal, 1994. (Marathi)

Kalelkar, Kaka. *Stray Glimpses of Bapu*. Ahmedabad: Navjivan Publishing House, 1950.

———. *Gandhiwad-Samajwad: Ek Tulanatmak Adhyayan*. Delhi: Sasta Sahitya Manda, 1939. (Hindi)

Kapadia, Pranlal. 'Relationship between Central and State Boards'. *Khadi Gramodyog* 1, no. 3 (December 1954): 19.

Kumarappa, Bharatan. (Compiled and edited). *Sarvodaya*. Ahmedabad: Navjivan Publishing House, 1954.

Kripalani, J. B. *The Gandhian Way*. Bombay: Vora & Co. Publishers, 1938.

———. *The Plan: A Gandhian Critique*. Bombay: Janata Prakashan, ND.

———. *Gandhian Thought*. New Delhi: Gandhi Smarak Nidhi/ Orient Longman, 1961.

'Letter from C. Bradford of Dharchula, U. P.' *Indian Social Reformer* 40, no. 3 (21 September 1929): 40–41.

Majumdar, Dhirendra. *Varg-heen Samajachya Dishene: Lok-Ganga Yatra*. Kolhapur: Mahatma Gandhi Chair/Shivaji University, 2010. (Marathi)

———. *Samagra Gram-Seva ki Aor*. Varanasi: Sarva Seva Sangh, 2001. (Hindi)

Mashruwala, K. G. 'Some Danger-Spots of Yarn Currency'. *Harijan* 9, no. 14 (19 April 1942): 118–119.

———. 'Controls for Sarvodaya'. *Harijan* 12, no. 38 (21 November 1948): 320–321.

———. *Gandhi and Marx*. Wardha: Sarva Seva Sangh, 1956.

Mashruwala, K. G. 'Facing Realities'. *Harijan* 12, no. 40 (5 December 1948).

Mehta, Vaikunth L. *Decentralised Economic Development*. Bombay: Khadi & Village Industries Commission, 1964.

———. *Towards a Co-operative Socialist Commonwealth*. Bombay: Maharashtra State Co-operative Union, 1965.

———. 'Sources of Inspiration'. *Khadi Gramodyog* 1, no. 1 (October 1954): 5.

Mira Behn. 'Some Reflections on the Bhoodan Movement'. Reprinted in *Vicarious Living*, Appendix I, 55–59.

Narayan, Jayaprakash. *Prison Diary*. Pune: Abhay Prakashan, 1977.

———. *Towards Total Revolution*, Vols. I–IV, edited by Brahmanand. Bombay: Popular Prakashan, 1978.

———. *Selected Works of Jayaprakash Narayan*, Vol. 1 (1929–1935), edited by Bimal Prasad. New Delhi: Manohar Publishers, 2000.

Nehru, Jawaharlal. *Jawaharlal Nehru on Community Development, Panchayati Raj and Cooperation*. New Delhi: Ministry of Community Development, Panchayati Raj and Cooperation, Government of India, 1965.

Sundaram, J. C. 'Common Production Programme'. *Khadi Gramodyog* 1, no. 3 (December 1954): 52–55.

Thakurdas, Purushottam. *A Brief Memorandum Outline: A Plan of Economic Development of India* (2 Vols.). London: Penguin, 1945.

Secondary Sources

Books, Pamphlets and Articles

Achuthan, R. *Taking Gandhi to People through Seminars*. New Delhi: National Committee for Gandhi Centenary, ND.

Agarwal, Shriman Narayan. *One Week with Vinoba*. New Delhi: All India Congress Committee, 1956.

———. *Vinoba: His Life and Work*. Bombay: Popular Prakashan, 1970.

Ahmad, Aijaz. *Lineages of the Present: Political Essays*. New Delhi: Tulika Books, 1996.

Allen, Douglas, ed. *The Philosophy of Mahatma Gandhi for the Twenty-First Century*. New Delhi: Oxford University Press, 2008.

Arnold, David. *Science, Technology and Medicine in Colonial India*. New York, NY: Cambridge University Press, 2000.

Bagchi, Amiya Kumar. 'Colonialism and the Nature of Capitalist Enterprise in India'. *Economic & Political Weekly* 23, no. 31 (30 July 1988): 38–50.

Bajaj, Radhakrishna, and Sudhakar Tare. *Kishorelalbhai Mashruwala*. Sevagram: Sevagram Ashram Pratishthan, 1991. (Hindi)

Bakshi, Rajni. *Civilizational Gandhi*. Gateway House Research Paper No. 6. Mumbai: Indian Council on Global Relations, 2012.

Bandyopadhyay, Sekhar, ed. *Nationalist Movement in India: A Reader*. New Delhi: Oxford University Press, 2009.

Banerjee, Debdas. 'Science, Technology & Economic Development in India: Divergence in Historical Perspective'. *Economic & Political Weekly* 23, no. 20 (16 May 1998): 1199–1206.

Banerjee, Samir. *Notes from Gandhigram: Challenges to Gandhian Praxis*. New Delhi: Orient BlackSwan, 2009.

Bapat, Ram. *Swarajya ani Rajyasanstha*. Kolhapur: Mahatma Gandhi Chair/Shivaji University, 2003. (Marathi)

Basole, Amit. *Gandhi, Kumarappa and Non-modern Challenge to Economics*. January 2005. www.facstaff.bucknell.edu/ab044/Gandhi-Kumarappa.pdf (accessed on 2 May 2006).

Beaud, Michel. *A History of Capitalism, 1500–2000*. Delhi: Aakar Books, 1981.

Bedekar, D. K. *Towards Understanding Gandhi* (ed. by Rajabhau Gawande). Bombay: Popular Prakashan, 1975.

Bhargava, Rajeev. 'History, Nation and Community: Some Reflections on Nationalist Historiography of India and Pakistan'. *Economic & Political Weekly* 35, no. 4 (22–28 January 2000): 193–200.

———. *Individualism in Social Science: Forms and Limits of a Methodology*. New Delhi: Oxford University Press, 2008.

———. *What is Political Theory and Why Do We Need It?* New Delhi: Oxford University Press, 2010.

Bhatia, B. M. 'Growth and Composition of Middle Class in South India in Nineteenth Century'. *The Indian Economic and Social History Review* 2, no. 4 (October 1965): 343–344.

Bhattacharya, S. 'Cotton Mills & Spinning Wheels: Swadeshi and the Indian Capitalist Class, 1920–22'. *Economic & Political Weekly* 47, no. 20 (20 November 1976): 1828–1834.

Bhole, L. M. *Essays on Gandhian Socioeconomic Thought*. New Delhi: Shipra Publications, 2000.

Bilgrami, Akeel. 'Occidentalism, the Very Idea: An Essay on Enlightenment and Enchantment'. *Critical Enquiry* 32, no. 3 (Spring 2006): 381–411.

Blackburn, Stuart, and Vasudha Dalmia, eds. *India's Literary History: Essays on the Nineteenth Century*. New Delhi: Permanent Black, 2004.

Bondurant, Jean V. *Conquest of Violence: The Gandhian Philosophy of Conflict*. Bombay: Oxford University Press, 1955.

Brown, Judith M. *Modern India: The Origins of an Asian Democracy*. New Delhi: Oxford University Press, 1984.

Brown, Judith M., and Anthony J. Parel, eds. *The Cambridge Companion to Gandhi*. New Delhi: Cambridge University Press, 2011.

Calvocoressi, Peter. *Who's Who in the Bible*. London: Penguin Books, 1988.

Carver, T. N. 'Review of Gandhian Economic Thought by J. C. Kumarappa'. *The Journal of Political Economy* 60, no. 2 (April 1952): 166–167.

Chakkanatt, John Dilip. *Of God and Mammon: J. C. Kumarappa's Religious Theory of Economics as a Counterpoint to the Religion of Economics*. New Delhi: Intercultural Publications, 2001.

Chakrabarty, Dipesh. *Provincializing Europe: Postcolonial Thought and Historical Difference*. New Delhi: Oxford University Press, 2001.

Chandavarkar, Rajnarayan. *Imperial Power and Popular Politics: Class, Resistance and the State in India, C.1850–1950*. New York: Cambridge University Press, 1998.

Chandoke, Neera. 'Indigenous Social Sciences'. *Economic & Political Weekly* 26, no. 21 (25 May 1991): 1357.

Chandra, Bipan. *Essays on Colonialism*. New Delhi: Orient BlackSwan, 1976.

Chatterjee, Margaret. *Gandhi and the Challenge of Religious Diversity: Religious Pluralism Revisited*. New Delhi: Bibliophile South Asia, 2005.

———. *Inter-religious Communication: Gandhian Perspective*. New Delhi: Bibliophile South Asia, 2009.

Chatterjee, Partha. *Nationalist Thought and the Colonial World: A Derivative Discourse*. New Delhi: Oxford University Press, 1985.

Chaudhury, Sushil, and Michel Morineau, eds. *Merchants, Companies and Trade: Europe and Asia in the Early Modern Era*. New York: Cambridge University Press, 1999.

Chibber, Vivek. *Locked in Place: State Building and Late Industrialisation in India*. Princeton, NJ: Princeton University Press, 2003.

Chousalkar, Ashok. *Hind Swaraj ani Atma Balachi Prapti*. Kolhapur: Shivaji Vidyapeeth, 2008. (Marathi)

Claerhout, Sarah, and Jacob de Roover. 'The Question of Conversion in India'. *Economic & Political Weekly* 40, no. 28 (9 July 2005): 3048–3055.

Coats, A. W. 'Seligman, Edward Robin Anderson'. In *The New Palgrave Dictionary of Economics*, Vol. 4, edited by J. Eatwell, M. Milgate, and P. Newman. London: Macmillan Press, 1987, 300.

Cohn, Bernard S. *Colonialism and Its Forms of Knowledge: The British in India*. New Delhi: Oxford University Press, 1997.

Dabholkar, Devdatta. *Gandhijinche Arthashastra*. Nasik: Gandhi Smarak Nidhi, ND. (Marathi)

Dasgupta, Ajit K. *A History of Indian Economic Thought*. London: Routledge, 1993.

———. *Gandhi's Economic Thought*. London: Routledge, 1996.

Datta Roy Choudhury, Uma. 'Technological Change in the Indian Economy, 1950–1960'. *Economic & Political Weekly* 1, no. 1 (20 August 1966): 37–48.

Davenport, H. J. *Economics of Enterprise*. New York, NY: Augustus M. Kelley, 1913. http://www.cooperativeindividualism.org/davenport_economics_of_enterprise.html (accessed on 12 March 2008).

Desai, Mahadev (M. D.). 'An Economic Survey'. *Young India* 11, no. 48 (28 November 1929): 389–390.

———. 'Interpretation of the Wardha Education Scheme'. *Harijan* 6, no. 11 (12 February 1938): 1–2.

Desai, Maganbhai P. 'Village Shoe-Maker vs. Shoe-Making Factories', *Harijan* 23, no. 18 (3 April 1954): 40.

Desai, M. B. 'Gandhiji and Village Economy'. *Journal of MSU Baroda* (Gandhi Centenary Special Number) 18, no. 1–2. (April–July 1969): 79–88.

Desai, Narayan. *The Fire and the Rose: Biography of Mahadevbhai*. Ahmedabad: Navjivan Publishing House, 1995.

Dharampal. *Collected Writings* Vols. I–V. Goa: Other India Press, 2000.

Dhawan Shankardas, Rani. *The First Congress Raj: Provincial Autonomy in Bombay*. New Delhi: Macmillan India, 1982.

Diwan, Romesh, and Mark Lutz, eds. *Essays in Gandhian Economics*. New Delhi: Gandhi Peace Foundation, 1985.

Diwan, Romesh K. 'Total Revolution and Appropriate Technology'. *Gandhi Marg* 4, no. 7 (October 1982): 631–645.

Doctor, Adi H. *Sarvodaya: A Political and Economic Study*. Bombay: Asia Publishing House, 1967.

Dube, Saurabh. 'Colonial Registers of a Vernacular Christianity: Conversion to Translation.' *Economic & Political Weekly* 39, no. 2 (10 January 2004): 161–171.

Dube, Saurabh, and Ishita Banerjee-Dube, eds. *Unbecoming Modern: Colonialism, Modernity & Colonial Modernities*. New Delhi: Social Science Press, 2006.

Epstein, S. J. M. *The Earthy Soil: Bombay Peasants and the Nationalist Movement: 1919–1947*. New Delhi: Oxford University Press, 1988.

Farinelli, Franco. *Capitalist Form of Production in South Asia: Consequences of British Policies*. New Delhi: Manohar Publishers, 1991.

Fisher, Margaret W., and Joan Bondurant. 'The Impact of Communist China on Visitors from India: Review of Various Pamphlets'. *The Far Eastern Economic Quarterly* 15, no. 2 (February 1956): 249–265.

Fox, Richard G. *Gandhian Utopia: Experiments with Culture*. Boston, MA: Beacon Press, 1989.

George, S. K. *Gandhi's Challenge to Christianity*. Ahmedabad: Navjivan Publishing House, 1947.

Ghosh, B. N. *Gandhian Political Economy: Principles, Practices and Policy*. Hampshire: Ashgate Publishing, 2007.

Ghosh, Saila Kumar. *Colonial Modernization and Gandhi*. Calcutta: Papyrus, 2008.

Gidwani, Vinay. 'The Quest for Distinction: A Reappraisal of the Rural Labour Process in Kheda District (Gujarat)'. *Economic Geography* 76, no. 2 (April 2000): 145–168.

———. *Capital Interrupted: Agrarian Development and the Politics of Work in India*. Ranikhet: Permanent Black, 2008.

Govindu, Venu Madhav, and Deepak Malghan. 'Building a Creative Freedom: J. C. Kumarappa and His Economy Philosophy'. *Economic & Political Weekly* 40, no. 52 (24 December 2005): 5477–5485.

———. *The Web of Freedom: J. C. Kumarappa and Gandhi's Struggle for Economic Justice*. New Delhi: Oxford University Press, 2016.

Green, Martin. *The Origins of Non-violence: Tolstoy and Gandhi in Their Historical Settings*. New Delhi: Harper Collins, 1986/1998.

Gregg, Richard B. *A Philosophy of Indian Economic Development*. Ahmedabad: Navjivan Publishing House, 1958.

Gregg, Richard. *The Power of Non-violence*. Hartford: Greenleaf Books, 1935/1959. Reprinted in *Journal of American History* 91, no. 4 (2005): 1318–1348.

Gutiérrez, Gustavo. *A Theology of Liberation: History, Practice and Salvation*. New York: Orbis Books, 1973.

Guha, Ramachandra. *Mahatma Gandhi and the Environmental Movement*. Pune: Parisar, 1993.

———. *Varieties of Environmentalism: Essays North and South*. New Delhi: Oxford University Press, 1998.

———. *Environmentalism: A Global History*. New Delhi: Oxford University Press, 2000.

———. *An Anthropologist among the Marxists and Other Essays*. New Delhi: Permanent Black, 2000.

Guha, Sumit. *The Agrarian Economy of the Bombay Deccan 1818–1947*. New Delhi: Oxford University Press, 1985.

Gupta, Shaibal. 'Potentials of Industrial Revolution in Pre-British India'. *Economic & Political Weekly* 15, no. 9 (1 March 1980): 471–474.

Habib, Irfan. *Indian Economy 1858–1914*. A People's History of India Series, No. 28. New Delhi: Tulika Books, 2006.

———. *Technology in Medieval India c. 650–1750*. A People's History of India Series, No. 20. New Delhi: Tulika Books, 2008.

Haksar, Vinit. *Rights, Communities and Disobedience: Liberalism and Gandhi*. New Delhi: Oxford University Press, 2001.

Hardiman, David. *Peasant Nationalists of Gujarat: Kheda District, 1917–1934*. New Delhi: Oxford University Press, 1981.

———. *Feeding the Bania: Peasants and Usurers in Western India*. New Delhi: Oxford University Press, 1996.

Harvey, David. *A Brief History of Neoliberalism*. Kolkata: Update Publication, 2010.

Heehs, Peter. 'Shades of Orientalism: Paradoxes and Problems in Indian Historiography'. *History and Theory* 42, no. 2 (May 2003).

Heller, Henri. *The Birth of Capitalism: A Twenty-First Century Perspective*. London: Pluto Press, 2011: 169–195.

Iyer, Raghavan. *Moral and Political Thought of Mahatma Gandhi*. New Delhi: Oxford University Press, 1973/2000.

Jaju, Shrikrishandas. *Akhil Bharat Charakha Sangh ka Itihas*. Sevagram: Akhil Bharat Charakha Sangh, 1950. (Hindi)

Joseph, Sarah. 'Indigenous Social Science Project: Some Political Implication'. *Economic & Political Weekly* 26, no. 15 (13 April 1991): 959–963.

Joseph, Sarah. 'An Agenda for Political Theory in India'. *Social Scientist* 20, no. 12 (December 1992): 42–52.

———. 'Society versus State? Political Society and Non-Party Political Process in India'. *Economic & Political Weekly* 37, no. 4 (26 January–1 February 2002): 299–305.

Kantowsky, Detlef. *Sarvodaya: The Other Development.* Bombay: Vikas Publishing House, 1980.

Kappen, Mercy, ed. *Gandhi and Social Action Today.* New Delhi: Sterling Publishers, 1990.

Karnik, Ajit. 'Transformations, Then and Now: The Appeal of Karl Polanyi'. *Economic & Political Weekly* 43, no. 48 (29 November 2008): 101–109.

Kolge, Nishikant. *Gandhi against Caste.* New Delhi: Oxford University Press, 2017.

Kosambi, Meera. 'Indian Response to Christianity, Church and Colonialism: Case of Pandita Ramabai'. *Economic & Political Weekly* 27, no. 43–44 (24–31 October 1992): WS-61–WS72.

Kripalani, J. B. *My Times: An Autobiography.* New Delhi: Rupa & Co., 2004.

Kulke, Hermann, ed. *The State in India 1000–1700.* New Delhi: Oxford University Press, 1995.

Kumar, Devendra. *Dr. Kumarappa: Jeevan ani Karya.* Pune: Gandhi Smarak Nidhi, 1992.

———. 'Kumarappa: Visionary of Sustainability'. *Gandhian Perspective* 10, no. 1–2 (1997): 34–39.

Kumar, Dharma, ed. *The Cambridge Economic History of India 1757–1979 Vol. II.* Cambridge, UK: Cambridge University Press, 1983.

Laggers, G. G., and E. Wang. *Global History of Modern Historiography.* Noida: Pearson, 2010.

Lenin, V. I. *Imperialism: The Highest Stage of Capitalism.* New Delhi: Left Word Books, 2000.

Liebl, Maureen, and Tirthankar Roy. 'Handmade in India: Preliminary Analysis of Crafts Producers and Craft Production'. *Economic & Political Weekly* 38, no. 51–52 (27 December 2003 and 2 January 2004): 5366–5376.

Liew, Tat-siong Benny. *Postcolonial Interventions: Essays in Honour of R. S. Sugirtharajah*, Vol. 23 of *The Bible in the Modern World.* Sheffield: Sheffield Phoenix Press, 2009.

Lindley, Mark. *J. C. Kumarappa: Mahatma Gandhi's Economist.* Mumbai: Popular Prakashan, 2007.

Lindley, Mark. 'Kumarappa: A Giant or Midget?' *Economic & Political Weekly* 42, no. 21 (26 May 2007): 1975–1981.

Linton, Erica. *Fragments of a Vision: A Journey through India's Gramdan Villages.* Varanasi: Sarva Seva Sangh Prakashan, 1971.

Loomba, Ania. *Colonialism/Postcolonialism.* London: Routledge, 2007.

Loomis, Mildred. 'Four Worlds in Economics'. *Gandhi Marg* 4, no. 1 (1 April 1982): 50–55.

Magdoff, Harry. *Imperialism: From the Colonial Age to the Present.* New Delhi: Aakar, 1978/2009.

Mallampalli, Chandra. *Christians and Public Life in Colonial South India 1863–1937: Contending with Marginality.* London: Routledge Curzon, 2004.

Major, Rafael. 'The Cambridge School and Leo Strauss: Texts and Context of American Political Science'. *Political Research Quarterly* 58, no. 3 (September 2005): 477–485.

Mahajan, Gurpreet. *India: Political Ideas and Making of a Democratic Discourse.* London: Zed Books, 2013.

Markovits, Claude. *Indian Business and Nationalist Politics 1931–39: The Indigenous Capitalist Class and the Rise of the Congress Party.* Cambridge, UK: Cambridge University Press, 1985.

Marsh, David, and Gerry Stöker, eds. *Theory and Methods in Political Science.* New York, NY: Palgrave Macmillan, 1995.

Mathur, J. S. *Essays on Gandhian Economics.* Allahabad: Chaitanya Publication House, 1960.

McGowan, Abigail. *Crafting the Nation in Colonial India.* New York, NY: Palgrave Macmillan, 2009.

Mehta, Vadilal Lallubhai, *Equality through Trusteeship: An Alternative for Full Employment along Gandhian Lines.* New Delhi: Tata McGraw Hill Publishing, 1977.

Mehta, V. R. *Foundations of Indian Political Thought.* New Delhi: Manohar Publishers, 1996.

Mehta, V. R., and Thomas Pantham, eds. *Political Ideas in Modern India: Thematic Explorations (History of Science, Philosophy and Culture in Indian Civilization*, Vol. X, Part 7). New Delhi: SAGE, 2006.

Menon, Dilip. 'Religion and Colonial Modernity: Rethinking Belief and Identity'. *Economic & Political Weekly* 37, no. 17 (27 April 2002): 1662–1667.

———. 'The Many Spaces and the Times of Swadeshi'. *Economic & Political Weekly* 46, no. 42 (20 October 2012): 44–52.

Mielants, Eric H. *The Origins of Capitalism and 'The Rise of the West'*. Philadelphia, PA: Temple University Press, 2007/New Delhi: Munshiram Manoharlal Publishers, 2013.

Mira Behn (Madeleine Slade). *The Spirit's Pilgrimage*. London: Longman, 1960.

Mohanty, Manoranjan. *Contemporary Indian Political Theory*. New Delhi: Sanskriti, 2000.

Moore, R. J. *The Crisis of Indian Unity: 1917–1940*. New Delhi: Oxford University Press, 1974.

Mukherjee, Aditya. 'Indian Capitalist Class and the Public Sector 1930–1947'. *Economic & Political Weekly* 9, no. 3 (17 January 1976): 67–73.

———. *Imperialism, Nationalism and the Making of the Indian Capitalist Class, 1920–1947*. New Delhi: SAGE Publications, 2002.

Mukherjee, Dhurjati. 'Planning and Rural Development: The Gandhian Perspective'. *Gandhi Marg* 4, no. 6 (August 1982): 601–610.

Mukherjee, Tilottama. 'Markets in Eighteenth Century Bengal Economy'. *The Indian Economic and Social History Review* 48, no. 2 (2011): 143–176.

Nand, Brahma, ed. *Village Communities and Land Tenure in Western India under Colonial Rule*. New Delhi: Manohar Publishers, 2009.

Nanda, B. R. *In Gandhi's Footsteps: The Life and Times of Jamanalal Bajaj*. New Delhi: Oxford University Press, 1990.

Natarajan, L. *American Shadow over India*. Bombay: People's Publishing House, 1952.

National Seminar on J. C. Kumarappa. Madras: Dr. J. C. Kumarappa Centenary Committee, 1992.

Ning, Wang. 'Orientalism versus Occidentalism?' *New Literary History* 28, no. 1 (Winter 1997): 57–67.

Oddie, G. A. 'Protestant Missions, Caste and Social Change in India, 1860–1914'. *The Indian Economic and Social History Review* 6, no. 3 (September 1969): 259–291.

Omvedt, Gail. *Dalits and the Democratic Revolution: Dr. Ambedkar and the Dalit Movement in the Colonial India*. New Delhi: SAGE Publications, 1994.

Ostergaard, Geoffrey, and Melville Currell. *The Gentle Anarchists: A Study of the Leaders of the Sarvodaya Movement for Non-violent Revolution in India*. London: Oxford University Press, 1971.

Overstreet, Gene D., and Marshall Windmiller. *Communism in India*. Berkeley, CA: University of California Press, 1959.

Palmer, Richard E. *Hermeneutics: Interpretation Theory in Schleiermacher, Dilthey, Heidegger, and Gadamer*. Evanston: Northwestern University Press, 1969.

Pantham, Thomas. *Political Theories and Social Reconstruction: A Critical Survey of the Literature on India*. New Delhi: SAGE, 1995.

Pantham, Thomas, and K. L. Deutsch, eds. *Political Thought in Modern India*. New Delhi: SAGE Publications, 1986.

Papers and Proceedings of the Round Table on Research Programme on Gandhian Thought. Bombay: Khadi and Village Industries Commission, 1970.

Papola, T. S., and V. N. Mishra. 'Some Aspects of Rural Industrialisation'. *Economic & Political Weekly* 41, no. 43 (October 1980): 1733–1746.

Paranjape, Makarand. *Decolonization and Development: Hind Swaraj Revisioned*. New Delhi: SAGE Publications, 1993.

Parekh, Bhikhu. *Gandhi's Political Philosophy: A Critical Examination*. London: Macmillan Press, 1989.

———. *Colonialism, Tradition and Reform: An Analysis of Gandhi's Political Discourse*. New Delhi: SAGE, 1989/1999 (revised edition).

Parekh, Bhikhu, and R. N. Berki. 'The History of Ideas: A Critique of Q. Skinner's Methodology'. *Journal of the History of Ideas* 34, no. 2 (April–June 1973): 163–184.

Parekh, Bhikhu, and Thomas Pantham, eds. *Political Discourse: Explorations in Indian and Western Political Thought*. New Delhi: SAGE Publications, 1987.

Parel, Anthony J. *Gandhi: 'Hind Swaraj' and Other Writings*. New Delhi: Cambridge University Press, 1997.

———. *Gandhi, Freedom, and Self-Rule*. New Delhi: Vistaar, 2000.

Pasricha, Ashu. *Rediscovering Gandhi Vol. 4: Consensual Democracy—Gandhi on State, Power and Politics*. New Delhi: Concept Publishing Company, 2010.

Patel, Sujata. 'Construction and Reconstruction of Woman in Gandhi'. *Economic & Political Weekly* 23, no. 8 (February 1988): 377–387.

Patnaik, Utsa. 'The Agrarian Question and Development of Capitalism in India'. *Economic & Political Weekly* 21, no. 18 (3 May 1986): 781–793.

Pateman, Carole. 'Criticising the Empirical Theorists of Democracy: A Comment on Skinner'. *Political Theory* 2, no. 2 (May 1974): 215–218.

Phadke, Y. D. *Vyakti ani Vichar*. Pune: Shree Vidya Prakashan, 1979. (Marathi)

Pillai, P. V. 'Hind Swaraj in the Light of Heidegger's Critique of Modernity'. *Gandhi Marg* 4, no. 4 (July 1982): 445–458.

Pinto, Vivek. *Gandhi's Vision and Values: The Moral Quest for Change in Agriculture*. New Delhi: SAGE, 1998.

Polanyi, Karl. *The Great Transformation: Political and Economic Origins of Our Times*. Boston, MA: Beacon Press, 1957.

———. 'Ports of Trade in Early Societies'. *The Journal of Economic History* 23, no. 1 (March 1963): 30–45.

Prakash, Gyan. 'Subaltern Studies as Postcolonial Criticism'. *The American Historical Review* 99, no. 5 (December 1994): 1475–1490.

Prasad, Bimal, ed. *Socialism, Sarvodaya and Democracy: Selected Works of Jayaprakash Narayan*. Bombay: Asia Publishing House, 1964.

Prasad, Madho. *A Gandhian Patriarch: A Political & Spiritual Biography of Kaka Kalelkar*. Bombay: Popular Prakashan, 1965.

Prasad, Rajendra. *Autobiography*. Bombay: Asia Publishing House, 1957.

Pratap, Abhay. *Ahimsa ke Prayog: Gandhi Seva Sangh ka Itihas* (compiled by Kanakmal Gandhi and Parag Cholkar). Varanasi: Sarva Seva Sangh, 2011.

Prayer, Mario. 'The Vatican Church and Mahatma Gandhi's India, 1920–1948'. *Social Scientist* 37, no. 1–2 (January–February 2009): 39–63.

Pyarelal. *Towards New Horizons*. Ahmedabad: Navjivan Publishing House, 1959.

———. *The Last Phase* (3 Vols.). Ahmedabad: Navjivan Publishing House, 1956–1958.

Raghuramaraju, A., ed. *Debating Gandhi: A Reader*. New Delhi: Oxford University Press, 2006.

Rahman, A. *History of Indian Science, Technology and Culture AD 1000–1800*. New Delhi: Oxford University Press, 1998.

Rajendran, N. *National Movement in Tamil Nadu 1905–1914: Agitational Politics and State Coercion*. Madras: Oxford University Press, 1994.

Rajagopalachari, C. *Gandhi's Teachings and Philosophy* (lecture delivered at University of Pune). Bombay: Bharatiya Vidya Bhavan, 1967.

Ramagundam, Rahul. *Gandhi's Khadi: A History of Contention and Conciliation*. New Delhi: Orient Longman, 2008.

Ramachandran, G. *Promotion of Gandhian Philosophy* (special lecture). Mysore: Prasaranga University of Mysore, 1966.

Ranson, Rev. C. W. 'The Growth of the Population of Madras'. In *The Madras Tercentenary Commemoration Volume*. London: Humphrey Milford/Oxford University Press, 1939.

Raychaudhuri, Tapan, and Irfan Habib, eds. *The Cambridge Economic History of India*, Vol. 1. Cambridge, UK: Cambridge University Press, 1982.

Richter, William L., ed. *Approaches to Political Thought*. New Delhi: Rawat Publications (Lanham: Rowman & Littlefield Publishers), 2009.

Rothermund, Indira. 'Gandhi in Maharashtra: Some Ideological Perspective'. *Gandhi Marg* 4, no. 7 (October 1982): 663–679.

Rowland, Christopher, ed. *The Cambridge Companion to Liberation Theology*. New York, NY: Cambridge University Press, 1999.

Roy, Tirthankar. 'Development of Distortion': "Powerlooms" in India 1950–1997'. *Economic & Political Weekly* 33, no. 60 (April 1998): 897–911.

———. *Traditional Industry in the Economy of Colonial India*. New York, NY: Cambridge University Press, 1999.

———. *The Economic History of India 1857–1947*. New Delhi: Oxford University Press, 2006.

Rudolph, L. I., and S. H. Rudolph. *The Modernity of Tradition: Political Development in India*. Chicago, IL: University of Chicago Press, 1967.

Samuels, W. J. 'Davenport, Herbert Joseph'. In *The New Palgrave Dictionary of Economics*, Vol. 1, edited by J. Eatwell, M. Milgate, and P. Newman. London: Macmillan Press, 1987: 749.

Sanyal, Amal. 'The Curious Case of Bombay Plan'. *Contemporary Issues and Ideas in Social Sciences* 6, no. 10 (2010). http://journal.ciiss.in/index.php/ciiss/article/view/78 (Accessed on 15 September 2014).

Sardar, G. B. *Mahatma Gandhi ani Maharashtra*. Pune: Samvad Prakashan, ND. (Marathi)

Schöettli, Jivanta. *Vision and Strategy in Indian Politics: Jawaharlal Nehru's Policy Choices and the Designing of Political Institutions*. Oxon: Routledge, 2012.

'Christian Friedrich Schwartz: Apostle to South India'. In William Carey University's Donnell Hall Research Collection. http://

www.wmcarey.edu/carey/schwartz/schwartz.htm (accessed on 7 April 2008).

Seligman, E. R. A. 'The Economic Interpretation of History'. *Political Science Quarterly* 16 (1901): 612–640; 17: 71–98, 284–312. http://www.efm.bris.ac.uk/het/seligman/econinte.htm (accessed on 12 March 2008).

Public Debate between Prof. ERA Seligman and Prof. Scott Nearing. Verbatim Report by Convention Reporting Co. Fine Arts Guild, Inc. New York, 1921. University of Toronto Online Archives of Roberts Library. http://www.archive.org/details/debatebetween-era00seliuoft (accessed on 19 October 2011).

Sharma, Yogesh Chandra. *Cotton Khadi in Indian Economy.* Ahmedabad: Navjivan Publishing House, 1970/1999.

'Brief History of Sashtriyars'. http://sastriars.org/brief_history_01.html (accessed on 4 March 2008).

Shivdatta, ed. *Samagra Nai Talim: Vichar, Darshan, Yojana evam Pathyakram.* Wardha/New Delhi: Nai Talim Samiti and Gandhi Smriti Darshan Samiti, 2006. (Hindi)

Skinner, Quentin. 'Meaning and Understanding in the History of Ideas'. *History and Theory* 8 (1969): 3–53.

———. 'Some Problems in the Analysis of Political Thought and Action'. *Political Theory* 2, no. 3 (August 1974): 277–303.

———. *Visions of Politics Vol. I: Regarding Method.* Cambridge: Cambridge University Press, 2002.

Southard, Barbara. 'The Feminism of Mahatma Gandhi'. *Gandhi Marg* 3, no. 7 (October 1981): 404–422.

Srivatsan, R. 'Concept of "Seva" and the "Sevak" in the Freedom Movement'. *Economic & Political Weekly* 41, no. 5 (4 February 2005): 427–438.

Stepelevich, Lawrence S., ed. *The Capitalist Reader.* New York, NY: Arlington House Publishers, 1977.

Strauss, Leo. 'Political Philosophy and History'. *Journal of History of Ideas* 10, no. 1 (January 1949): 30–50.

Studdert-Kennedy, Gerald. *British Christians, Indian Nationalists and the Raj.* New Delhi: Oxford University Press, 1991.

Subrahmanyam, Sanjay. *The Political Economy of Commerce: South India, 1500–1650.* Cambridge, UK: Cambridge University Press, 1990.

———. *Money and the Market in India.* New Delhi: Oxford University Press, 1996.

Sugirtharajah, R. S. *Asian Biblical Hermeneutics and Postcolonialism: Contesting Interpretations.* Maryknoll, NY: Orbis Books, 1998.

———. *The Postcolonial Biblical Reader.* Oxford, UK: Blackwell Publishing, 2006.

———. *Exploring Postcolonial Biblical Criticism: History, Method, Practice.* London: Wiley-Blackwell, 2011.

Suinian, Liu, and Wu Qungan, eds. *China's Socialist Economy: An Outline History 1949–1984.* Beijing: Beijing Review, 1984.

Sumant, Yashwant. *Mahātma Gāndhi Yānchi Vichār Srushti: Kāhi Alakshit Pailu.* Pune: Sadhana, 2016. (Published posthumously, Marathi)

———. *Adhunik Bharataatil Dharama Chintan.* Pune: Sadhana. (Forthcoming Marathi)

Sykes, Marjorie. *The Story of Nai Talim: Fifty Years of Education at Sevagram, 1937–1987.* Wardha: Nai Talim Samiti, 1988.

Tekumalla, Viswanathan, ed. *Cottage Industries of India.* Madras: Silpi Publication, 1948.

Terchek, Ronald. *Gandhi: Struggling for Autonomy.* New Delhi: Vistaar, 1998.

Thomas, P. *Christians and Christianity in India and Pakistan: A General Survey of the Progress of Christianity in India from Apostolic to the Present Day.* London: George Allen & Unwin, 1954.

Thorner, Alice. 'Semi-Feudalism or Capitalism: Contemporary Debates on Classes and Mode of Production in India'. *Economic & Political Weekly* 26, nos. 49, 50 and 51 (December 1982): 1961–1968, 1993–1999 and 2061–2065.

Tilak, Raghukul. 'Needed a Blueprint for Gandhian Socialism'. *Gandhi Marg* 4, no. 4 (July 1982): 471–477.

Tyabji, Nasir. 'Capitalism in India and the Small Industries Policy'. *Economic & Political Weekly* 15, nos. 41 and 43 (October 1980): 1721–1732.

Vinaik, M., *The Gandhian Crusader: A Biography of J. C. Kumarappa.* Gandhigram: Gandhigram Trust, 1956/1987.

———. *J. C. Kumarappa and His Quest for World Peace.* Ahmedabad: Navjivan Publishing House, 1956.

Vasaniya, P. C. 'Palm Sugar: A Plantation Industry in India'. *Economic Botany* 20, no. 1 (January–March 1966): 40–45.

Veervalli, Anuradha. *Gandhi in Political Theory: Truth, Law and Experiment.* Surrey: Ashgate Publishing, 2014.

Victus, Solomon. *Religion and Eco-Economics of Dr. J. C. Kumarappa: Gandhism Redefined.* New Delhi: ISPCK, 2003.

———. *Jesus and Mother Economy: An Introduction of the Theology of J. C. Kumarappa.* New Delhi: ISPCK, 2008.

Vidal, Denis. 'Markets'. In *The Oxford India Companion to Sociology and Social Anthropology,* Vol. 2 edited by Veena Das. New Delhi: Oxford University Press, 2003, pp. 1342–1360.

Viswanathan Peterson, Indira. 'Between Print and Performance: The Tamil Christian Poems of Vedanayaka Sastri and the Literary Cultures of Nineteenth Century South India'. In *India's Literary History: Essays on the Nineteenth Century,* edited by Stuart Blackburn and Vasudha Dalmia. New Delhi: Permanent Black, 2004, pp. 25–59.

Warrender, Howard. 'Political Theory and Historiography: A Reply to Professor Skinner of Hobbes'. *The Historical Journal* 22, no. 4 (December 1979): 931–940.

Weber, Thomas. *Gandhi, Gandhism and the Gandhians.* New Delhi: Lotus Collection, 2006.

Yang, Anand A. *Bazzar India: Markets, Society, and the Colonial State in Bihar.* Berkeley, CA: University of California Press, 1998. http://arkcdlib.org/ark:/13030/ft4779n9tq/ (accessed on 12 February 2013).

Zacharia, Benjamin. 'In Search of the Indigenous: J. C. Kumarappa and the Philosophy of Gandhian Economic'. In *Colonialism as Civilizing Mission: Cultural Ideology in British India,* edited by Harald Fischer-Tiné and Michael Mann. London: Anthem Press, 2004, pp. 248–269.

———. *Developing an Intellectual and Social History of India.* New Delhi: Oxford University Press, 2005.

Zaidi, A. M., and S. G. Zaidi, eds. *The Encyclopaedia of the Indian National Congress,* Vols. 10–12. New Delhi: S. Chand & Co., 1980.

Online Audio Sources

Goshiben Captain's Interview by Uma Shanker (16 June 1970). Centre for South Asian Studies, University of Cambridge Oral History Archive Interview No. 122. (Audio) http://karachi.s-asian.cam.ac.uk/archive/audio/captain.html (accessed on 10 August 2011).

G. R. Rao's (Gora) Interview by Arun Gandhi (February 1969). Centre for South Asian Studies, University of Cambridge Oral History Archive Interview No. 232. (Audio) http://karachi.s-asian.cam. ac.uk/archive/audio/rao.html (accessed on 10 November 2012).

Jayaprakash Narayan's Interview by Arun Gandhi (March 1969). Centre for South Asian Studies, University of Cambridge Oral History Archive Interview No. 235. (Audio) http://karachi.s-asian.cam.ac.uk/archive/audio/narayanj.html (accessed on 20 May 2011).

Shankarlal Banker's Interview by Uma Shanker. (22 December 1972). (Audio) http://karachi.s-asian.cam.ac.uk/archive/audio/banker. html (accessed on 22 May 2011).

Shankarrao Deo's Interview by Uma Shanker (27 March 1970). Centre for South Asian Studies, University of Cambridge Oral History Archive Interview No. 121. (Audio) http://karachi.s-asian.cam. ac.uk/archive/audio/deo.html (accessed on 23 May 2011).

U. N. Dhebar Interview by Uma Shanker (12 August 1970). Centre for South Asian Studies, University of Cambridge Oral History Archive Interview No. 156. (Audio) http://karachi.s-asian.cam. ac.uk/archive/audio/dhebar.html (accessed on 10 November 2012).

Index

Ecumenical Association of the Third World (EATWOT), 174
Emmanuel, Arghiri, 83
environmentalism, 15
equilibrium, 13

Federation of Indian Chamber of Commerce and Industry, 47
feminism, 15
First World War (also known as European War), 56
Fox, Richard, 4
freedom, 2, 5, 6

Gandhi Memorial Fund (Gandhi Smarak Nidhi), 73, 76, 145
Gandhi–Irwin Pact, 55
Gandhian political economy (GPE), 13
Gandhism, 7, 8, 15, 18, 21, 22, 23, 25, 27, 134
General Agreement on Trade and Tariff (GATT), 164
Ghosh, B. N., 13, 14
Gram Sevak Vidyalaya, 64, 66
Gram Udyog Patrika, 28, 67, 70, 78, 110, 116, 144, 151
Gram-dan (donation of the entire village land and its redistribution through Gram Sabha), 17
Gramodyog Sanghs, 140
Grave Yard Peace, 105
Green, Martin, 3
Gregg, Richard, 3

Guha, Ramachandra (also known as Green Gandhian), 28, 149
Gujarat Vidyapeeth, 48

Harijan, 28, 70, 110, 114, 117, 135, 151
Harijans, 60
Hind Swaraj, 69
Hinduization, 171
Hindustani Talimi Sangh, 124
hindutva (Hindu-ness), 6
hindutvaization, 171
Hirachand, Seth Walchand, 72, 109
human economic organizations, types of, 84
human rationality theory, 13
Hussain, Zakir, 65
Hypnotic Peace, 105
hypocrisy, 11

ideal polity, 15
idleness, 11
Indian National Congress, 135
    Earthquake Relief Committee for Bihar (1934), 58
    Karachi session of, 55
Indian Social Reformer, 162, 163
individualistic human economic organization, 84
Industrial Survey Committee, 66
industrialization, 9
    Gandhi's hostility to, 12
initiative, 9
inner character, 5
Islam, 18

plural societies
  inter-religious communication in, 6
  provision for public space, 6
pluralism, 5
political economy, 13
political independence, 17
Political Science Quarterly, 41
poverty, 6, 11, 34, 45, 78, 79, 97, 111, 166
Prasad, Rajendra, 58, 72
Press Act (1910), 47
private property, 9
progressive capitalism, 42
proselytization, 16
purity of end and means, 2

Rajputs, 50
Ram Raj, concept of, 1
Ramine Commission of 1898, 32
Ranade, Mahadev Govind, 47
Rawls, John, 4
Raz, Joseph, 4
religious discourse, 150
religious mysteries or miracles, 3
religious thought, 6
Report of the Industrial Survey Committee, 103
revolution, 16
Round Table Conference, Second (1931), 56
Roy, M. N., 109

sadhak, 16
sadhana, 16
samanya dharma (routine religious practices), 16
Sampatti-dan (donation of wealth), 17

Samyukta Maharashtra Movement (or the anti-emergency agitations), 18, 21
Sarabhai, Ambalal, 109, 111
Sarda Bill, 163
Sarva Seva Sangh, 25, 74
sarvesham avirodhen (renunciation from every contradiction and confrontation), 18
Sarvodaya, 107, 134, 147
  economics, 19–21
  Samaj, 20, 21
Satya-nishtha (faith in and commitment to truth), 19
Satyagraha, 2, 3, 17, 22
scarcity, 13
Schumacher, E. F., 164
Second World War, 66
secularism, 15
self-confidence, 9
self-discipline, 9
self-ownership, notion of, 9
self-purification, 22
self-respect, 9
Seligman, E. R. A., 40–44, 82
Shapurjee, Shoorji, 72
sheep-flock or herd type nationalism, 82
Shram-dan (donating one's labour), 17
Shroff, A. D., 109
Sikhism, 18
Sitaramayya, Pattabhi, 62
social human economic organization, 84
social revolution, 26
social welfare, maximization of, 14
socialism, 9

About the Author

Chaitra Redkar is Associate Professor in the Department of Political Science at SNDT Women's University, Mumbai. She holds a PhD in Politics from Savitribai Phule Pune University. Dr Redkar specializes in Modern Indian Political Thought and Social Movements, with more than two decades of research and teaching experience in these areas. She has been closely associated with the Gandhian movement in Maharashtra. Dr Redkar has written broadly in the area of political ideas and Indian politics. She has many publications to her credit, including books, book chapters, journal articles, newspaper columns and translations. Among these, her political biography of a lesser known Gandhian activist, Sane Guruji, in her mother tongue, Marathi, should be especially mentioned.